Theology and the University

Theology and the University

EDITED BY

John Apczynski

THE ANNUAL PUBLICATION OF THE
COLLEGE THEOLOGY SOCIETY
1987
VOLUME 33

UNIVERSITY
PRESS OF
AMERICA

Lanham • New York • London

Annual Publication • 33

University Press of America®, Inc.
4720 Boston Way
Lanham, Maryland 20706

3 Henrietta Street
London WC2E 8LU England

Library of Congress Cataloging-in-Publication Data

Theology and the university / edited by John Apczynski.
      p.   cm. — (Annual publication of the
      College Theology Society ; v. 33)
      Includes bibliographical references.
  1. Theology—Study and teaching—United States.
  2. Universities and colleges—United States—Religion.
3. Theology—History. I. Apczynski, John V. II. Series.
BX905.T44   1989   207'.73—dc20   89–14703 CIP

ISBN 0–8191–7472–6 (alk. paper)
ISBN 0–8191–7473–4 (pbk. : alk. paper)

 The paper used in this publication meets the minimum requirements of
American National Standard for Information Sciences—Permanence
of Paper for Printed Library Materials, ANSI Z39.48–1984.

CONTENTS

ACKNOWLEDGMENTS

The editor wishes to thank his colleagues who unselfishly shared their time and wisdom to assist in the preparation of this volume.

The essays by William Shea and James Heft have appeared in *Current Issues in Catholic Higher Education*, volume 8 (Winter, 1988), pp. 35–44 and volume 9 (Summer, 1988), pp. 26–38, respectively. The editor thanks the Association of Catholic Colleges and Universities for permission to include them in this volume.

Finally a word of thanks is due to Sandy Goodliff whose secretarial skills have helped to bring this volume to press.

PREFACE

Among the more vexing problems posed by the modern academy to scholars of religion is the legitimacy of their very presence in the university. The contemporary academic community is dominated by a critical temper that is empirically oriented, open to a plurality of views, and chary of absolute claims. While perhaps not quite antithetical to religion, such a posture appears, in the minds of many academicians, to be inhospitable to religion and its traditional scholarly apparatus. The resultant conviction that, except for antiquarian curiosity, religion and its study have no place in the modern academy is still too often encountered.

Those who study religion professionally know, of course, that such an understanding is a simplistic caricature which thoroughly distorts matters. Unfortunately such presumptions about what inquiry in the university requires and what inquiry in religion permits are cloaked sufficiently enough in verisimilitude to make the problem persistent. And there is the rub. How does one express clearly and convincingly in the contemporary academic context the legitimacy of the study of religion? To complicate matters further, the evolution of the legal and political traditions in the United States requires that the question be posed within the distinctive settings of both publicly funded state universities as well as private universities which often have (or have had) some denominational affiliation.

Since the middle of this century state institutions have seen the steady rise of the analysis of religion in the form of "religious studies." Yet in spite of the demonstrable success of such programs, particularly their enthusiastic acceptance by many students, the precise delineation of what ought to be happening here is still hotly disputed.[1] Should the study of religion be limited to the descriptive

---

[1]See, for example, the proposal defended by Robert N. Minor and Robert D. Baird ["Teaching about Religion at the State University: Taking the Issue Seriously and Strictly," *Bulletin CSSR*, 14 (1983), 68–72] and the responses by Julia B. Mitchell and David B. Annis ["Teaching about Religion at the State University: A Reply," *Bulletin CSSR*, 14 (1983), 113–141 and by Philip Boo Riley ["Teaching about Religion at the Religiously Affiliated University: Taking the Issue Seriously and Strictly; A Reply to

task? What role do interpretative theories play? Is "religious studies" more of a "field" than a "discipline"?[2] To what extent must one become like an "insider" or devotee in order to understand a tradition accurately? Can students expect professors of religion to assess evaluative claims and defend normative positions in the classroom?

As such questions move from the more descriptive toward the more normative end of the spectrum, the scholarly study of religion begins to resemble the traditional form of inquiry called theology. At this point rather heated discussions within the profession often occur.[3] Some, fearing that religious commitments would not permit a genuinely critical inquiry would bar theology from the university, while others would admit a "practitioner" of a particular tradition on the analogy of departments of literature including creative poets or novelists among their ranks. To a certain extent the problem here reflects a concern over the form or character of theological inquiry. Partly as a result of the challenge posed by the modern university setting several theologians have revisioned theology so that its arguments and criteria are public and open to academic scrutiny.[4] When conceived in this way, must not the theological enterprise be a constitutive part of any thoroughgoing study of religion, even on state university campuses?

However that is resolved, one might be tempted to suppose that at private, religiously affiliated colleges and universities at least, this sort of problem would not emerge. That is not quite the case, however. To be sure, there is a general acceptance of the place of

Robert Baird and Robert Minor," *Bulletin CSSR*, 14 (1983), 145–46. For another example, see N. Ross Reat, "Insiders and Outsiders in the Study of Religious Traditions," *Journal of the American Academy of Religion*, 51 (1983), 459–476 and the responses it elicited from Edwin Gerow, Charles Vernoff, Langdon Gilkey, and Edmund Perry (pp. 471–91).

[2]Charles Vernoff, "Naming the Game: A Question of the Field," *Bulletin CSSR*, 14 (1983), 109–13.

[3]See Ivan Strenski's challenge ["Our Very Own 'Contras': A Response to the 'St. Louis Project' Report," *Journal of the American Academy of Religion*, 54 (1986), 323–35] and Walter Capp's vigorous rejoinder ["A Response to Dr. Strenski," *Ibid.*, 55 (1987), 125–26].

[4]See, for example, the recent work of these theologians: Schubert M. Ogden, *On Theology* (San Francisco: Harper & Row, Publishers, 1986); David Tracy, *The Analogical Imagination: Christian Theology and the Culture of Pluralism* (New York: Crossroad, 1981); Edward Farley, *Ecclesial Reflection: An Anatomy of Theological Method* (Philadelphia: Fortress Press, 1982); and Gordon D. Kaufman, *The Theological Imagination: Constructing the Concept of God* (Philadelphia: Westminster Press, 1981).

theology and biblical study in the curriculum, so that the question would not emerge in that form. But precisely what that place is, whether on the graduate, professional level[5] or in the undergraduate curriculum,[6] is by no means settled.

In this context the nexus of problems surrounding the study of religion is just as vexatious. What role might the methodologies employed in religious studies play in theological reflection? Can they be accommodated by theology without the loss of its own proper form of reflexivity? What if the use of such methodologies leads to the challenging of enshrined formulations of the community of faith? To what extent should such probings be made part of professional ministerial training or the liberal arts undergraduate curriculum?

Within the Roman Catholic tradition such issues have arisen with increasing urgency. The recent efforts by the Vatican to remove theologians from their positions in seminaries and to subject the teaching of theology in the undergraduate curriculum to the direct juridical control of ecclesiastical authorities are not merely matters of internal religious politics. They are in addition practical manifestations of theological claims and positions which, under the pressing needs of the moment, are often allowed to escape the proper scrutiny that might challenge their adequacy.

In the midst of this historical moment, the College Theology Society decided to devote its 1987 annual meeting, held at Loyola College in Baltimore, to the theme of "theology and the university." The essays collected in this volume provide a representative sampling of the sort of reflection that occurred at that meeting. While presupposing the broader American context, they address primarily questions of theology and its place in Catholic institutions of higher learning. As we survey their contents, however, it will be clear that their relevance is much broader and that they make a substantive

---

[5]See Edward Farley, Theologia: The Fragmentation and Unity of Theological Education (Philadelphia: Fortress Press, 1983) and Max L. Stackhouse, Aplogia: Contextualization, Globalization, and Mission in Theological Education (Grand Rapids: William B. Eerdmans Publishing Company, 1988).

[6]See the report on the "St. Louis Project" published in the Journal of the American Academy of Religion, 52 (1984): Walter H. Capps, "Religious Studies/Theological Studies," pp. 727–30; Laurence J. O'Connell, "Religious Studies, Theology, and the Humanities Curriculum," pp. 731–37; Jacob Neusner, "Why Religious Studies in America? Why Now?" pp. 738–41; P. Joseph Cahill, "Theological Studies, Where Are You?" pp. 742–47; and William F. May, "Why Theology and Religious Studies Need Each Other," pp. 748–57.

contribution that will be instructive to all who are concerned with
the aims and goals of higher education today.

In the first part of this volume the essays focus on the character of
theological reflection in light of specific historical examples. James
Hennesey uses his historian's wit to illustrate the importance of
historical fact for any theologian aspiring to understand a tradition,
as well as the importance of knowing how to distinguish and relate
them. One of the most common misapprehensions about theology,
particularly in its medieval manifestations, is that it is monolithic
and subject to strict ecclesiastical control. Gary Macy surveys facets
of the theological debate surrounding the eucharist initiated by
Bonaventure and Aquinas, thereby providing a case of theological
inquiry that fostered a divergent set of views on a crucial doctrinal
issue which occupied several generations of theologians without
external ecclesiastical interference. An important source often
claimed for theology today is "experience." Lillian Bozak-DeLeo
explores how Julian of Norwich, on the basis of her mystical experience, developed a soteriology dominated by divine love which stood
in sharp contrast to Anselm's dominant version based on divine
justice; she then suggests how Julian's position may be more congru-
ent with contemporary insights. Terence Martin explores the dialogues of Erasmus in order to portray the qualities of genuine
conversation that are required of theological practice. These historical perspectives on theological inquiry show it to be a more open,
dynamic, and pluralistic sort of inquiry than it frequently is presumed to be—by academics as well as ecclesiastical authorities.

The essays in the second part of this volume continue to probe the
character of theological inquiry, but now in ways appropriate to the
contemporary university setting. Phyllis Kaminski explores how
feminist insights into the nature of knowledge and the employment
of root metaphors of relationality might contribute to a transformation of theological inquiry. In his essay Patrick O'Connell argues that
the critics of the recent U.S. bishops' pastorals on peace and on the
economy differ not only in their political agendas but more importantly in their theological presuppositions on the kingdom of God.
It demonstrates that a theological defense of ecclesiastical authority
need not be based on servile submission but can operate through
openly accountable forms of rationality. Using contemporary literary
theory on the reality of fictional characters beyond the written text,
John McCarthy explains how this may shed light on the power of the
biblical texts to evoke the presence of Jesus. David Tracy tackles the

problem of the role of theology in education by retrieving the way in which the soul was understood to be capable of transformation in the classical dialogues of Plato. McCarthy's and Tracy's essays are instructive not only as models of theological reasoning but also through their offering substantive contributions to the way in which *theologia* could function in the contemporary university.

The next set of essays in the third part of this volume explore explicitly what function theology ought to fulfill in a university. William Madges surveys the issue as it arose for Catholicism in nineteenth century Ireland and Germany in order to draw out the lessons that theology's purpose is to search for truth about ultimate reality through open and critical dialogue and in this way be of service to both Church and society. The contemporary malaise affecting universities in part reflects the shaking of what is being called the modern, Enlightenment model of rationality. Steven Ostovich proposes some suggestions for the role of theology in a post-modern university by outlining the elements of Juergen Habermas' notion of communicative reason and its application to theology by Helmut Peukert. A good example of such a shift from a "modern" understanding of the role of theology is offered by Alice Gallin's reconstruction of the emergence of theology on Catholic campuses during the 1950's and its collapse in the aftermath of the 1960's. Her concluding observations suggest that the integration of theological activity into the undergraduate curriculum must be a critical element of Catholic higher education.

The essays in the fourth and final part of this collection pick up the question of the character of Catholic higher education. James Heft traces the development of the notion of "academic freedom" in the United States and the attendant tensions brought about as it was received within Catholic higher education. On the basis of this careful reading he offers tentatively several suggestions for preserving academic freedom in a specifically Catholic setting. In the context of the fragmentation and specialized professionalization that plague American higher education, William Portier argues for the place of a distinctive point of view informing an educational institution and for the value of Catholicism in informing the ideals of liberal education. Finally William Shea argues that Catholic higher education ought to play an important role not only for the Church, but also for the culture at large. A Catholic college can serve this wider purpose to the extent that it takes pluralism seriously enough to engage in responsible dialogue with the entire range of cultural options. In this way a Catholic college can move beyond mere tolerance of pluralism toward the kind of growth that offers and expects public accountability of fundamental values. If such a suggestion were acted upon theology and the university would indeed perform an invaluable service for the American public.

John V. Apczynski

Part One

THEOLOGICAL INQUIRY:
HISTORICAL PERSPECTIVES

THE SCHOLAR IN THE CHURCH: A HISTORIAN's VIEW

James Hennesey, S. J.

"Christianity, because of the type of religion which it is, *necessarily* has one foot in the past. It is not a timeless truth; it is rooted in history." The words are those of Daphne Hampson of the University of St. Andrews, discussing with Rosemary Ruether the topic, "Is There a Place for Feminists in a Christian Church?"[1] Hampson takes the negative side in the debate and concludes that Christianity is impossible for women because its story is so ineradicably sexist. Ruether rightly, I think, finds the root of Hampson's assessment in her platonic spirituality, and the debate goes on. I prefer to leave it to my philosophical betters. But not until I have expressed my agreement with Daphne Hampson's premises, if not her conclusions. She puts the premises well: "In recounting to another what christianity was about you would have to relate to [its] story and [its] history." Or, even more simply, "there is always this past dimension."[2] There is, and it makes Christianity different from other religious forms preoccupied rather with an exclusive concentration on what they understand as "nature" or perceive as "personal experience."

Writing recently on the theology of marriage, Lisa Sowle Cahill set some parameters: "A Christian perspective on any moral issue derives from the interaction of a number of insights. . . . These are Scripture, tradition, philosophy, and descriptive or empirical information about human persons or communities." Amen to that! Amen also to Cahill's further remarks about "tradition." It "includes not

---

[1]Daphne Hampson and Rosemary Ruether, "Is There a Place for Feminists in a Christian Church?" *New Blackfriars* 68 (1987) 9.
[2]*Ibid.*, 9, 10.

only authoritative church teachings, but also the faith and practice of the whole believing community more broadly understood."[3]

Here I should like to narrow my sights and talk about what I define as the specifically "Catholic" understanding of Christianity, the one which insists, in a way that its "Protestant" counterpart does not, on "tradition" as central to its belief-system. In my written text, I have put those adjectives, "Catholic" and "Protestant" within inverted commas. I am not here talking about denominational belonging, but about where one meets the self-revelation of God. I am talking of "tradition" as it was described in the second chapter of Vatican II's constitution on divine revelation, arising from and discerned in the historical as well as the ongoing life, thought and worship of the people of God which is the church, the tradition of which German theologian Joseph Ratzinger wrote that it "is identified, and thus defined, with the being and faith of the church."[4]

The dynamic understanding of tradition accepted by Vatican II has been for church historians the same sort of magna carta that in 1943 *Divino Afflante Spiritu* was for biblical scholars. But we are twenty years behind them in our magna carta and even further behind in making our discipline truly serviceable to the total theological enterprise. It was in 1967 that the Vorgrimler-edited *Commentary on the Documents of vatican II* appeared, in which Ratzinger declared: "All that is certain is that from now on it will be impossible to ignore the critical historical method."[5] After Vatican II, that bête-noir of the historical in theology, Vincent of Lérins, "no longer appears," so Ratzinger wrote, "as an authentic representative of the Catholic idea of tradition." His "static *semper*"—the adage setting as norm of Catholicity "what has been believed everywhere, always and by all"—"no longer seems the right way of expressing [the nature of historical identity and continuity]."[6]

The two areas in which Ratzinger recognizes the historical revolution sanctioned by Vatican II are (1) acceptance of historical critical method; and (2) realization of the pervasiveness and consequences of change. Dutch historian Peter Geyl distinguished them years ago as "dry-biscuit" history and "plum-cake" history, the one

---

[3]Lisa Sowle Cahill, "Divorced from Experience: Rethinking the Theology of Marriage," *Commonweal* (27 March 1987) 171.

[4]Herbert Vorgrimler, gen. ed., *Commentary on the Documents of Vatican II* (New York: Herder & Herder 1969; orig. German ed. 1967) 3:184–185.

[5]*Ibid.*, 158.

[6]*Ibid.*, 187.

the field of the research historian, the other of the metahistorian looking beyond the facts, but, one hopes, not ignoring them, to see and synthesize the "big picture."[7] The historian-as-such is properly a dry-biscuit type, whose contribution to metahistory is to testify to the fact of change. Beyond that can safely be left to the philosophers and theologians of history, but always with a wary eye on their tendency to skimp the facts and proceed from inadequate premises.

I do not disagree with Peter Meinhold, for whom, as a reviewer summarized him, "the real subject of church history is . . . the eschatological congregation of God's people, called by Christ, in which He Himself is present, intending to give her participation in His divine kingdom."[8] I am sure that my own religious understanding of "church" affects me at every stage of the historical process from initial selection of topic to final interpretation. But I believe I must try to avoid confusing the two orders of knowledge and set myself to discovering the human history of the people who are the church, their understanding of God, their common humanity and the physical world, their institutions, their ethical norms and behavior, their ways and understanding of worship, their sense of themselves precisely as Christians and, in my particular area of interest, as Catholic Christians.

What happens beyond that is for others to analyze and philosophize about. Walter Kasper has long since written that "we are experiencing a radical historicization of all reality," marked by "metamorphoses and developments in the church's pattern of faith" taking place "not only in accordance with the laws of organic growth," but proceeding "by leaps and bounds, shifts, anticipations and retardations."[9] All of which, I suspect, reads better in the original German! But the theme is a common one, sounded long ago by Robin Collingwood when he wrote of movement away from what he termed the substantialist position of "history frozen solid."[10] Rebutting Daphne Hampson, Rosemary Ruether chides her for holding just such a "thoroughly unhistorical" view of Christianity as a historical religion, one she shares with those who use it to resist

---

[7]Ved Mehta, "Onward and Upward with the Arts: the Flight of the Crook-Taloned Birds," The New Yorker 8 December 1962.

[8]Journal of Ecclesiastical History 22 (1971) 86–88.

[9]"Are Church and Theology Subject to Historical Law?" in Walter Kasper et al., The Crisis of Change (Chicago: Argus, 1969) 7, 9.

[10]R. G. Collingwood, The Idea of History (New York: Oxford University Press 1956) 43.

change. For Ruether being historical means: (1) being a living community of people, who have a present and a future, not just a past;
and (2) that "the search for absolutes in past historical experience is
unhistorical, since history is ever partial, relative and limited."[11]

Finishing a study on "The Frequency of the Eucharist throughout
History," Robert Taft makes a crucial distinction. He has pointed in
the article to the "shifting sands" of historical evidence. His final
lines read:

> What the judgement should be today is not for the historian to say.
> For history shows the past to be always instructive, but never normative.
> What is normative, is tradition. But tradition, unlike the past, is a living
> force whose contingent expressions, in liturgy or elsewhere, can
> change."[12]

Vatican II's *Dei Verbum* situates tradition in the "life, thought and
worship" of the church community. There I find the justification for
my existence as a church historian who studies the church community's life, thought and worship. But I do not confuse what I do with
even the tentatively final word on what the tradition is. I think this
is where we avoid one of the Modernist pitfalls. Church history, like
biblical study, is only a partner in a complex theological enterprise.
It offers the result of its research; it testifies to the pervasiveness of
change. Others take up from there.

Historians are not without enemies. A small catalogue will make
that plain. Foremost are those of our own house, the antiquarians,
the antique dealers who use history to resist change. They pre-empt
good words like "orthodox," "conservative," and "traditionalist,"
when they are none of these. They are rather the Catholic fundamentalists of whom Patrick Arnold has written so tellingly.[13] They are
the latter-day gnostics, both timid and arrogant, whose institutional
and personal insecurity has led them, as Gabriel Daly pointed out,
to take refuge in a fideistic authoritarianism. The Irish Augustinian
is talking there about the nineteenth century, and it is to that century
that we now turn for the next entry in the catalogue of history's
enemies.[14]

---

[11]Hampson and Ruether 14–15.
[12]Robert Taft, "The Frequency of the Eucharist throughout History," *Concilium* 152 (1982) 24.
[13]Patrick M. Arnold, "The Rise of Catholic Fundamentalism," *America* 11 April 1987 297–302.
[14]Gabriel Daly, review of *How the Pope Became Infallible: Pius IX and the Politics of Persuasion*, *Studies* 72 (1983) 104.

The nineteenth was a century in which, as Daly indicates, "rejection of historical imagination and procedures" within Catholic thought left the field to "a certain type of purely essentialist metaphysics." Deduction from the supposed "nature" of this or that was "in"; induction, the historical method, was "out." It was all helped along by the authoritarian part of "fideistic authoritarianism," and, as John Acton suggested, by an emphasis on piety, which provided "a respectable and impenetrable cloak for all kinds of errors and false tendencies."[15] That was not Acton's style. For him, Kathleen Keating wrote, "neither an anti-intellectual spirituality nor a formal scholastic philosophy provided answers to the learned errors of the day."[16] John Acton was obsessed by "the need to tell the truth about the church."[17] He saw that approach being replaced in his own time by a system which "made the teaching of the church the sole foundation and test of certain knowledge, a criterion alike of the records of history and of the arguments of unbelief. . . . It supposed the part of ignorance and malice to be so large, and the powers of unaided reason so minute, that ecclesiastical authority could be the only guide, even in matters foreign to its immediate domain." In the process, Acton regretted, "the cultivation of those original studies which are needed for [theology's] advance" was abandoned.[18]

What is involved here, of course, is the nineteenth century development of a centralized teaching and governing authority in the Catholic Church that has successfully eclipsed the reality that preceded it and made it extremely difficult for friend and foe alike to imagine what the situation was before "Catholic" and "Roman" came practically in some quarters to be treated as synonyms.

Much of the change that happened was owed to the political and social upheaval of the years of European revolution. That needs a whole book for itself. A theological trend was also hastened, that of logical explication as the primary theological method. Historical inquiries became superfluous. To demand "due and diligent inquiry into scripture and tradition" was to sail in the face of the prevailing

---

[15]John Acton to Richard Simpson, Munich, 8 March 1859, in Josef L. Altholz and Damien McElrath, eds., *The Correspondence of Lord Acton and Richard Simpson* (Cambridge: Cambridge University Press, 1971) 1: 157.

[16]Kathleen C. Keating, "John Acton and the Church of Pius IX," unpublished Ph.D. dissertation, Fordham University (1973) 83–84.

[17]*Ibid.*, 29 (Cambridge University Library, add. mss. 4910, 98).

[18]John Acton, "Ultramontanism," *Home and Foreign Review* (July 1863), reprinted in Douglas Woodruff, ed., *Essays on Church and State by Lord Acton* (London: Hollis & Carter 1952) 49–50.

theological wind blowing up from below the Alps.[19] The school reached new heights with the re-establishment of the Society of Jesus at the Gregorian University by Pope Leo XII in 1824. Historians like Aubert and Congar, Kasper, Mackey and Sanks have rehearsed the story.[20] Perhaps it is best capsulized in the quip reported of Pius IX after Cardinal Filippo Guidi alleged serious difficulties from tradition against the prospective definition of papal infallibility. "Tradition," the pope replied, "I am tradition." The authenticity of the tale has been questioned, but it fits well in a theological world where one Roman Jesuit theologian remarked that the treatise on the church was nothing but a treatise on authority,[21] and another wrote that indeed the church was a royal priesthood, as 1 Peter 2:9 has it, because it was "a kingdom ruled by priests."[22] The introduction of the notion of a "living" or "active" tradition, and its practical identification with papal magisterium, minimized, if they did not eliminate the need for historical study. The temptation to fall into what can aptly be described as ecclesiastical positivism was strong.

The advent late in the nineteenth century of Thomistic revival only strengthened the trend. Yves Congar long ago did a comparison between ultramontane textbooks on the church and those tagged as "Gallican" or "Febronian." The biggest difference he noted was that the latter began with historical facts and attended to history's complexity, while ultramontane authors used texts from the past to illustrate their affirmations.[23] They proof-texted. They alleged exempla. They began with a prioris and found the facts to fit them.

The French Jesuit Louis Billot dominated the scene at the Gregorian from 1885 until 1910. He was "the prince of theologians," a powerful force in anti-Modernist days and, until for political reasons Pius XI dismissed him from the cardinalate in 1927, prominent on the Roman scene. His theological influence was felt well into the

---

[19]Owen Chadwick, *From Bossuet to Newman: The Idea of Doctrinal Development* (Cambridge: Cambridge University Press 1957) 44.

[20]Roger Aubert, "La Géographie ecclésiologique au XIXe siécle," in Maurice Nédoncelle *et al.*, *L'Ecclésiologie au XIXe siècle* (Unam Sanctam 34; Paris: Éd. du Cerf 1960) 11–55; Yves Congar, "L'Ecclésiologie de la Revolution française au Concile du Vatican sous la signe de l'affirmation de l'autorité," *ibid.*, 77–114; J. P. Mackey, *The Modern Theology of Tradition* (New York: Herder & Herder 1963); T. Howland Sanks, *Authority in the Church: A Study in Changing Paradigms* (Missoula: Scholars' Press 1974).

[21]Congar, *supra* (n. 20) 100.

[22]Domenico Palmieri, *Tractatus de Romano Pontifice* (2nd ed.; Prati: Giachetti, 1891) 71: "Est enim Ecclesia regale et sanctum sacerdotium, quia est regnum quod a sacerdotibus regitur. . . ."

[23]Congar, *supra* (n. 20) 93.

1950s. It is in his thought that there is the clearest identification: tradition = magisterium. And magisterium = papal magisterium, for all practical purposes. Edgar Hocedez's judgment on Billot comes as no surprise: "History and its methods were beyond his horizon."[24]

There were other facets to the Thomistic revival, at Louvain, for example, where church-historical study has always flourished. Systematicians know better than I of the efforts now made to reincorporate attention to both scripture and tradition in the overall theological enterprise. But not everyone sees it that way. At the annual meeting in New York City last September of the Fellowship of Catholic Scholars, the keynote speaker, Bishop Edward Egan, gave a lesson in how to prepare a talk to be given "in successful seminaries," that is, in seminaries which are maintaining enrollment and moving their candidates on toward the priesthood:

> Take a clear Catholic position on just about anything, develop it with philosophical and theological precision and illustrate the development with citations from Scripture, the fathers, the classic theologians and the encyclicals of the popes.

As Bishop Egan said, his is a "Theology very similar in structure and style to the theology manuals of the 30s, 40s and 50s."[25]

The picture for the historian, however, is not totally bleak. Dei Verbum's emphasis on the growing, developing, dynamic nature of tradition and its identification with the life, thought and worship of the church, its being and faith—both vertically and horizontally, diachronically and synchronically—commands our attention. It is a concept of tradition so immensely more rich than that of Louis Billot. Other conciliar themes contribute. Yves Congar singles out the use of the term "People of God" as highlighting the church's historicity, its incarnation in human beings who exercise the freedom so proper to them in the world and in time.[26] There is the notion of the church as "pilgrim people," "not," as the English and Welsh bishops have put it, "an army marching in formation, but more like a group of travellers in a desert."[27] Cardinal Ratzinger has

[24]Sanks, supra (n. 20) 77–90; Edgar Hocedez, Histoire de la théologie au XIXe siècle (3 vols.; Brussels/Paris: L'Édition universelle/Desclée de Brouwer 1947–1952) 3: 370.
[25]Edward Egan, "Trends in American Spirituality," Origins 16 (30 October 1986) 35.
[26]John H. Miller, ed., Vatican II: An Interfaith Appraisal (Notre Dame IN: University of Notre Dame Press 1966) 202.
[27]The Tablet (London) 24 May 1986 527.

fastened on the way in which the term expresses "the historicity of
the church which is still underway and will first become itself when
the ways of time have been traveled."[28] Bishop Christopher Butler's
Theology of Vatican II describes from the perspective of an energetic
and involved participant how the council moved Catholic thought
from an almost exclusively conceptual approach—the one that dominated the sixty seven draft *schemata* drawn up by its preparatory
commissions—to one that is historical and biblical.[29] A recent writer
in *The Downside Review* remarked on the efforts of theologians like
Tracy, Groome and Schillebeeckx to relate ordinary human experience and "the story or text of Christian tradition."[30] The historian's
task is to assist the enterprise by making the story known.

My title suggests a historian looking at scholars. I have in fact
looked at a sub-group of scholars, namely historians. It has been, I
hope, a pardonable narcissism. But now, I should like to offer a few
suggestions as to how history can help in the common effort.

Stephan Kuttner has gloried in that profoundly anti-historical
happening, the twelfth-century triumph in western Christianity of
the canon lawyers: "It is by this sublime disregard of history (or we
may say, by the primacy of reason over history)," he wrote, "that the
medieval lawyers were able to make a system out of the conflicting
data they found in the experience of reality."[31] Historians have fared
no better at the hands of Platonic and Stoic philosophers, nor at
those of counter-Reformation Jesuits promoting theories of logical
explication. Nineteenth-century essentialists and their twentieth-
century heirs think us at best suited to illustrate their treatises. But
they are no more pesky than the omnipresent presentists who twist
legitimate concern for attention to experience both personal and
scientific into the nihilism that proclaims the past irrelevant and the
future essentially different.

Whatever the source, neglect of history's help in establishing the
tradition contributes to our common impoverishment.

History's help may aid understanding of how Christians have in

[28]Joseph Ratzinger, "The Ecclesiology of the Second vatican Council," *Communio*
13 (1986) 249.
[29]Christopher Butler, *The Theology of Vatican II* (rev. ed., Westminster MD: Christian Classics 1981).
[30]John Sullivan, "Blondel and Apologetics," *The Downside Review* 105 (1987) 1.
[31]Stephan Kuttner, *Harmony from Dissonance: An Interpretation of Medieval Canon
Law* (Wimmer Lecture 10; Latrobe PA: Archabbey Press 1960) 35; and in *id.*, *The
History of Ideas and Documents of Canon Law in the Middle Ages* (London: Variorum
Reprints 1980) 11.

fact been religious; how we have set behavioral norms; how we have structured and governed our communities.

Considerable light, for example, is shed on the nature of Catholicism in Ireland by students of the nineteenth-century devotional revolution spearheaded in that island by Cardinal Paul Cullen. One such student has concluded that the Irish Catholic's life "was governed by the God of Justice and not by the God of Love or Mercy . . . not in fact [by] the God of Catholic tradition in Ireland . . . [but] instead [by] the God of Victorianism, a British and Protestant God." A shibboleth or two are being challenged there! The explanation continues: "The stringent social norms of nineteenth century Britain became entangled with a fervent and essentially non-intellectual form of Catholicism. The resultant mix became the religion of the Catholic Irish who, in their innocence, imagined it to be the faith of Patrick, Brigid and Columcille."[32] I wonder, must we not take another look at the much maligned Jansenists and to factor into our estimate of that Catholic sect so undoubtedly rigid in its origins the mounting evidence that it gave birth perhaps not so much to the Irish and other Catholicism just described, but to its nineteenth-century Liberal Catholic opposite?

It is a commonplace to note how historical study puts paid to myths of homogeneity in Catholic thought and practice. John Hickey Wright marshalled such arguments some years back in a pair of articles which directly addressed themselves to the controversy over birth control, citing as examples of papal teaching reversed Gregory XVI's stricture on the primacy of individual conscience; Pius IX's negative view of separation of church and state and his insistence on Catholic exclusivity; and the differences on membership in the body of Christ between Pius XII's *Mystici Corporis* and Vatican II's *Lumen Gentium*.[33] He might have added the differing attitudes on modern ecumenism found in St. Pius X's *Editae Saepe* and Pius XI's *Mortalium Animos* and documents of the latest ecumenical council.

We know the substantial service John Noonan provided with his historical study called *Contraception*. His conclusions there about the 1931 encyclical letter *Casti Connubii* bear repetition:

---

[32]Louis McRedmond, "The Church in Ireland," in John Cumming and Paul Burns, eds., *The Church Now: An Inquiry into the Present State of the Catholic Church in Britain and Ireland* (Dublin: Gill and Macmillan 1980) 39.

[33]John Hickey Wright, "An End to the Birth Control Controversy?" and "The Birth Control Controversy Continued," *America* 7 March, 22 August 1981.

As distillation of past doctrinal statements, the encyclical was a masterpiece. At the same time, its composers were indifferent to the historical contexts from which their citations came, and uninterested in the environmental changes which differentiated the present context. The encyclical was a synthesis, it was not history.[34]

What if it, or its successor-encyclical in 1968, *had* been history? If they had been written out of the idea of tradition incorporated in its constitution on divine revelation by the second Vatican Council? James Brundage, in his 1985 presidential address to the American Catholic Historical Association, made just such an historical study for the period ending in the early middle ages.[35] It makes interesting reading.

A headline in *The Tablet* of London, April 4, 1987, read: "Tribal Rancour at Choice of Bishop." The difficulty had arisen in the Gulu diocese of Uganda. Four African priests were suspended because of the vigor of their protests at the appointment of a new auxiliary bishop from another tribe. Our interest here is in the statement made on February 16, 1987 by Archbishop Karl-Josef Rauber, apostolic pro-nuncio in Uganda, as he explained the process by which the new bishop had been chosen. "The responsibility for appointing a bishop," the nuncio explained, was "exclusively that of the pope," but the choice was made "after a long, careful and impartial process of consultation" which was conducted only in part by the local nunciature.[36]

From Uganda the scene shifts to California and the November 1986 celebration at the University of San Francisco of the seventy-fifth anniversary of Maryknoll. In the course of the discussions, I raised the sensitive question of the relationship of local churches to the see and bishop of Rome. China has insisted on the "Three Selfs" movement: churches must be self-governing, self-propagating and self-financing. One must not be naive. Any slogan needs its content investigated. But on the face of it, the "Three Selfs" rhetoric could be equally expressive of the mind of the first bishop of the United States, John Carroll of Baltimore. He surely had an understanding of communion with Rome more sharply nuanced than that allowed in

<hr>

[34]John T. Noonan, Jr., *Contraception: A History of Its Treatment by Catholic Theologians and Canonists* (Cambridge MA: Harvard University Press 1966) 427.
[35]James A. Brundage, " 'Allas! That Evere Love Was Synne': Sex and Medieval Canon Law," *Catholic Historical Review* 72 (1986) 1–13.
[36]*The Tablet* 4 April 1987 380.

the People's Republic of China today, but it is equally true that he did not consider that he was running a branch operation of a Roman central office. He neither was, nor wanted to be, a "vicar apostolic," either in title or concept. "A refined Roman political contrivance," he termed that office.[37]

The fact is, that as the nineteenth century began, the pope nominated bishops only in mission countries and in the Papal States. Everywhere else, his role was that of instituting those who had been chosen by others. Since the second Lateran Council in the year 1139, that choice was supposed to rest with cathedral chapters. The system had, of course, suffered great abuse. But, again the historical datum that theologians might want to consider, it was only in 1884 that the papacy laid formal claim to the right to name all bishops everywhere in the world.[38] That should be kept in mind as the church meditates on the consequences of renewed collegiality, on the principle of subsidiarity, and on the thoughts of Pope John Paul II, recently reported as having recalled that Vatican II used the title "vicar of Christ" of all bishops, that it was a title he preferred to reserve in his own case for the most solemn moments. He would rather use the title, "successor of St. Peter," or, better still, "bishop of Rome."[39]

The uses of history in the theological enterprise are many. Its service is to assist the community, its theologians, its leaders, to know more accurately, to sense more faithfully, what has been, down the centuries, the life, the thought and the worship of the Christian community, the "tradition" on which Catholic Christianity places such reliance.

[37]James Hennesey, "An Eighteenth-Century Bishop: John Carroll of Baltimore," Archivum Historiae Pontificiae 16 (1978) 171–204; and id., "The Vision of John Carroll," Thought 54 (1979) 322–333.
[38]Garrett Sweeney, "The 'Wound in the Right Foot': Unhealed," in Adrian Hastings, ed., Bishops and Writers: Aspects of the Evolution of Modern English Catholicism (Wheathamstead: Anthony Clarke 1977) 207–234.
[39]The Tablet 11 April 1987 399.

RECEPTION OF THE EUCHARIST ACCORDING TO THE THEOLOGIANS: A CASE OF THEOLOGICAL DIVERSITY IN THE THIRTEENTH AND FOURTEENTH CENTURIES

Gary Macy

Ever since Paul admonished the Corinthians for their overly enthusiastic celebration of the breaking of the bread, Christian writers have distinguished between worthy and unworthy reception. This admonition gradually moved toward theological clarification and codification during the dispute over the eucharistic teaching of Berengar of Tours in the eleventh century. The majority of the opponents of Berengar held to a theology of the sacrament based on the teaching of the ninth century monk, Paschasius of Corby. In their understanding of that theology, reception of the Body and Blood of the Lord was necessary in order that the natural Body of the Lord might mingle with the body of the recipient, thus granting immortality.

The question then necessarily arose of why the bodies of sinners or infidels or even animals do not become immortal once in contact with the risen Body of the Lord through reception. Beginning with Lanfranc, the most intelligent of Berengar's foes, it was customary for theologians to speak of two modes of reception in the Eucharist. Basing themselves on Augustine, worthy reception was described as spiritual communion, and unworthy reception became known as either corporeal or sacramental reception. Both forms of reception assumed that the believer actually consumed the consecrated species. It was agreed that all believers, sinners or not, received the true Body and Blood. Only the just, however, received the saving effect of this reception. Theologians disagreed about animals and infidels. Some argued all received the true Body of the Lord, mice and men alike. Others insisted that only believers received; unbelievers and animals ate only the species of bread and wine.[1]

In the twelfth century, works associated with the school of Anselm at Laon introduced a third form of communion, spiritual reception alone. According to these theologians, one could receive the full benefits of the Eucharist by devotional acts which demonstrated a union with God in faith and love[2]. Thus three forms of reception were imperfectly associated with the three elements of the Eucharist. Sacramental reception entailed reception of both the *sacramentum* (the species alone) and of the *sacramentum et res* (the Body and Blood of Christ), while spiritual communion entailed reception of the *res* only (a union of faith working in love or according to some writers, the Church as mystical Body). Of course, one could also receive both sacramentally and spiritually when one consumed the species in worthy reception.

By the beginning of the thirteenth century, the question of who might receive the Eucharist, and how he or she might receive it, had been fairly carefully explored and several different theories had been put forward regarding reception by, for instance, animals.[3] The discussion was to undergo one further and significant development, however, during the first half of the thirteenth century.

Basing himself on earlier writers, and especially Pope Innocent III, the secular master and later convert to the Franciscans, Alexander of Hales, argued that reception depended upon the recognition of the sign value of the sacrament by the recipient.[4] In Alexander's

---

[1]Gary Macy, *Theologies of the Eucharist in the Early Scholastic Period* (Clarendon Press: Oxford, 1984), p. 47 et passim.

[2]Macy, esp. pp. 86–96.

[3]For a discussion of this entire issue, cf. Artur Landgraf, "Die in der Frühscholastik klassische Frage *quid sumit mus*," *Dogmengeschichte in der Frühscholastik*, vol. 3, part 2 (Regenburg, 1955) and Gary Macy, "Of Mice and Manna: *Quid mus sumit* as a Pastoral Question," *Recherches de Théologie Anciénne et médiévale* (to appear).

[4]Ideas similar to those espoused by Alexander exist in late twelfth and early thirteenth century writers. Cf., for instance, Innocent III, *De Sacro Altaris Mysterio, liber IV,* cap. 16: Nam in quo similitudo deficeret, in eo sacramentum non esset, sed ibi se proderet, et fidei locum aufferret, neque jam crederetur quod ita fieri non oportet. Itaque quantum ad nos servat per omnia corruptibilis cibi similitudinem, sed quantum ad se non amittit inviolabilis corporis veritatem. *PL* 215:867. See also Peter of Capua, *Summa "Uetustissima ueterum"* (1201–2): "Et potest dici quod etiam in ipso sumente manet materiale corpus donec in eo est aliqua forma ipsius panis. Non tamen incorporatur ei quia cibus est anime non corporis ut dicit Augustinus." Vatican City, Biblioteca Vaticana, Vaticana latina MS 4296, fol. 70r1 and Jacques de Vitry, *Historia occidentalis* (c. 1219–1225): "Forma igitur gustatur, sentitur, dentibus atteritur. Corpus autem non in uentrem descendit, sed ob ore ad cor transit. Comeditur sed non consumitur." Edited by J. F. Hinnebusch, (Fribourg, 1972), p. 231. I am planning a complete study of this earlier material.

commentary on Peter Lombard's *Sentences*, written c. 1222–23[5] he explained that since the Body of Christ is spiritual food, only an intellectual nature is capable of receiving it. As Augustine had pointed out, the outward sign leads to the inner reality and only the intellect can so reach beyond the sign to the reality behind it. Animals then receive simply the outer forms, the taste of bread and wine. Only humans can understand symbols, and therefore only humans can access the presence of the Lord underlying the symbol *(sacramentum)* of bread and wine.[6]

Writing between 1220 and 1236 in a work now known as the *Quaestiones disputatae 'Antequam esset frater'*, Alexander offered a fuller explanation of this form of sacramental theology. There are three kinds of union possible in the Eucharist, according to Alexander. One can be united in thought, in love and in nature to Christ. Those who existed before the coming of Christ could be united in thought and love, but not in nature. Angels, too, having a different nature than Christ, cannot receive him naturally. Then, too, Christ can be received with more or less love, and more or less understanding. This means there are different degrees of reception of Christ. Perfect reception would take place only in heaven, Alexander intimated. Those who receive the sign alone, like Jews and pagans, are united only to the sign, as if it were mere bread. Again there is a union of those who both believe and understand the reason for the sign. Finally, there is the greater union of those who believe and love, and this is spiritual reception.[7]

Alexander discussed the question of whether only rational creatures have the ability to receive this sacrament. It would seem that irrational creatures must be able to receive since, once transubstan-

---

[5]On the dating of Alexander's works, see Alexander of Hales, *Quaestiones disputatae 'Antequam Esset Frater'* edited by PP. Collegium S. Bonaventuræ (Quaracchi: Florence, 1960) pp. 34*–36*.

[6]E.G., "Quaestio est propter quid, si corpus Christ ibi est, non sumitur a brutis animalibus. —Responsio est ad hoc, quod differt sensus in brutis et in nobis. Est enim in nobis ordinatus ad rationem, in brutis vero non. Quia ergo corpus Christi sub sacramento non dicit tantum quod ad sensum pertinet, sed quod ad rationem, quod sensus est a brutis sumitur, scilicet species panis; quod in ordine ad rationem est non sumitur, scilicet corpus Christi." Alexander of Hales, *Glossa in quatuor libros sententiarum (Bibliotheca franciscana scholastica medii aevi*, vol 15) (Quaracchi: Florence, 1957), p. 204. Cf. also p. 161–2.

[7]*Quaestiones disputatae*, pp. 966–7 (no. 199), esp. p. 967: "Item, alia est unio speciei tantum, ut in iis qui manducant secundum quod est sacramentum solum, sicut panem aliquem, ut ludaei vel pagani. —Item est unio secundum rationem signi, ut in eo qui credit et intelligit; et maior adhuc est eo qui credit et diligit, ut in iis qui spiritualiter accipiunt; et sic secundum quod maior unio, maior manducatio".

tiation takes place, the body of Christ remains as long as the species of bread remains. If an animal receives the species of bread, it ought as well to receive the body of Christ. If, however, by sacramental reception is meant that the recipient touches the reality behind the sign as well as the sign alone, then neither animals, nor Jews, nor pagans can be said to receive sacramentally. True to the principles established earlier, Alexander asserted that to receive sacramentally, properly speaking, is to be united either in nature or faith or charity with Christ. Certainly animals cannot then receive. Even Jews and pagans, however they might share in the same human nature as Christ, do not receive sacramentally since they do not understand the reality underlying the signs.[8]

Alexander's discussion of reception is extremely important. Not only do I know of no earlier author who had so explicitly argued that reception was dependent on the intentionality of the receiver, but Alexander's theology would be very influential. At least four important theologians of the next generation would directly or indirectly follow Alexander's theology. The Franciscans, William of Militona and St. Bonaventure, and the Dominicans, Guérric of St. Quentin, and Guérric's most famous student, Albert the Great, all followed Alexander in asserting the importance of a true theology of sign in the reception of the Eucharist.

William of Militona, writing c. 1245–1249, followed Alexander in his lengthy and elaborate explanation of reception. Because it is a sign, understood only by reason or faith, only rational creatures are capable of reception of the *sacramentum et res* of the Eucharist. Irrational animals are only capable of receiving the accidents of the species, that is the *sacramentum*.

Humans can actually consume the Body of Christ, although it is not digested. The Body does enter the stomach so long as the species exist. The species when vomited contain only the accidents, although it is possible that the substance of the bread is miraculously

---

[8]*Ibid.*, p. 699–700 (no. 205–210). E.g.: "Respondeo: manducare sacramentaliter, ut proprie dicitur, est attingere rem sub sacramento; ergo ubi nullo modo attingitur, nec perm modum crediti, nec per modum cogniti, nullo modo est manducatio sacramentalis.vel sacramentaliter; sed est quodam modo manducatio carnalis, et adhuc, proprie non est ibi manducatio carnalis, quia non est ibi divisio substantiae, cum non sit ibi nisi divisio accidentium solum. . . . Ad hoc quod obicitur de Iudaeo vel pagano, dico quod plus est in hac manducatione quam in manducatione irrationalis creaturae, quia unio est ibi in natura. Tamen quia non est ibi cognitio rei sub specie, et cum manducatio sacramentalis importet accipere species et attingere rem quae est sub sacramento fide, non manducant sacramentaliter."

returned.[9] Only rational creatures can receive, though, because the content of the sign can only be reached by faith or knowledge. Animals receive only the accidents with no substance, so it cannot even be called eating. Further, William argued that reception by unbelievers is only accidental as well, but with the potential for sacramental reception.[10]

William summarized his thought in the following manner: "Therefore an animal is united with the accidents alone; for unbelievers, who inwardly believe nothing, is added an aptitude for sacramental or spiritual reception; for those having a deformed faith is added a knowledge of that to which they are united; to those having a true faith, in which charity is included, is added a union of love."[11]

The Dominican master, Guérric of St. Quentin, offered a very similar, although much briefer, discussion of reception in his commentary on the *Sentences*. Guérric held the Dominican chair of theology from 1233–1245, and so it is possible that William used Guérric's discussion in forming his own thought[12]. Guérric held, as did Alexander and William, that only human beings are capable of receiving the Eucharist, as only they are capable of using signs.[13] Further, some of sort of faith is necessary for sacramental reception.[14] Finally, animals are incapable of reception because they lack the necessary intelligence.[15]

---

[9]This is the opinion of Pope Innocent III, *De sacro altaris mysterio libri sex. Liber IV* (PL 215: 863).

[10]William of Militona, *Quaestiones de sacramentis* (ed. C. Piana and G. Gál) (Bibliotheca scholastica medii aevi, vol. 23) (Quaracchi: Florence, 1961), pp. 695–700. For the dating of this work, see the introduction, pp. 5*–33*

[11]*Ibid.*, 701: "Unde brutum unitur solum accidentibus; infidelis nihil penitus credens superaddit quandam aptitudinem ad sacramentalem vel spiritual manducationem; habens fidem informem superaddit quod unitur cognito, habens formatum credito, in quantum habet caritatem unitur ut dilecto."

[12]On the dating for Guérric's reign as master, see James Weisheipl, *Friar Thomas D'Aquino: His Life, Thought & Works* (Catholic University of America Press: Washington, D.C., 1974), pp. 65–66.

[13]"Respondeo secundum diuinam naturam est cibus angelorum. Secundum ultramque Christus est cibus hominum. In Christo enim duplex est natura, humana scilicet et diuina. Et simila in homine duplex, corporalis et spiritualis. Unde homo in ipso plenam inuenit refectionem. Item cibus est hominum secundum duplicem statum, uie scilicet comprehensionis. In utraque enim statu uidetur sed differentur quia in statu comprehendoris, fidem sine uelamine. In statu uero uie sub uelamine fides. Enim accepitur sub speculo et enigmate quia uero uiator non cognoscit sine sensu. Oportet quod uelamen subiectum sit sensui quia uero signum eius quod uelatur oportet quod ducat in illud ideo non sumitur nisi a rationalis, scilicet homo. Ideo solum ab homine sumitur." Guérric of St. Quentin, *Sentences*, Paris, Bibliothéque Nationale, nat. lat. 1604, fol. 36r2. Cf. William of Militona, *op. cit*, p. 702–3.

[14]"Item altera sunt qui habent fidem formatam, aliqui qui habent fidem informem,

These theologians were not the first to suggest that animals con-
suming the species receive only the accidents. This had already been
the teaching of the authors associated with the School at Laon in the
twelfth century.[16] Their contribution was to offer an explanation for
this teaching based on intellectual intention. Only humans can
understand symbols, and therefore only humans can make contact
with the presence of the Lord underlying the symbols (sacramentum) of bread and wine.

Bonaventure, perhaps the greatest of the Franciscan theologians,
followed his predecessors in emphasizing the importance of the
disposition of the recipient in the Eucharist. A long discussion of
this issue occurs in his commentary on the Sentences. Probably
written in the late 1240's or early 1250's, although it is possible that
he revised the commentary during his teaching career which ended
with his election as minister general in 1257.[17] Three conditions are
necessary for true reception: first, one must be capable of intending
the res of the sacramentum; secondly, one must believe; thirdly, one
must understand the significance of the sacrament in order to receive. It is because mice and angels cannot meet these requirements,
that they are incapable of reception.[18]

Bonaventure pointed out that true sacramental reception involves
reception of the sacramentum (the species) as a true sign. First, this
means that the species must be received as food with the intention
of eating them as food. Secondly, the recipient must be capable of
understanding a sign, and in fact of understanding this sign. The
recipient must intend to receive the Body and Blood of Christ as the
Church believes. Therefore, only humans can receive sacramentally.
Bonaventure disagreed slightly with William of Militona over the
question of heretics. Bonaventure conceded that a heretic might

---

aliqui qui neutrum. Si plus accedit ad manducationem secundum susceptionem
sacramenti habens fidem formatam quam habens fidem informem. Ergo qui nullo
modo habent fidem nullo modo accedunt. Ergo nullo modo accepint non habens
fidem formatem uel informem. Ergo tota sumendi est fides non natura. Unde non quia
homo uel rationalis sed quia fideles." Ibid. Cf William, op. cit., p. 716.

[15]"Quod oblicitur de mure. Dico non commedat quia solum sumatur ad illo qui
habet sensum ordinatum ad intelligentiam." Ibid., fol. 36v1.

[16]A. Landgraf, "Die in der Frühscholastik klassiche Frage", p. 207.

[17]See, for instance, David Burr, Eucharistic Presence and Conversion in Late Thir-
teenth-Century Franciscan Thought (Transactions of the American Philosophical
Society, vol 74, part 3) (The American Philosophical Society: Philadelphia, 1984), p.
8.

[18]Bonaventure, Commentaria in quatuor libros sententiarum in Opera Omnia, vol.
4, (Quaracchi: Florence, 1889), p. 204.

receive sacramentally if the heretic intended to accept what the Church believes to be present. With this one exception, Bonaventure's presentation is very similar to William's. Bonaventure, however, articulated more clearly the central role which intention plays in accessing the presence of the Lord by the recipient.[19]

Bonaventure also made clear the distinction between *situs* and *actum* in sacraments. If one objects that the species cannot be separated from the substance of the Body and Blood after the consecration, Bonaventure argued that while this might be true as far as *situs*, that is that the Body and Blood are united to the place of the species, the two may be separated *ad actum*, that is to say that whatever happens to the species does not also happen to the Body and Blood contained under the accidents. Just as the species are broken by the priest and nothing happens to the Body and Blood, so too the species can be received by an animal or infidel without touching the Body and Blood which are contained under this sign. Only through the intention of the recipient to receive what is believed to lie under the species can the Body and Blood be attained.[20]

In his commentary on Distinction 13 of Lombard's fourth book, Bonaventure discussed what would happen if a mouse ate the consecrated species. First, he argued that a mouse receives some food, but does not receive sacramentally or spiritually. Secondly, he argued that just as a mouse cannot be baptized, so a mouse cannot receive the Eucharist.[21] Bonaventure then went on to discuss two different opinions as to what a mouse eats in the sacrament. First he describes the thought of those who argue that since the presence of the Body and Blood lasts as long as the species, therefore as long as the species subsist in the stomach of the mouse, the Body and Blood are also present. The mouse is not truly said to eat the Body and Blood in this case, however, for the mouse cannot reach the Body and Blood either in nature, nor through knowledge nor in love. Bonaventure rejects this opinion for it is an offense to piety to think that the Body and Blood of the Lord might be in the stomach of a mouse.[22]

Bonaventure next discussed the opinion of those who argue that the mouse could never eat the Body and Blood of the Lord, for Christ

---

[19]*Ibid.*, p. 204–5.
[20]*Ibid.*, p. 205.
[21]*Ibid.*, p. 307.
[22]*Ibid.*, p. 308.

is only under the sign in so far as this sign is directed to human use,
and since a mouse is incapable of this, the Body and Blood disappear
and substance of the bread returns. Bonaventure called this opinion
"more common, more honest and more reasonable."[23] Bonaventure
then asked whether the Body and Blood of Christ might descend
into the stomach of a human. He clearly states that in so far as the
effect of the sacrament is concerned, the Body and Blood never
descend into the stomach, but pass into the mind of the believer.
Whether the *substance* of the Body and Blood descends into the
stomach is a more doubtful issue, however. Bonaventure cites four
different opinions here. The first argues that wherever the species
subsist, the substance of the Body and Blood exists, even in the
stomach of a mouse. The second opinion states that the Body and
Blood descend into the stomach of humans alone, and that the
substance remains there as long as the species are suitable for
reception. A third opinion also holds that the substance descends
into the stomach of a human in so far as that act is part of reception,
but the substance does not remain in the stomach of the recipient.
The final opinion recorded by Bonaventure describes the presence
as lasting as long as any part of the species is sensed. After the
species are no longer sensed, the further presence of the Lord is
spiritual, not physical.[24]

Bonaventure pointed out that all four opinions have reasons to
support them, and that it is difficult to judge between them. He
rejected the first opinion again because it would be impious to think
of the Body of the Lord in the stomach of a mouse. He also rejected
the fourth opinion for it lacks tightness of thought. A human being,
after all, can also sense food in his or her stomach. Bonaventure
would, however, accept both of the other positions as probable. It is
probable, therefore, that the Body and Blood are present only so long
as the eating takes place, but that they do not remain in the stomach
of the recipient. It seemed to Bonaventure more probable, and more
reliable to say, however, the Body and Blood remain in the stomach
of the recipient so long as the species have their proper form and are
suitable for human consumption. In opposition to William of Militona, therefore, Bonaventure argues that when the species are vomited up by a sick person, the Body is still present if the species are

---

[23]"Et haec opinio communior est et certe honestior et rationabilior." *ibid.*
[24]*Ibid.*, pp. 310–311.

still recognizable as human food, and so great care must be taken in giving communion to a sick person.[25]

Bonaventure clearly carried on the teaching of both the Franciscans and the Dominican theologians who preceded him. The faith and reason of the recipient determined whether the Body and Blood of the Lord would be present, even in unworthy reception, for that individual recipient.

Bonaventure's contemporary, the Dominican Albert the Great discussed this question at least twice during his long career. His earliest treatment, that contained in his *De sacramentis,* was written c. 1240. In this short discussion, he followed the teaching first expounded by Alexander of Hales. He explained that since the Body of Christ is spiritual food, only an intellectual nature is capable of receiving it. As Augustine had pointed out the outward sign leads to the inner reality and only the intellect can so reach beyond the sign to the reality behind it. Animals then receive only outer forms, the taste of bread and wine. Only humans can understand symbols, and therefore only humans can make contact with the presence of the Lord underlying the symbol *(sacramentum)* of bread and wine.[26]

A much longer and more important discussion of the reception of the Eucharist takes place in Albert's commentary on the *Sentences,* written in 1249.[27] Albert distinguished two ways in which the Eucharist might be said to be received sacramentally, as opposed to spiritually. One could say that in one sense, only the sign is received, with no understanding of what the sign meant. On the other hand, one could receive the sign while understanding its meaning. Infidels can only receive in the first sense.[28] In discussing the requirements for either sacramental or spiritual reception, Albert specified more clearly his concerns in this matter. It is necessary for sacramental reception that some sort of relationship exist between the recipient and thing received. Therefore, at least some sort of faith is required, and so infidels cannot be said to receive. Yet, Albert did not wish to deny that the Body of Lord must be present wherever the species of the bread and wine exist.[29]

---

[25]*Ibid.,* p. 311.

[26]*De Sacramentis* in *Opera omnia,* vol 26 (Aschendorff: Münster, 1985), pp. 65A–B, 66A.

[27]On the dating of Albert's works, see Burr, p. 16.

[28]*Commentarii in Sententiarum,* vol. 29 of *Opera omnia,* ed. August and Emil Borgnet (Paris, 1890–99), *Liber IV, Dist.* 9, *art.* 3 (p. 218).

[29]*Ibid., art.* 4 (p. 219).

Albert attempted to resolve his dilemma in discussing the further question of whether the Body of the Lord can be said to pass into the stomach in reception. He answered by arguing that there are two ways that the Lord's Body can be said to enter into the stomach. The Body could enter the stomach and be digested like any other food, and this is clearly impossible. Secondly, the Body could be said to merely exist in the place where the bread happens to be, that is, in the stomach. In this case, one might say that the Lord's Body does enter the stomach. Albert's problem here has to do with the metaphysics involved in the change. "I do not see, rationally, how the Body of Christ cannot pass into all places into which the species of bread and wine pass, they being the sign under which the whole Christ is contained, according to the truth of the reality signified (res)."[30] In saying this, however, Albert was aware that his opinion ran counter to that of at least some of the other masters, and he was careful to put his ideas forward cautiously. He ended his discussion with the caveat, "And I say this without prejudice, because some masters say the opposite."[31]

Albert made explicit in his commentary that a tension existed between a true sacramental theology and the metaphysics involved in the eucharistic change. If the Eucharist is truly a sign, then only those capable of understanding such a sign can be said to be capable even of unworthy reception of the Body and Blood of the risen Lord. Yet if a true substantial change takes place in the Eucharist, then the Body and Blood must be present wherever the species of bread and wine exist. Albert's solution would seem to be similar to that of Bonaventure. The Body and Blood exist as long as the species can be sensed, but no connection exists between the recipient and the risen Lord except in faith. Albert did go further than any of his predecessors, however, in emphasizing the importance of metaphysics over the theology of sign by insisting that the Body and Blood must be present *everywhere* the species exist. This at least implies that the Body and Blood must be present in the stomach of an animal or infidel, a suggestion Alexander, William and Bonaventure reject. It is no wonder that Albert made this suggestion tentatively.

---

[30]". . . quia non video rationaliter qualiter corpus Christi non transit ad omnem locum, ad quem transeunt species panis et vini, sub quibus secundum veritatem rei continetur totus Christus." *Ibid.*, *art.* 5 (p. 220).

[31]"Et hoc dico sine praejudicio: quia quidam Magistri dicunt oppositum." *Ibid.*

These tentative suggestions would find a full-fledged defense in the work of the most famous of Albert's students, and indeed the most famous of the Dominicans, Thomas Aquinas. Thomas first tackled the subject of eucharistic reception in his commentary on the Lombard's *Sentences*, thought to reflect his teaching in Paris from 1252 to 1256.[32] Thomas accepted two forms of reception, sacramental and spiritual. Sacramental reception entails reception both of the species and of the Body and Blood. Thomas was aware that some theologians admitted forms of reception that included either reception of the species alone or participation in the Mystical Body alone. He accepted the latter, but the former he rejected as inappropriate to the Eucharist, for this would entail a purely accidental reception.[33]

In discussing whether a sinner can receive the Body of Christ, Thomas abandoned the usual arguments in favor of such a reception based on the faith of the sinner. Instead Thomas firmly insisted that sinners receive because the change of the substance of the bread and wine into the Body and Blood of the Lord, once it takes place, cannot be reversed except by another substantial change. As long as the accidents of bread exist, the Body and Blood of the Lord continue in the sacrament. Only when digestion so changes the species that they are unrecognizable, are the Body and Blood separate from the species. Thomas clearly followed Albert on this point, "As long as the species are not changed, there is no way for the Body of Christ to cease to be here."[34] This principle made Thomas' further discussions of this question awkward, for it would assume then that both animals and infidels receive the sacrament, both difficult positions to maintain.

Thomas answered these problems by distinguishing, as Bonaventure had before him, between reception as understood in terms of the thing received and reception in terms of the receiver. In terms of what is received, anyone who receives the species receives the Body and Blood of Christ. In terms of the receiver, however, only those receive who understand this food to be a visible sign of the spiritual reality underlying it. In this sense, neither infidels nor animals can be said to receive the Body and Blood. Thomas explicitly rejected

---

[32]On the dating of Thomas' works, see Weisheipl, pp. 358 ff.

[33]Thomas Aquinas, *Scriptum super sententiis magistri Petri Lombardi* (ed. M.F. Moos) (P. Lethielleux: Paris, 1947), pp. 365–366.

[34]*Ibid.*, p. 368–9. Cf. p. 369: ". . . ideo quamdiu species non mutatur, nullo modo desinit ibi esse corpus Christi: . . .".

the opinion of Bonaventure, however, that animals cannot receive
the Body and Blood as it exists under the signs of bread and wine.
"This reason is not valid because of two things," Thomas insisted.
First, the species are not changed immediately in the stomach of the
animal, and therefore no change can take place in the substance
supporting these accidents. The host could be removed and still be
used. Secondly, just because a thing is not used for its intended
purpose, it does not cease to exist. Therefore, Thomas explained,
the Body and Blood of the Lord are received into the mouth of
animals and descend into their stomach.[35]

Even Thomas seemed somewhat uneasy with this rather disgust-
ing conclusion and in one passage Thomas seemed momentarily to
forget that he had rejected reception of the accidents alone based on
his own metaphysical principles. "Irrational creatures in no way
spiritually eat, nor sacramentally, because they neither use this
eating as a sign, nor eat the sign for the reason that it is a sign.
Therefore infidels are not said to eat sacramentally who intend to
receive what the Church receives, but believe nothing to be here.
And similarly someone who eats a consecrated host, not knowing
that it is consecrated, does not eat sacramentally in that way, because
he does not eat the sign except *per accidens*."[36]

Writing some twenty years later, Thomas, in one of his last
writings, would merely repeat his insistence that the metaphysics of
the sacrament outweigh the importance of the intentionality of the
believer. In the *pars tertia* of the *Summa theologiae*, Thomas presented virtually a repetition of his arguments in the *Commentary on
the Sentences*, and once again, Thomas explicitly rejected Bonaventure's argument against reception by animals.[37]

The significance of this difference has not gone unnoticed by
historians. As early as 1939, the brilliant young Dominican, Yves de

---

[35]*Ibid.*, pp. 370–371.

[36]"Ad tertium dicendum quod creatura irrationalis nullo modo spiritualiter manducat, neque sacramentaliter; quia neque utitur manducato ut sacramento, neque
manducat sacramentum dicitur manducare infidelis qui intendit recipere hoc quod
recipit Ecclesia, quamvis hoc credat nihil esse. Et similiter etiam ille qui manducaret
hostiam consecratam, nesciens eam consecratam esse, non manducaret sacramentaliter aliquo modo, quia non manducaret sacramentum nisi per accidens; nisi quod
plus accederet ad sacramentalem manducationem, inquantum est aptus natus sacramentum ut sacramentum manducare: quod bruto non competit. Nec tamen oportet
quod sit alius modus manducationis tertius a duobus praedictis; quia hoc quod est
per accidens, in divisionem non cadit." *Ibid.*, p. 371.

[37]*Summa theologiae tertia pars*, q. 80 (ed. P. Caramello) (Marietti: Rome, 1956), pp.
488–491.

Montcheuil, pointed out the significantly different understanding of a sacrament that underlies this divergence between Thomas and Bonaventure. More recently the importance of this disagreement has been pointed out by the great liturgist and historian, Pere Pierre-Marie Gy.[38] In summary, Thomas' theology differs significantly from that of not only Bonaventure, but other thirteenth century theologians in insisting that any reception of the accidents also includes reception of the Body and Blood. The necessary metaphysical connection between the accidents of the bread and wine and the substance of the Body and Blood overrode the theological understanding of the Eucharist as a true sign. Like his mentor, Albert, however, he was reluctant to speak of reception by animals or infidels as true sacramental reception. It was more precisely, no reception at all. If metaphysically, the connection between the accidents of bread and wine and the substance of the Body and Blood could not be broken by the intention of the recipient, neither could it be said that there was any connection, even a sacriligious one, between an unintentional recipient and the Body of the risen Lord contained in the sacrament.

Thomas' approach to this question is extremely important. First, his arguments would, of course, carry great weight during and after the Reformation in debates about the Eucharist. Secondly, and more interestingly for historians perhaps, he was outspokenly in disagreement with several prominent predecessors and contemporaries. His was certainly the minority opinion when he taught it, and it seems, remained the minority opinion at least until end of the thirteenth century, and, outside the Dominican order, beyond.

At least two thirteenth century Dominicans who discussed this question either explicitly or implicitly reject Thomas' opinion. Hugh of Strasbourg, a student of Albert writing c. 1265–1270, argued that neither heretics nor infidels nor brute animals can receive the Body and Blood.[39] Nicholas Gorran, the Dominican exegete writing before

---

[38]Yves de Montcheuil, "La Raison de la Permanence du Christ sous les Espéces Eucharistiques d'apres Saint Bonaventure et Saint Thomas," *Mélanges théologiques*, 3rd. ed. (Aubier: Paris, 1951), pp. 71–82.and Pierre-Marie Gy, O.P., "La Relation au Christ dans l'Eucharistie Selon S. Bonaventure et S. Thomas d'Aquin," *Sacrements de Jésus Christ* (J. Dore et al., eds.) (Institut Catholique de Paris: Paris, 1983), pp. 70–106.

[39]"De modis sumendi eucharistiam" Cap. xvi: Corpus Christi quatuor modis sumitur. Quidam accipiunt illud spiritualiter tantum vt qui accipiunt esse sacramenti. id est. gratiam et non sacramentum corporis Christi. De hoc modo sumendi dicit Augustinus Crede et manducasti. id est. corpori Christi mystico incorporatus es.

1285[40] explicitly rejected Thomas' teaching. "It is known," Nicholas stated, "that the Body of Christ is not consumed by animals. Against this (it is argued) that whoever consumes the species containing (it) consumes as well the Body contained therein. I respond that animals do not consume the species as species, that is, according to the relation that they have to that which they contain, but only as (the species) themselves absolutely."[41]

This is not to say that no Dominican authors defended the teaching of Thomas. Peter of Tarentaise, the later Pope Innocent V, writing between 1256 and 1259 accepted as truer Thomas' opinion that animals receive the Body contained under the accidents of bread and wine while rejecting the opinion of Bonaventure. The rest of Peter's discussion of reception, however, depends fairly heavily on Bonaventure rather than Thomas.[42] With John Quidort of Paris, writing in the 1290's, however, a clear defense of Thomas' theology appears. In discussing whether infidels, children or animals receive, John appears to accept Thomas' argument: "Some have said concerning this matter that sinners do not receive. Rather, however, when (the sinner) touches the species of this sacrament with his lips, he touches the substance because as long as the species remain, so long does the true Body of Christ remain nor is there any way in which the substance of the bread is able to return. Therefore whoever receives the *sacramentum*, ought to receive the *rem*, but not the effect. It follows that an infidel receives the *sacramentum et rem* but not sacramentally because they do not receive the sacrament as a signifier."[43]

Quidam sacramentaliter tantum vt communicantes in mortali peccato: quia licet Deus sit vbique per essentiam, non tamen per gratiam. Quidam spiritualiter et sacramentaliter, vt qui accipiuntur rem et sacramentum .id est. communicantes in gratia. Quidam neutro modo, vt qui nec rem nec sacramentum accipiunt vt heretici qui nichil conficiunt. Primi non manducantes manducant. Secundi manducantes non manducant. Tercii manducantes manducant. Quarti non manducantes (non) manducant." Hugh of Strasbourg, *Compendium theologice veritatis* (Paris, 1515), fol. 142v. On Hugh's dates, see Burr, p. 25.

[40]On Nicholas' dates, see the *New Catholic Encyclopedia* (New York, 1967), vol. 10, p. 453.

[41]"Item ibidem glossa. Sciendum quod a brutis corpus Christi non sumitur. Contra. quicumque sumit species continentes sumit contentum corpus. Respondeo bruta non sumant species ut species, scilicet, secundum ordinem quem habent ad contentum sed secundum se absolute." Nicholas of Gorran, *Commentaria ad I Corinthianos*, Paris, Bibliothéque Mazarine, MS 270, fol. 199r2.

[42]Peter of Tarentaise, *Innocentii Qvinti . . . In IV. Librum Sententiarum Commentaria . . .* (Toulouse, 1651; reprinted Gregg Press Inc., Ridgewood, N.J., 1964), pp. 100–103, 142. Cf. Bonaventure, *op. cit.*, pp. 201–2, 310–311. On the dating of this work, see Burr, p. 25.

[43]"Item juxta hoc utrum infideles, pueri et bruta animalia. Ad hoc dixerunt aliqui

John followed Thomas' argument fairly closely. He accepted the teaching of Thomas that it was metaphysically impossible for the species to be separated from the Body and Blood of the Lord without some intervening change in the species, but he was reluctant to follow Thomas further, and remove purely accidental reception as a form of reception.

Meanwhile, Franciscan theologians continued to develop their own theology. John Duns Scotus, surely one of the most famous and influential of the Franciscan masters, taught both in Paris and Oxford. We have reports of the lectures which he gave on the *Sentences* of Peter Lombard in both universities. In Oxford and later in Paris, Scotus consistently taught what might be called the Franciscan line. He did however add his own clarifications. Debate continues on the dating of Scotus' works, but in all likelihood, the two works considered here took final form in last years before his death in 1308.[44] In the Oxford lectures, Scotus described four kinds of reception: 1) one can receive the sacrament, but not sacramentally, 2) one can receive sacramentally, but not spiritually, 3) one can receive the sacrament, both sacramentally and spiritually and finally, 4) one can receive spiritually, but not sacramentally. Scotus was the first, to my knowledge, to admit a separate form of reception as *sacramentum, et non sacramentaliter.* It does describe quite neatly what Albert seems to have had in mind, but Scotus is the first to argue for these four ways to receive the Eucharist.

The subtle doctor went further than his predecessors, too, in determining the importance of intentionality in reception. For Scotus, those who receive only the species includes all who recognize the host only as common food, including heretics and Christians who hold the Eucharist in contempt. The second form of reception includes all who believe the Body of Christ to be present and wish to be joined in union with Christ, whether good or evil Christians.

---

quod peccator non suscipit. Immo substantiam cum labiis tangit species huius sacramenti quia quamdiu maneret species tamdiu manet uerum corpus Christi nec est via quando substantia panis possit redire. Ideo quere recipit sacramentum debet quod recipiat rem sed non effectum. Sequitur infidelis suscepit sacramentum et rem sed non sacramentaliter quia non reficit signum ad signatum." John of Paris, *Sententia,* Paris, Bibliothéque Mazarine 889, fol. 82r1. On the dating of this work, see the introduction to *Jean de Paris (Quidort) O.P., Commentaire sur les Sentences. Reportatio. Livre I* (ed. Jean-Pierre Muller) (Pontificum Institutum S. Anselmi: Rome, 1961) and the *Dictionary of the Middle Ages,* Joseph Stryer (ed.), vol. 7 (Charles Scribners: New York, 1986), pp. 136–7.

[44]On the controversy surrounding the dating of Scotus' works, see Burr, p. 76.

The faithful can receive spiritually whether they receive the consecrated host or merely desire to do so, and thus the four forms of
reception are complete.[45]

In his commentary on the *Sentences* given in Paris, Scotus modi-
fied his position to follow more closely that of the earlier Franciscan
theologian, Richard of Middleton. Scotus here describes three kinds
of reception, 1) *sacramentum et non sacramentaliter* as before, 2)
sacramentum et sacramentaliter, and 3) *sacramentaliter et spiritualiter*. He dropped here the fourth form of reception, spiritual
reception alone. In describing the first two forms of reception, he
closely followed Richard. Anyone, man or beast, who receives without faith, receives only the species. On the other hand, all who
receive with the intention of receiving the Body of Christ do so, and
again Scotus listed the different form of intentionality which this
may take.[46]

Herveus Natalis, writing c. 1301–2, would be the first Dominican
theologian since Thomas to discuss the question of reception at
length. His discussion is an interesting and intelligent blend of the
teachings of Bonaventure, Thomas and Albert.[47]

Herveus began his discussion by modifying slightly the by then
well-known distinction of Bonaventure. One can distinguish between sacramental reception on the part of the sign and sacramental
reception on the part of the recipient. According to the first distinction, all receive sacramently: mice, dogs, and good and evil persons.
According to the second distinction, one can receive in two ways,
either with devotion, and hence spiritually, or without devotion and
hence merely sacramentally.

Whoever receives the consecrated host, whether he or she accepts
it as a sign or not, whether men or animals, all receive the true Body
of Christ because it is impossible that a new substance could come
to exist here unless some further change takes place. Even more
carefully than Thomas, Herveus laid out the metaphysical reasons
why this must be so. He followed Albert, however, in distinguishing
between receiving the sacrament sacramentally, and receiving the
sacrament but not sacramentally. Herveus argued that this distinction applies only to the Eucharist, where it is possible to receive the

---

[45]*Opus Oxoniensis* in *Opera omnia*, vol 17, (Vives: Paris, 1894), p. 75.

[46]*Reportatio Parisiensia* in *Opera omnia*, vol. 24 (Vives: Paris, 1894), pp. 27–8.

[47]On the dating of Herveus' work, see Fredrick J. Roensch, *Early Thomistic School*
(Priory Press: Dubuque, Iowa, 1964), pp. 106–117.

sacrament, but not sacramentally.[48] The discussion of reception by Herveus demonstrates the marked tendency on the part of both Franciscan and Dominican theologians to integrate the most valuable insights of earlier theologians into a coherent whole with a wholesome disregard for factionalism. This tendency will become more apparent in later writers.

Peter of La Palu, the Dominican master whose commentary on the *Sentences* dates from 1310–1312, seems to have lacked his fellow Dominican's subtlety, at least on this point.[49] Peter began his discussion of the modes of reception by asserting two modes of reception, spiritual and sacramental. He based this distinction on canon law. He then went on, however, to describe four modes of reception. The first, both sacramental and spiritual, describes those who receive worthily. The second, neither sacramental nor spiritual, describes those sinners who do not communicate at all. The third, sacramental but not spiritual, describes the reception of sinners who do communicate. Finally, the fourth form of reception describes those who receive spiritually, but not sacramentally.[50]

Peter absolutely insisted that Body and Blood persisted in the sacrament as long as the species remained unchanged. Some of the conclusions Peter drew from this probably would have greatly embarrassed Thomas. Peter not only agreed that sinners and animals really receive the true Body of Christ, but that if the species are vomited up, Christ ought to be considered still present. The fact that such things are not really useable by humans does not touch the implacable Peter.[51]

---

[48]Herveus Natalis, *Hervei Natalis Britonis In quatuor Libros sententiarum Commentaria . . .*, (Paris, 1647; Republished by Gregg Press Limited, Farnborough, Hants. England, 1966), p. 345:1A–2C.

[49]On the dating of Peter's work, see Roensch, pp. 124–131.

[50]"Secunda conclusio est quod est duplex modis manducandi, scilicet spiritualiter et sacramentaliter. *De cons.* d. 3 c. "Quia passus, etc" et "Qui manducat cum multis aliis". Unde aliquis manducat sacramentaliter et spiritualiter vt in fide et charitate comunicans. Alius neutro modo nec sacramentaliter nec spiritualiter, sicut peccator non communicans. Quartus spiritualiter et non sacramentaliter vt iustus non communicans. Sed si habet actu deuotionem ad sacramentum vt deuote audiens missam tunc magis, si tunc magis, si autem desideret communicare aut celebrare nece possit, tunc maxime." *Exactissimi et quorum probati a clarissimi doctoris Petri de Palude predicatorii ordinis . . . quartus sententiarum liber . . .* (Paris, 1514), fol. 35v2.

[51]"Secunda conclusio est quod potest istud sacramentum suscipere: quia eius essentia est materie consecratio quam brutum vere sumit quia vere manducat species sub quibus vere est corpus Christi. Et dato quod per hoc reddantur inhabiles ad vsum hominis propter quem sunt: nihilominus non propter hoc desinit ibi esse benedicta: sed per accidens est: sicut si homo comederet hostiam consecratam quam crederet simplicem: quam si brutum manducare non potuit miraculum est: sicut asinus heretici manducare non potuit: sed flexis genibus hostiam adorauit." *Ibid.*

Peter even went so far as to insist that if it is possible, a mouse which has nibbled the sacred species ought to be trapped, burned and the ashes dumped down the piscina.[52] He did not mention whether the offending mouse was given a chance to repent before taken to the fire. Peter would go further than any thirteenth or fourteenth century theologians with whom I am familiar in asserting a nearly corporeal presence of the risen Lord in the Eucharist. He certainly also rejected the notion that the intentionality of the receiver could in any way affect the presence for that recipient, be he mouse or man. Peter seems to have been the exception, however, in his extremely physicalist interpretation of Thomas.

Nicholas of Lyra, the Franciscan exegete, became a master at the University of Paris in 1309. He wrote his famous commentary on scripture between 1322 and 1339, and died while teaching at Paris in 1349. The commentaries are not the only works ascribed to him, however. A short work entitled *Dicta de sacramento* is also attributed to him. It was published in Cologne in 1480, and then reprinted in 1485, 1490, 1495 and a final time in Paris in 1513. Although the work appears to be genuinely that of Nicholas, little or nothing has been written about it.[53]

The work is a discussion of the conditions necessary for worthy reception of the Eucharist, and clearly relies on the discussion of the Franciscans outlined so far. Nicholas suggested twelve requirements for a worthy reception. One must be a human, a viator (that is still in this life), a believer, an adult, mentally competent, fasting devotely, without awareness of mortal sin, not guilty of notorious crimes, having a clean body, not prohibited by the appearance of a miracle, having a proper minister and finally having a right intention.[54]

Fascinating as some of these requirements might be, my discussion will be limited to the two conditions most interesting for this study, that the recipient be a human and that he or she be a believer. The

---

[52]"Respondeo. si mus potest exenterari debet: et mus quidem debet conburi et cinis in poscina periici." *Ibid.*, fol. 36v2.

[53]For a recent summary of what is known about Nicholas' life and works, see the *Dictionary of the Middle Ages*, vol. 9, p. 126.

[54]"He sunt conditiones necessaria requisite ad idoneum susceptorem sacramenti eucharistie per quas potest responderi ad plures questiones consuetas fieri. Requiritur enim quod sit homo, viator, fidelis, adultus, mente preditus, ieiunus deuotus, sine conscientia peccati mortalis, crimine non notatus, corpore mundus, apparitione miraculosa non prohibitus, a ministro ydoneo tempore debito, intentione recta." Nicholas of Lyra, *Dicta de sacramentis* (Cologne, 1495) The edition is unfoliated.

first condition, according to Nicholas, immediately excludes both animals and angels. If one asks what an animal receives when it eats the sacrament, Nicholas responded that some argue that the Body of Christ ceases to be here. This is the opinion of Bonaventure, although Nicholas does not name him. Nicholas rejects this opinion, however, both on the grounds of authority, and because God has made a special pact with the church that as long as the species exist after consecration the Body of Christ will remain united to them. Nicholas then posited that animals receive really but not sacramentally.[55]

Nicholas explained further when he discussed why the recipient must be a believer. If one asks what unbelievers receive in the sacrament, Nicholas responded that they receive as animals do. Here using the terminology of Albert, Herveus and Duns Scotus, Nicholas argued that there is a difference between receiving the sacrament, and receiving sacramentally. To receive sacramentally, one must understand the signified reality under the sign, and this neither unbelievers nor animals can do.[56]

Nicholas is consistent in his use of these distinctions. Children before the age of reason can receive really, but not sacramentally, just like animals and infidels. In the same way, those who are

---

[55]"Prima conditio est quod sit (homo) per quod statim excluditur omne brutum animal et angelis siue bonus siue malus. Sed si queratur Numquid brutum animal suscipit sacramentum. Dixeratur aliqui quod immediate quando brutum suscepit sacramentum desinit ibi esse corpus Christi. Sed hoc reprobatur a magistro sententiarum in quarto de consecratione. Et similiter in decretis de conse. di.ii.ca. Qui bene non custodierit. Et ideo dicitur ab aliis aliter et melius ut videtur quod quamdiu species ille sacramentales mutare non fuerint per calorem naturalem stomachi: tamdiu remanet ibi corpus Christi. Vnde sicut habemus ex speciali facto diuino quod ad vltimam dispositionem corporis humani deus infundit creando ipsam animam et eam tenet in corpore durante tali dispositionem: sic etiam deus statuit pactum cum ecclesia quod tamdiu esset ipsum corpus Christi sub sacramento quamdiu permanent ille species quam prius afficiebantur et aspiciebant panem sicut subiectum a quo postea miraculose separantur et manu tenentur et propter illud est ut redderet deus ecclesiam certam quando ibi esset corpus Christi et quando non. Recipit ergo brutum realiter et non sacramentaliter et hoc exponam inferius in tercia conditione."Ibid.

[56]"Tertio dixi (fidelis) et intelligo non illum qui de fide solum instructum est sed illum qui iam accepit sacramentum baptismi et factus est per hoc de familia Christi. Ex quo statim patet quod cathecumino quamtamcumque habenti fidem perfectam non debet hoc sacramentum administrari. Sed si queratur Numquid infidelis recipiendo sacramentum recipit corpus Christi dicendum de ipso sicut de bruto supra tactum est quod sumit realiter sed nullio modo sacramentaliter inquantum infidelis. Si queras Numquid idem est sumere sacramentum et sacramentaliter sumere. Dico quod non quia sumere sacramentaliter addit supra sumere sacramentum modum sumendi videlicet quod referat signum in signatum credendo et si opus est confidendo ore quod sub illis speciebus veraciter contincatur corpus Christi quod non facit infidelis nec etaim brutum." Ibid.

mentally incompetent should only receive if they are capable of
giving some sign of devotion, or if they were recently capable of
such a sign. In short, there must be some evidence that these people
are capable of understanding the signification of the species. If not,
they are not capable of sacramental reception.[57]

Nicholas stated the importance of asserting the real presence of
the Body and Blood of the Lord in the Eucharist somewhat more
strongly than earlier Franciscan theologians. As long as the species
exist, so does the Body and Blood, despite what happens to the
species. He equally strongly asserts, however, that the presence is
only there for those capable of understanding that presence. Neither
animals, nor infidels, nor children, nor the mentally incompetent
can understand the sign value of the sacrament, and therefore they
do not have access to the real presence. For them, this might as well
be ordinary food.

Nicholas' presentation is a thoughtful integration of the theologically important insight of Bonaventure and others that since the
Eucharist is a sign, only those capable of understanding this sign are
capable of any form of relationship with the Body of Christ really
present under the accidents of bread and wine. On the other hand,
he was willing to accept Thomas' philosophical insight that as long
as the accidents of bread and wine persist, the substance of the Body
and Blood must continue to underlie the species.

A similar integration of Franciscan and Dominican theology appears in the writing of the Dominican Durand of Saint-Pourçian.
Three versions of his commentary on the Sentences exist, and I have
used the third recension completed c. 1313–1327.[58] Durand would
go further than any previous Dominican writer to reconcile the
insights of both Bonaventure and Thomas. Durand started his dis-

---

[57]"Nunc autem pueri ante annos discretionis et si possunt eucharistiam realiter
sicut quemcumque alium cibum comedere, non tamen possunt hoc sacramentum
sacramentaliter manducare nec eo uti ut sacro signo, referendo significandum in
signatum sed ut communio signo, et sic propter carentiam discretionis non percipiunt
ibi veraciter continere corpus Christi." Ibid. See also: "Si autem sit amentes sic quod
non fit furiosus sed tantummodo loquens inania et a vero sensu alienatus. Adhuc
distinguendum est, quia vel pretendit actus et signa deuotionis tunc potest ei
ministrari, si vero nullum actum aut signum deuotionis pretendit, recurredum est ad
tempus precedens passionem quia si tunc petierit et deuotionem pretenderit et obstet
aliquid aliud periculum, licite potest sibi dari." Ibid.

[58]On the dating of this work, see Weisheipl, p. 343, the New Catholic Encyclopedia,
vol. 4, pp. 1114–16, The Oxford Dictionary of the Christian Church, (2nd ed.) (Oxford
University Press: Oxford, 1974), pp. 433–4, and the Dictionary of the Middle Ages,
vol. 4, pp. 313–4.

cussion of reception by insisting, like Bonaventure, that this sacrament is ordained only to the use of humans. Neither animals, nor even the good angels are capable of reception. Only humans have the capacity and necessity of using temporal signs to reveal veiled spiritual realities, and as the Eucharist functions in just such a way, only humans are capable of reception. Infidels also are incapable of receiving this sacrament per se and the same may be said of the faithful who accept the consecrated host as unconsecrated. Only humans who understand this sign are able to receive it as it is meant to be received. Others receive only the accidents of the bread and wine.[59]

So far Durand would seem a staunch advocate of the theology of Alexander of Hales, William of Melitona and Bonaventure. Durand was, however, also faithful to Thomas' thought. He argued that although animals and infidels only receive per accidens, the true Body and Blood remain under the accidents as long as they are recognizable as bread and wine. Like Thomas, Durand clearly rejected Bonaventure's argument that the presence ceases when animals receive.[60]

Durand, like Nicholas of Lyra, seemed to be searching for some way of expressing the theologically important truth that the Eucharist is really a sign, a sacrament. Those who are incapable of understanding that sign do not participate in the saving action of the Church. Metaphysically, however, it was impossible that the substance of the bread and wine underlying the accidents of bread and wine should disappear without some further transmutation taking place. Durand, like his Franciscan contemporary, Nicholas, went a long way in reconciling these two truths. They both suggested, in their own way, that there are two relationships here. The theologically important relationship between the risen Lord and the believer is determined by the intention and faith of the recipient. The metaphysical relationship between the accidents of the bread and wine and the substance of the Body and Blood was not determined by the faith of the recipient, but then, neither had this relationship, in itself, any saving power.

This compromise, reached at least by the middle of the fourteenth century, is important for two reasons. First, and most importantly, it

---

[59]Durand of Saint-Pourçian, D. Durandi a Sancto Porciano, . . . in Petri Lombardi Sententias Theologicas Commentariorum libri III, (Venice, 1571; Reprinted by The Gregg Press Incorporated, Ridgewood, New Jersey. 2 vols), fol. 312vA–B.
[60]Ibid.

has often been thought (and said and written) that the medieval theologians had lost a true theology of sign, a theology that would only be recovered in the Reformation. This is clearly not the case. Without denying the metaphysical presence of the risen Lord in the sacrament, theologians came to insist that that presence was meaningless unless the recipient understood the signs which pointed to it. This is a true theology of symbols; a theology which focuses not so much on the presence of the Lord in the Eucharist, but rather emphasizes the purpose and function of that presence. Catholics in particular might do well to keep this teaching in mind when in dialogue with their brothers and sisters in the Protestant tradition.

Secondly, the history of the theology of reception rehearsed here would demonstrate once again the toleration for diversity which existed during the central middle ages. Thomas and Bonaventure, at least, certainly disagreed about the relative importance of metaphysical and theological concerns in understanding the real presence. Yet, the diversity of their opinions was not only tolerated, but, on the whole, accepted and developed by later theologians. Condemnations were hurled by neither ecclesiastical officials nor by the competing theological schools. And this could have easily happened. Dominicans were urged by their superiors to support Thomas' thought, and the magisterium was not loathe to step in to settle theological disputes during these centuries.[61]

If there are lessons to be learned from this theological toleration, they surely must include the insight that the history of theology is at its best a history of toleration and diversity; and even such disputed issues as the real presence have a tradition of more breadth than a narrow reading of post-Reformation theology would lead one to believe.

---

[61]The Dominican General Chapter of Paris in 1279 held that no attack on Thomas' work would be tolerated within the order. For details, see Weisheipl, pp. 341 ff.

THE SOTERIOLOGY OF JULIAN OF NORWICH

Lillian Bozak-DeLeo

The theological insights of Julian of Norwich seem to be the direct result of her mystical experience. This is particularly true of her understanding of Redemption. Her perception of sin and of God's reaction to it did not corespond to what she knew as the Church's teaching on this issue. She found herself unable to reject the insight that came as a result of her visions, but she also found it impossible to substitute her own view for that of the received theology, since she was convinced that the Church's position must be accepted. By her own account, this conflict troubled her for years. The Long Text of her *Showings*, composed twenty years after the visions them-selves, reflects the resolution of this conflict. It contains the two important aspects of her thought which relate precisely to this point and which are not found in the Short Text, written just after her visions: the parable of the Lord and the Servant, and the image of the Motherhood of Christ.

It is particularly instructive to compare Julian's soteriology to that of Anselm's *Cur Deus Homo*, for two reasons; because Anselm's explanation of the redemption has dominated theological thought from his century to our own, and secondly because the interpretation that gave Julian so much trouble, since it seemed incompatible with her own insight, was apparently that of Anselm. They provide an interesting contrast: two quite different ways of interpreting the Redemption. The difference between them seem to flow from differ-ences in theological method (although Julian would probably object to such a term being applied to her writing), and in the fundamental insight into the nature of God. It is an intriguing example of the theology of the Schools coming into conflict, or apparent conflict, with a more personalistic theology.

Anselm, like all Scholastics, sought to explain in a logically satisfying way the truths accepted in faith: *fides quaerens intellec-*

tum. The *Cur Deus Homo* is entirely based on the presupposition that, beginning with the doctrines of the Incarnation and Redemption, purely rational arguments could be found to demonstrate their truth and necessity, convincing even to an unbeliever. Such reasoning, to be sure, must be subordinated to the authority of the Church: he insisted that any argument, however conclusive it seemed, was to be taken as only his personal opinion unless it were corroborated by higher authority.[1]

Although she would have agreed with the last point, Julian's approach was quite different; a search for logical arguments was not her primary concern. The bases for her theology were the insights, particularly her perception of God, that resulted from her mystical vision. This she could not set aside, being convinced that it was a direct revelation from God. She spoke of it as "the higher judgment which God himself revealed . . . and therfore I had of necessity to accept it."[2] Her insights had to be explained and their implications developed but, unlike Anselm, Julian did not feel the need to fit her insights into a logical and legalistic system. As a result, her views, although consistent in themselves and with Scripture, do not have the same logical completeness as those of the Scholastics. This would have been seen as a flaw in the Middle Ages; today it can be seen as an asset. Nevertheless, like Anselm, Julian could not take her own insight as absolute; she did feel obligated to find it in correspondence with the teachings of the Church, so she was greatly disturbed when she was unable to do so.

If Julian and Anselm were not in agreement on the method to be used in interpreting the Redemption, neither were they in agreement on the primary attribute of the deity. Anselm's writings make it clear that, for him, divine justice was the one attribute to which all others must be subordinated. Thus, his entire explanation of the Redemption and the resultant necessity for the Incarnation was based completely on the requirements of divine justice. God's mercy, God's love, God's compassion, all took second place. Julian, on the other hand, perceived divine love to be God's predominant attribute. The whole of the divine activity in Incarnation and Redemption was determined by God's love for us. The requirements of divine justice,

---

[1]Anselm of Canterbury, *Cur Deus Homo,* Book I, Chap. 2, in *St. Anselm: Basic Writings,* trans. S. N. Deane (La Salle, Ill.: Open Court, 1961), p. 181.
[2]Julian of Norwich, *Showings,* trans. Edmund Colledge and James Walsh (New York: Paulist, 1978), Chap. 45, p. 256. All references to the *Showings* are to the Long Text.

divine honor, even divine omnipotence, were subordinated to divine love.

Naturally, one's focus on either justice or love as the primary attribute of God would determine one's interpretation of sin and redemption: precisely the issue that caused Julian such great difficulty for so many years. She was very much aware of her own sinfulness, and very clear that a sinner deserves nothing but divine wrath and blame. She knew from the teaching of the Church that God was constantly angered by human sins and ready to punish the sinners severely. She lived in the late fourteenth century when much of Europe had just been devastated by the Black Death, the time of the Hundred Years War, economic depression, the Avignon Papacy and the Great Western Schism. It is incredible that she would not have viewed the calamities overwhelming Europe as divine punishment for the sins of the Church and the world. But she did not. Her revelations gave her a vision of God that simply was not compatible with such an explanation. She saw human evaluation of sin and sinners as stern and judgmental, but the divine judgment she saw as always "good and lenient."[3] God assigns to humans "no kind of blame," since he constantly sees us in the light of "his own great endless love."[4] In fact, Julian saw the very being of God as love and goodness, so much so that she could find in God no room at all for anger or blame. Her frustration came from her inability to reconcile this perception of God with the contemporary theological view of God's anger at sin which required punishment or propitiation. This commonly accepted interpretation was certainly based largely on Anselm's soteriology, even though his understanding of God's impassivity left no place for divine anger at sin. Still, Anselm's God was too distant to be angry, Julian's was too involved.

Anselm's stress on the demands of divine justice and dignity led him to consider sin solely as an offense against the honor of God, as "nothing else than not to render God his due."[5] In this context, every sin requires satisfaction: the honor stolen from God must be restored but, since every sin involves contempt directed toward one of infinite dignity, the restoration must be greater than what is owed for the initial offense. This puts mankind into a double bind. Since every human owes everything to God anyway, there is no way for any

---

[3]Ibid.
[4]Ibid., p. 257.
[5]Anselm, Bk. I, Chap. 11, p. 202.

human to pay God more than is owed. Also, since Adam's sin
corrupted human nature, no human can avoid sin, so with each
additional sin our debt increases and the possibility of adequate
recompense decreases. Furthermore, humans are blameworthy both
for their sins and for their inability to repay God the debt owed him.
Anselm uses an image of a slave to illustrate this point, an image
which provides an interesting contrast to a similar image in Julian's
writing. Anselm speaks of a master giving a specific task to a slave
and warning him about a ditch from which he could not extricate
himself, were he to fall into it. If the slave went out and threw
himself into that ditch so that he was unable to complete the task he
was given, he would be doubly guilty: guilty of not doing the task he
was assigned and also guilty of doing what he was warned not to do.
Thus Anselm concluded that humans are doubly guilty: for not
paying the debt they owe to God and for their incapacity to do so.[6]
Hence, of course, the necessity for atonement by the God-man who
alone does not owe the debt of death to God, so his death alone
could be the super-eminent recompense.

From Anselm's perspective, the necessity of such repayment is
absolute. It would be contrary to divine justice, and therefore contrary to the divine nature, for God to forgive sin without receiving
sufficient satisfaction for the sin. For Anselm, divine compassion
and even divine omnipotence are constrained by the requirements
of divine justice. He argues that it would not be proper or fitting "for
God to put away sins by compassion alone, without any payment of
the honor taken from him" because to do so would leave no distinction between the guilty and the not-guilty, which would not be
fitting for God.[7] Indeed, Anselm argues that such an action would be
impossible for God: "Even God cannot raise to happiness any being
bound at all by the debt of sin, because he ought not to."[8] The
requirements of justice limit God's omnipotence, as well as his
compassion. The compassion of God, in Anselm, is shown by his
willingness to send the Son to fulfill the demands of divine justice,
so that God's work in creating humans would not be wasted. And,
as we have seen, it is precisely the death of Christ that is needed to
satisfy divine justice. The Resurrection and the resultant unity of
Christians with Christ have no essential role in Anselm's logical
argument.

---

[6]Ibid., Chap. 24, pp. 233–34.
[7]Ibid., Chap. 12, pp. 203–04.
[8]Ibid., Chap. 21, p. 230.

Julian focuses on exactly those elements that Anselm ignores. It is quite understandable why his approach gave her such trouble. She simply could not see how it could be compatible with her own perception of the centrality of divine love. Her view of the necessity of the Incarnation and of the death of Christ are quite different. At first, she did concentrate on the Passion and death of Christ, which would be expected considering the prevalence of devotion to the Passion in the late medieval period. Her initial prayer was that God give her a vision of the Passion so that she could experience the sufferings of Jesus.[9] Her visions were almost all of the suffering and dying Christ. The surprising thing is that she did not draw from this experience a sense of God's anger at sin, nor the idea that God was somehow pleased by suffering. Instead, her entire discussion of her visions, even in the Short Text, centers on God's great love for humans and even on God's delight in us.

The Short Text contains no resolution of Julian's problem of correlating her perception of God's love with what she understood to be the Church's teaching about God's anger at sin. Whenever she tried to confront this problem, God simply revealed to her that "all will be well," but she was unable to perceive how it would be so.[10] In the Long Text, she tells us that after twenty years of being troubled by this, God finally gave her the answer she sought through a new insight into the Parable of the Lord and the Servant, apparently a part of her original series of visions which she did not fully understand at the time. This vision was of a Lord, seated upon his throne, looking with love upon his servant who stands before him, ready to do his bidding. So the Lord gives the servant a task, and the servant runs off, eager to do his Lord's will. But the servant falls as he runs and severely injures himself, so that he cannot rise or help himself in any way. His sufferings come from his physical hurt, but even more from the fact that he is unable to carry out the Lord's wishes and is unable to see the Lord's face. In the vision, Julian looked closely at the face of the Lord, to see if he blamed the servant in any way for falling, but she could find no blame nor anger directed toward the servant, but only love and concern. Indeed, the Lord thought it proper to reward the servant for his suffering in the service of the Lord. Julian at first identified the servant with Adam, and was puzzled by the fact that some of the servant's characteristics did not

---

[9]Julian, Chap. 2, p. 178.
[10]Ibid., Chap. 32, p. 233; cf. Short Text, Chap. xv, p. 151.

fit Adam. After twenty years when she was given the new insight,
she recognized that the servant represented both Adam and Christ:
Adam, inasmuch as the servant fell and was injured and in great
pain, unable to rise on his own and unable to look upon the face of
the Lord; and Christ, inasmuch as the servant stood ready to do the
will of the Lord, and loved the Lord and, upon receiving the
command, rushed off to do his bidding. Julian also realized, from
this, that Christ and Adam are united: both represent humanity.
When Adam and, with Adam, all mankind fell into sin and thus into
hell, the Son of God fell too, into the womb of the virgin in order to
remove all blame from Adam and to save him from hell.[11] Indeed,
Julian perceived this union of Christ with Adam as unbreakable:
"because of the true union that was made in heaven, God's Son
could not be separated from Adam, for by Adam I understand all
mankind."[12] So, in Julian's understanding, it is the Incarnation itself
that is salvific, not just the Passion and Death. We are redeemed
precisely by being brought into union with God through our participation in the one who unites the divine and human natures. Thus,
she says, the Father assigns no more blame to us than he does to his
Son.[13]

The contrast with Anselm's image is obvious, and amazing. For
Anselm, the servant sinned deliberately and is guilty both of not
completing his assigned task and of winding up in the ditch he had
been warned against. He, representing mankind, is still required to
pay the debt he owes, even though it is impossible for him to do so.
Throughout this discussion, the master, or God, seems to remain in
the role of a distant judge, evaluating the situation in the light of
strict legalistic justice.[14] In Julian's parable, however, the servant fell
inadvertently and was not blamed by the Lord. In fact, once the
servant had fallen and hurt himself, the Lord left his throne and sat
on the bare ground in the wilderness, waiting patiently and compas-
sionately for the servant's return. Julian explains this as showing
that God, having created the human soul to be the divine dwelling
place, was unwilling to provide another abode after Adam had fallen
and lost his ability to be that dwelling place. So the Father waited
patiently until the time when the Son took on human nature and
made it once again a thing of grace and beauty where God could

---

[11]Ibid., Chap. 51, pp. 267–78.
[12]Ibid., p. 274.
[13]Ibid., p. 275.
[14]Anselm, Bk. I, Chap. 23–24, pp. 232–33.

remain.[15] For Julian, as for Anselm, the Incarnation is absolutely necessary, but its necessity in her eyes is the result of God's love and compassion for humanity in its need, not the result of strict divine justice.

Julian's approach to sin, as seen in this parable, is also very different from Anselm's. She nowhere views sin as an offense against divine justice, a withholding of the honor due to God. Hers is a more personalistic approach, sin seen from the human perspective as an injury to human nature. It is our nature to be united to God, so sin, by separating us from God, is truly an unnatural state. We are entirely unable to remedy this situation. In Julian's images, we cannot heal the wound in our nature, restore our unity with God, or heal the blindness which prevents us from seeing God. We have an absolute need for redemption. And redemption, for Julian, is not the repayment of a debt owed to God, but the re-establishment of the union with God that can best be called mystical. We are one with Adam in his fall, which separated us from God, and we are reunited with God through our oneness with Christ. It is the Incarnation itself that brings humanity into union with divinity in the person of Christ. We are brought into that union by being brought into Christ as his members. Her stress on the Incarnation does not lead Julian to ignore or deny the importance of the Passion: in speaking of the Incarnation as the falling of the Son into human nature, she points out that this falling caused him great hurt. In his human flesh, Christ suffered all the pains of mankind in his Passion. But she does not view this suffering as demanded by the Father. She simply speaks of Christ's death as necessary before he could rise, and stresses the Resurrection as the point where human nature is restored to the beauty the Father willed for it.[16] The Passion and Death is not the central focus of Julian's soteriology, as it is in Anselm's. She places her emphasis on the Father's pleasure in the Son's bringing humanity back into union with God through the Resurrection.

Julian's Incarnational Soteriology is completed by the second image that is found only in the Long Text, that of the maternity of Christ. She introduces this image immediately after the Parable of the Lord and the Servant, and as the result of its insights. Christ is our mother because we are always united to him in his risen state (though at the same time we are always united to Adam in his sinful

---

[15]Julian, Chap. 51, pp. 271–72.
[16]Ibid., Chap. 51, pp. 277–78.

state), so we are enclosed constantly in God's love, just as a child is
enclosed constantly in its mother's love.[17] He is our mother in our
creation since we take our being from him: our nature, which can be
fulfilled only through our loving union with God, is taken from his
divine nature which is love itself. And this love never fails. Even
when humanity fell into sin, there was a part of our being, which
Julian calls a "godly will," that never turned away from God (at least
this is true of all those who are predestined to salvation).[18] More
importantly, God never turned from us and never ceased to love us.
Because of this constant divine love, Christ is also our mother in our
redemption: by grace he returns us to the place we belong, in union
with God in love. Julian describes the earthly life of Christ, and
particularly the Passion, as the process of his giving birth to us "for
joy and endless life."[19] At one point, she speaks of the entire life of
Christ from the Incarnation to the Resurrection as labor (though not
explicitly as the labor of childbirth);[20] at another, she does explicitly
compare the pains of his Passion to the pains of childbirth.[21] This
act of giving birth was an act of love on Christ's part, but his love
did not end there.

Julian's image of Christ's motherhood is not limited to giving
birth. In addition to giving us life, he nourishes us with his body
just as a mother feeds her child with milk from her own body.[22] But
Julian goes even farther: Christ also protects and comforts us. He
even allows us to fall into sin just as a mother sometimes allows her
child to fall and get hurt in order to learn something. When we do
fall into sin, we are made aware of our own weakness and of God's
great love for us. These two realities coexist within us: even when
we are so caught in "the darkness of sin that we cannot see clearly
the blessed face of our Lord God,"[23] we are still united to God in
Christ, sharing in his life and his love. The lack of love is only on
our side. The darkness and blindness is on our side. The anger is on
our side. God never changes, never stops loving us, never stops

---

[17]Ibid., Chap. 52–54, pp. 279–86.
[18]Ibid., Chap. 53, pp. 282–85.
[19]Ibid., Chap. 60, p. 298.
[20]Ibid., Chap. 23, p. 219.
[21]Ibid., Chap. 60, p. 298.
[22]Caroline Walker Bynum in *Jesus as Mother: Studies in the Spirituality of the High
Middle Ages* (Berkeley: Univ. of Calif. Press, 1962), pp. 150–54, points out that the
lactating mother was one of the most common maternal images applied to Christ in
the late medieval period.
[23]Julian, Chap. 72, p. 321.

wanting us to be united to him. So Christ never stops wanting us to run to him for comfort in our hurt, just as a child runs to its mother. He will comfort us, clean and heal our wounds, and again restore our true nature.[24] Throughout, he never ceases to love us and to delight in us.

The centrality of God's love in Julian's thought is obvious throughout, not merely in the content of her writings, but especially in their tone. She stresses love as the very being of God, as the core of human nature, as divine motivation for the redemption, and as the determining factor in our present relationship with God. This perception culminates in her image of the divine motherhood of Christ, which provides a sense of the warm, caring involvement of God with humanity that no abstract discussion could give. Julian's summary, as she concludes her development of the divine motherhood, shows this:

> . . . in accepting our nature he gave us life, and in his blessed dying on the cross he bore us to endless life. And since that time, now and ever until the day of judgment, he feeds us and fosters us, just as the great supreme lovingness of motherhood wishes, and as the natural need of childhood asks.[25]

The content, the imagery, the focus, the emotional tone of Julian's soteriology is very different from Anselm's. Yet both work from the same doctrines of Christianity: the seriousness of sin, the inability of humans to leave their sinful state, the absolute necessity for the Incarnation and Redemption. Anselm's summary of his argument clearly shows these points of contrast and similarity with Julian's:

> [it has been shown] by numerous and positive reasons . . . that the restoring of mankind ought not to take place, and could not, without man paid the debt which he owed God for his sin. And this debt was so great that, while none but man must solve the debt, none but God was able to do it; so that he who does it must be both God and man. And hence arises a necessity that God should take man into unity with his own person; so that he who in his own nature was bound to pay the debt, but could not, might be able to do it in the person of God.[26]

---

[24]Ibid., Chap. 61–63, pp. 300–04.
[25]Ibid., Chap. 63, p. 304.
[26]Anselm, Bk. II, Chap. 18a, pp. 278–79.

The logic is impeccable, the centrality of divine justice is evident. But, I think, ultimately unsatisfying.

Anselm's explanation of the absolute necessity for the Incarnation and Crucifixion, based on the demands of divine justice, was satisfying to his contemporaries because of its rational completeness. But the image of God that permeates the *Cur Deus Homo*, a God of justice and dignity who remains essentially untouched by human needs and whose concern is primarily his own honor, is much less appealing in today's world. Julian's Incarnational Soteriology, with her focus on a God of love who is as involved with us as a mother is with her own child, corresponds much more closely to current theological emphases. We too are inclined to focus on the loving nature of God and on the transformative nature of our union with Christ, more than on the juridical elements of the classical doctrine of expiation. We have lost sight of the extent to which this approach is also a part of our Christian tradition, a part which is well worth recovering. Julian provides us with one of its most beautiful and compelling expressions. The sense of divine love permeates her writing from beginning to end, and her final words show its centrality for her:

> What, do you wish to know your Lord's meaning in this thing? Know it well, love was his meaning. Who reveals it to you? Love. Why does he reveal it to you? For love . . . So I was taught that love is our Lord's meaning. And I saw very certainly in this and in everything that before God made us he loved us, which love was never abated and never will be. . . . In this love we have our beginning, and all this shall we see in God without end.[27]

---

[27]Julian, Chap. 86, pp. 342–43.

THEOLOGY AS UNIVERSITY: ERASMUS' CONVERSATIONAL IMPERATIVE

Terence J. Martin, Jr.

As a discipline in the university, theology holds an awkward, even tenuous, position. By the nature of the discipline as it has come down to us, every theologian is bound up with the demands and expectations of three distinct "publics": theological inquiry must be faithful to the church, credible to the academy, and responsible to society. As David Tracy notes, this complex social reality proper to theology precludes any simple or "wholesale" strategy.[1] Theology cannot afford to speak with a single voice, for it is obligated to speak fluently in the language of each public. Theologians must engage in several conversations at once. But in attempting this feat, the responsible theologian inevitably will be pulled and stretched by the rival, frequently conflicting questions, demands, and standards of accountability proper to each of these publics. Conflicts between ecclesiastical officials and academic theologians, debates about the differences between theology and religious studies, criticisms from social activists that academicians are over-intellectualized and under-involved, and the glaring differences in perspective between theologians and ordinary church people are symptoms of the fractured discourse which results when theologians face such varied audiences.

Given this social reality and the pressures it puts on theological inquiry, it is imperative that theologians discover and cultivate appropriately complex ways to deal clearly and persuasively with each of theology's three natural publics. Toward this end, I will present a rudimentary study of theological discourse, using the colloquies and dialogues of Erasmus as models of theological conversation. Literary dialogues, especially ones as lively as Erasmus'

---

[1]David Tracy, *The Analogical Imagination; Christian Theology and the Culture of Pluralism* (New York: Crossroad, 1981), p. 26.

colloquies, provide useful models for the analysis of discourse, since they graphically portray the possibilities, the obstacles, and the achievements of theological conversation.[2] As a genre of theological writing, the dialogue creates a world of discourse, filled with diverse characters whose interaction imitates (albeit in a highly stylized manner) the natural rhythms of actual discussion. Unlike the ordered, monological world of the treatise, the dialogue attempts to bring discourse down to earth, placing it squarely in a concrete social setting, where every utterance and every position must be hammered out in the give and take of social interaction. In this regard, Erasmus boasts that "whereas Socrates brought philosophy down from heaven to earth; I have brought it even into the games, informal conversations, and drinking parties."[3] As a result, these texts can prove to be particularly useful tutors: they can instruct us in the communicative virtues and skills (e.g., openness, criticism, persuasiveness, humor, etc.) which are necessary if theologians are to respond rationally to the different publics' challenges, that is, by creating and sustaining common space where the many voices and interests can converse together intelligently and productively.

I turn to Erasmus because he was acutely aware of the role of speech in the human project of building and sustaining civilized communities. For Erasmus, it is speech which makes us human, it is the failure of human discourse which makes us barbaric, it is speech (God's "sermo") which reconciles us to God, and it is good speech (conversation) which heals the burdened soul and reconciles human relationships.[4] So too for theology, which Erasmus portrays in his colloquies and throughout his correspondence as a colloquial enterprise in imitation of Christ's reconciling work. As Marjorie O'Rourke Boyle puts it, for Erasmus,

> The theologian is a colloquial man (sic). He converses with the Text and with its best commentaries. In imitation of Christ, God's own eloquent oration, he shares discourse with others in a renaissance of life and letters. The scholarship of Erasmus, standing bent over his manuscripts alone, is not solitary, but an imitative sermo, a textual

---

[2]Terence J. Martin, Jr., "The Social Rationality of Theological Discourse," *Horizons* 13 (1986), 23–42.

[3]Erasmus, "The Usefulness of the Colloquies" in Craig R. Thompson, ed. and trans., *The Colloquies of Erasmus* (Chicago and London: The University of Chicago, 1965), p. 630.

[4]Marjorie O'Rourke Boyle, *Erasmus on Language and Method in Theology* (Toronto: University of Toronto, 1977), pp. 40–47.

conversation with ancient and contemporary men. It flowers into a
"godly feast", a colloquy of devout men wisely explaining Scripture to
one another.[5]

Although Erasmus was extremely critical of the kind of theology
done in the universities of his own day—preferring the freedom of
the non-attached scholar and gravitating to small, familial "academies" like Aldus Manutius' Venetian publishing house—he was
utterly clear about the kind of discourse which is required in the
academy, in the church, or in society. I suggest, therefore, that
Erasmus offers us important lessons about the kind of theological
practices required today. He elucidates the ever-present reality of
adversarial situations, he tutors us in the art of conversation, and
thereby, he holds out the possibility that the interaction of the many
(the different publics, their interests, and their practices) will be
"turned toward the one," i.e., that the different voices will constitute
a "university" as a place and practice of turning co-operatively
toward common truth and welfare. I contend that theology will
function well in what we today call the university, only if it responds
to Erasmus' conversational imperative and hence becomes a university in its communicative practices.

In the next three sections, I will review examples of theological
discourse in the academy, in the church, and in the wider society,
drawing on the relevant fictional conversations from the colloquies
and dialogues of Erasmus. I will restrict my focus to these texts,
leaving analysis of Erasmus' correspondence (a record of his actual
practice of dialogue) to another study. My approach throughout will
be descriptive: listening in on the conversations of Erasmus' characters, I will try (1) to isolate the significant adversaries in each public,
thereby describing the challenges they present to theological speech,
and (2) to distill the various communicative strategies required for
theological response to these challenges, thereby outlining the shape
of rational theological discourse. The final section will examine
Erasmus' imperative to theological conversation and its importance
for theology today.

I. Theology in the Academy

In its efforts to be theoretically credible, theology has long made
use of the methods and wisdom of other academic disciplines.

---

[5]Ibid., p. 130.

However, in Erasmus' day, as in our own, significant voices disputed the intellectual marriage of theology and the secular disciplines. The "uneducated crowd," he reminds us in "The Antibarbarians," has a natural dislike of letters.[6] Even those with potential remain ignorant under the tutelage of local schoolmasters ("petty tyrants") who are dedicated to "the unteaching of everything which concerns Good Letters" (28); and people are naturally and easily swayed to abhor someone with learning by those monks "who dress up in the mask of religion" (36 and 34). "Beware," they say, "he's a poet, he's no Christian" (34). Anti-intellectual preachers "cry their wares by claiming to be men of religion" yet "think it the height of piety to know nothing" (32). They assume that "pure religion and consummate learning" are incompatible, since the former rests on faith while the latter ests on questions and argument. Abbots, it seems, "would rather rule over sheep than men," since educated monks are "less tractable than the ignorant" (25). Besides, retorts an abbot in one of Erasmus' colloquies, "Bookishness drives people mad."[7] Worst of all is the campaign against the humanities waged by the scholastic theologians of Paris and Louvain. They question the infusion of the new learning into the Christian world, charging the humanist theologians with "rejecting Christian writers and bringing in heathen ones."[8] Clearly, if theology is to have a place in the world of secular learning, then it must justify it and defend it.

In "The Antibarbarians", Erasmus sets out to defend the cause of learning against the various anti-intellectual voices of his day. He marshals a long series of counter-arguments to justify the use of pagan wisdom by Christian scholars: it is false piety (and envy) which praises hatred of other peoples' learning (49–51); if we are to take nothing from the pagan world, then much of Western culture will be lost (57); and critics confuse the misuse for the use of learning (63). Frequently, he takes a more offensive tack, suggesting that the authorities are simply bolstering their own rule by making sure no one can correct their ignorance (63 and 68); or boldly noting that the scholar's defence of the faith in times of stress has contributed more to the growth of the Christian religion than the blood of

---

[6]Erasmus, "The Antibarbarians," trans. Margaret Mann Philips, in Craig R. Thompson, ed., Collected Works of Erasmus, 23 (Toronto: University of Toronto, 1978), pp. 32 and 36.

[7]Erasmus, "The Abbot and the Learned Lady" in Thompson, ed., Colloquies, p. 222.

[8]Erasmus, "The Antibarbarians," p. 38.

martyrs (83). It is more significant, however, when the Erasmian
speaker (one of many lay theologians in these texts) claims that the
liberal disciplines (all of which have a pagan origin) fully "concern
Christ" (90). With Augustine, he argues that "everything in the pagan
world that was valiantly done, brilliantly said, ingeniously thought,
diligently transmitted, had been prepared by Christ for his society,"
(60) so that Christians may make free use of the wisdom and speech
of non-Christian culture (97). But Erasmus intends a stronger advocacy of the academic disciplines than Augustine: the Christian not
only "may" but "should" appropriate pagan learning, since classical
wisdom is fully Christ's work (60–1). There is no hint in the
Erasmian line of argument that classical learning was "stolen from
the Hebrews" or that it is an unimportant, merely passing stage of
revelation. Against the anti-intellectuals of his day, Erasmus fully
affirms the value of the secular disciplines for Christian reflection.[9]
Christians should imitate both "the moral virtues of the apostles
and at the same time the learning of Jerome."[10]

But while Erasmus argues vehemently for theological openness to
secular learning, he must contend with another group which uncritically and narrowly identifies itself with one or another school of
classical thought. In "The Ciceronian: A Dialogue on the Ideal Latin
Style," Erasmus engages a character named Nosoponus ("Mr. Work-
mad") who has dedicated himself to achieving perfect and complete
fidelity to Cicero's Latin style. He has, in fact, "touched no books
but Ciceronian ones" for seven years, all for the sake of gaining the
appellation of "Ciceronian" from the Italian Latinists he reveres.[11]
His devotion admits of "no exceptions. No one," he tells his interlocutors, "will be Ciceronian if even the tiniest word is found in his
works which can't be pointed to in Cicero's opus" (349). Slowly but
surely, in fine Socratic fashion, the Erasmian speakers lead Nosoponus to see that such an ideal is impossible to attain, since the
"whole Cicero" which he seeks to replicate is not even present in
Cicero's corpus (363, 369). Such an endeavor is, in fact, unfaithful to
Cicero, since Cicero was an orator who adapted his speech to the

---

[9]Marjorie O'Rourke Boyle, Christening Pagan Mysteries; Erasmus in Pursuit of
Wisdom (Toronto: University of Toronto, 1981), pp. 3–25.
[10]Erasmus, "The Antibarbarians," p. 112.
[11]Erasmus, "The Ciceronian: A Dialogue on the Ideal Latin Style," trans. Betty I.
Knott, in A.H.T. Levi, ed., Collected Works of Erasmus, 28 (Toronto: University of
Toronto, 1986), p. 346. Compare Erasmus, "The Echo," in Thompson, ed., Colloquies,
pp. 373–77.

subject (396) and to the situation (407), critically learning from
many different sources (399, 401) rather than narrowly imitating one
style from one source. The lead Erasmian speaker, Bulephorus
(meaning "Counselor"), advises Nosoponus to move beyond unimaginative imitation, for "it's inevitable that imitation falls short when
it tries only to follow a model, not to surpass it" (377; cf. 399 and
406). The true imitator of Cicero will "read all the best writers and
extract from the best the best they have to offer" (446; cf. 402). Then,
digesting their wisdom critically, he or she will speak creatively
from the heart "in the best and most appropriate way, even though
. . . in a manner very different from Cicero's" (399).

Erasmus finds Nosoponus' Ciceronian ideal narrow and suffocat-
ing. Indeed, as a habit of mind and a policy for thinking, he regards
this intellectual narrowness as thoroughly inappropriate for serious
Christian thinking. "It's paganism, believe me, Nosoponus, sheer
paganism, that makes our ears and minds accept such an idea"
(394). In making this charge, Erasmus is not rejecting Cicero because
he is pagan, for as we have seen, he affirms the inherent value of
classical learning.[12] What he rejects is not the paganism of Cicero,
but the paganism of these so-called Ciceronians. Their uncritical
and unimaginative devotion to Cicero's rhetoric blinds them from
appreciating wisdom from Christian sources: "how we gasp and gaze
in admiration if we get hold of a statue of one of the gods of the
ancient world, even a bit of statue; but the image of Christ and his
saints get hardly a glance from our prejudiced eyes" (395). Indeed,
their obeisance to Cicero even prevents them from profiting from
Cicero, since they are afraid to adapt his wisdom usefully and
persuasively to the needs of the Christian world. In a word, "anyone
who can be Ciceronian only by being unchristian is not even Ciceronian" (447). The true Ciceronian, the Erasmians counsel, is the one
who creatively adapts Cicero's ideals to Christian audiences, as
Cicero would himself do "if he were living today as a Christian
among Christians" (392). The Christian thinker should aspire to
combining Cicero's "supreme powers of expression with the faith of
Christ" (338; cf. 400).[13]

The Christian theologian who works in the academy must deal
with adversaries on two fronts: one which questions the propriety of

---

[12]Boyle, *Christening Pagan Mysteries.*
[13]See Geraldine Thompson, *Under Pretext of Praise: Satiric Mode in Erasmus'
Fiction* (Toronto: University of Toronto, 1973), p. 147.

serious intellectual inquiry and one which exclusively and uncritically adopts one favored conceptual system and its methods at the expense of everything else. As Erasmus shows us, the theologian's strategy must be appropriately nuanced. To the anti-intellectual, one must show the necessity and utility of critical inquiry, and to the loyal party-intellectual, one must show the virtue of evangelical awareness. Rhetorically, the Erasmian characters must work to make room for a distinction which neither of their adversaries can fathom: that there is a difference between proper and improper intellectual method in theology. The anti-intellectual must come to see that intellectual labor is proper to theology, while the narrow-minded intellectual must discover the limits to such work. For the most part, Erasmus proceeds through varied and careful argumentation, although sometimes his adversaries deserve "more to be laughed at than refuted by arguments."[14] The Erasmian characters do plenty of both. For the scholastic theologians of his day (Erasmus' third adversary in the academy), however, he has mostly laughter and ridicule. These Christian scholars fail to create a living integration of faith and learning, ending up instead, with "a kind of uneducated erudition" which curiously combines the worst from the barbarians and the Ciceronians (26).

II. Theology in the Church

Theology also seeks to serve the church: it helps to clarify the appropriateness of Christian belief and practice to the classic sources of the community's traditions. In doing so, theologians naturally and inevitably enter into discourse with ecclesial officials. Frequently, as we know from recent events, the discussion shifts in focus from the disputed issue at hand to a more fundamental inquiry into the nature and limits of authority for settling this or any other question. Erasmus portrays such a shift in "A Fish diet," a dialogue between a butcher and a fishmonger concerning the value of Catholic dietary laws.[15] The butcher (yet another Erasmian lay theologian) finds these laws to be "matters of choice, not of obligation" (323). If the "old law" is surpassed, then why are the same laws re-imposed now, especially when they cause such "bitter quarrels" between Christians (322–24)? Both speakers dream that the pope will miti-

---

[14]Erasmus, "The Antibarbarians," p. 119.
[15]Erasmus, "A Fish Diet" in Thompson, ed., *Colloquies*, pp. 312–57.

gate these conditions which keep so many people estranged from
the church and which place such a heavy burden on ordinary
people, hoping that he will devote himself truly and fully to "nothing other than the glory of Christ and the salvation of mankind"
(326–27). As it is, the butcher finds claims for papal and episcopal
authority confusing and confused: "how am I to tell whose interpretation is right, especially if the interpreters differ among themselves"
(329)? Surely there is room for doubt where papal judgments are
rescinded as errant by later popes (327), where entirely new laws are
fabricated without necessity (328), and where exceptions to laws are
assigned arbitrarily. In this line of inquiry, the butcher embodies the
theologian's critical (even prophetic) practice in dialogue with
church officials: theologians must question, even challenge, church
policy and practice by criticizing the inflation or distortion of
ecclesial power according to the measure of the gospels, for as the
butcher notes, it is "impious to transfer to men the honor due to God
alone" (342).

Where rational criticism proves ineffective, however, stronger
forms of critical dissent are in order. Erasmus illustrates this more
potent form of theological criticism in "Julius Excluded from
Heaven," a dialogue between Saint Peter and the recently deceased
Pope Julius II, known to history as the "warrior pope".[16] Reminiscent
of Lucian's dialogues of the dead, the dialogue takes place at the
gates of heaven, a forum where "only truth counts" (170). Julius
arrogantly demands entrance for himself and his army of "seasoned
cutthroats," threatening Peter with his "thunderbolt of excommuni-
cation" for not letting him enter at once (170). Wondering how such
threats could come from a man of Christ, Peter questions what kind
of life this pope has led. In response, Julius brags of his shady
procurement of the papacy, he touts the riches he accumulated
(192), he speaks with pride of his military conquests (174–77, 189–
90), and he boasts of his maneuvers to neutralize a council which
dared to criticize him (180–84). As this testimony proceeds, the
contrast between Julius' papacy and the life of a true disciple of
Christ is magnified: "Is this the role of the shepherd, the most holy
Father, the vicar of Christ" (191)? Clearly not, Peter concludes, for
this "man who wishes to be thought the closest to Christ, and even
his equal, is involved with all the most sordid things, money, power,

---

[16]Erasmus, "Julius Excluded from Heaven," trans. Michael J. Heath, in A.H.T. Levi,
ed., *Collected Works of Erasmus*, 27 (Toronto: University of Toronto, 1978).

armies, treaties, not to mention vices." Julius is "the furthest from
Christ," he is "truly Christ's enemy" (195). In this dialogue, we see
the full negative force of theological criticism at work: the contrast
between Julius' decadent, fraudulent papacy and Peter's ideal of
apostolic simplicity and virtue provides perfect leverage with which
to expose publically papal failures and shortcomings, without, however, giving up all hope that the ideal may be realized by a successor.

Theology also has a critical role to play in discourse with popular
piety. Several Erasmian dialogues take up the task of exposing the
inversion of value in popular religion, where trivial and surface
features of religious life are deemed more important than the essential and interior life of faith. In "The Fish Diet," once again, the
butcher and the fishmonger join together to lampoon the undue
significance attributed to ceremonies and petty regulations, at the
expense of a faithful and moral life. Popular religion is rife with
contradiction and hypocrisy:

> **Fishmonger:** . . . we see many persons trust so much in corporal rites
> that, relying on these, they neglect what belongs to true godliness:
> arrogating to their own merits what comes of divine bounty, standing
> still where they might have ascended to the more perfect, and slander-
> ing a neighbor on account of things neither good nor bad in themselves.
> **Butcher:** Indeed, when in the same affair there are two choices, one of
> which is better than the other, we always prefer the worse. The body,
> and what is of the body, are everywhere more esteemed than the things
> of the spirit. To have killed a man is considered a very serious crime—
> as it is; but to have destroyed a man's mind with pestilential doctrine,
> with poisonous ideas, is sport. If a priest lets his hair grow long, or
> wears a layman's garb, he is thrown into jail and punished severely; if
> he boozes in a brothel, if he whores, if he dices, if he corrupts other
> men's wives, if he never touches a Bible, he is nonetheless a pillar of
> the Church.[17]

In exchanges like this, Erasmus illustrates the negative moment in
the theologian's critical task: with a discriminating eye on what is
essential and what is not, theologians must expose the transfer of
significance from faith and charity to superstition and petty regulations, and they must highlight the perverted and destructive consequences this transfer entails. Nowhere is Erasmus' critical edge
sharper than in "A Pilgrimage for Religion's Sake," a dialogue filled

---

[17]Erasmus, "A Fish Diet," pp. 342–43.

with humorous but mocking derision for the cult of relics (e.g.,
Peter's knuckles, the Virgin's milk, and a martyr's skull!), superstition (don't look at these sacred things if you had intercourse last
night!), and the thievery of the monks who run the shrines.[18]
Throughout, pious explanations are offset with expressions of doubt
and ridicule.

There is, however, another more positive side to criticism. As John
Dewey points out, criticism is "not for its own sake, but for the sake
of instituting and perpetuating more enduring and extensive values."[19] Erasmus agrees, and many of his dialogues on popular
religion portray conversations where an ideal is held up as a beacon
for converting popular piety back to what is essential in Christian
life. In "The Shipwreck," for instance, the desperate passengers
aboard a sinking ship seek safety through superstitious appeal to the
Virgin Mary ("Port of Salvation"), incantations to the sea, and all
kinds of promises they could and would never keep. The interlocutors frown upon such behavior, but in the course of their conversation, two alternatives emerge: first, the narrator (who prays to God
alone) and second, a woman with child ("the only one who didn't
scream, weep, or make promises; she simply prayed in silence,
clasping her little boy.")[20] Both serve as exemplars for true piety,
and interestingly, both survive the ordeal. In this and similar dialogues, theological speakers not only parody the inverted values of
common superstition; they also hold up ideal models for conversion
to authentic piety.

Theology in the church also involves discourse with dissenters
and reformers. In this regard, Erasmus had planned to write three
dialogues between a Lutheran, a Roman Catholic opponent, and an
Erasmian arbitrator, in which "the affair will be discussed . . .
without accusations and strife, without deceit; simply naked truth
will be put forward, with such fairness and moderation that . . . the
opposite party (the Catholic) will be angrier with me than Luther,
interpreting my indulgence as collusion."[21] It is regrettable, indeed,
that these dialogues were never written. Nonetheless, "An Examination Concerning Faith" gives us a good idea of the kind of discourse

[18]Erasmus, "A Pilgrimage for Religion's Sake" in Thompson, ed., Colloquies, pp.
285–312.
[19]John Dewey, Experience and Nature (New York: Dover, 1958), p. 403.
[20]Erasmus, "The Shipwreck" in Thompson, ed., Colloquies, p. 143.
[21]Erasmus, quoted from Margaret Mann Phillips, Erasmus and the Northern Renaissance (New York: Collier, 1965), p. 177.

Erasmus hoped for between Catholic orthodoxy and reformers like Luther. In this dialogue, a Catholic (Aulus), who at first fears being spiritually infected, interrogates his Lutheran interlocutor (Barbatius) to see if his understanding of the Apostles' Creed is orthodox. Much to Aulus' surprise, Barbatius proves himself of sound doctrine.

> **Aulus:** When I was at Rome, I did not find everyone so sound in belief. **Barbatius:** No, and if you look around you'll find many elsewhere, too, who aren't equally convinced of these matters. **Aulus:** Since you agree with us in so many and so difficult questions, what hinders you from being wholly on our side? **Barbatius:** I want to hear about that from you, for I think I'm orthodox. Even if I wouldn't vouch for my life, still I try diligently to make it correspond to my confession. **Aulus:** Why, then, is there such conflict between you and the orthodox?[22]

That question need not be answered, for Erasmus' point lies in the question itself. It is an open, irenic question to Catholic and Lutheran, challenging both parties to come together peacefully around the shared core of the Christian faith, cautioning them not to let disputes over less important matters divide them.

The lesson of "The Examination," however is directed primarily to Catholic orthodoxy. It is, after all, Aulus who is converted from enmity to friendship, while Barbatius remains consistently tolerant. Indeed, as we saw earlier, Erasmus shares in dissenting from decadent and unchristian church officials. Catholic orthodoxy must reform (and hence be criticized) before it can accept Erasmus' invitation to join in tolerant and mutual understanding with its critics. Erasmus' irenicism does not, in short, nullify his dissent. Nor, I should add, does it rule out critical debate with the church's reformers. In "The Epicurean," for instance, Erasmus responds to Luther's hostile charge that he is drunk with the "folly of Epicurus," a phrase Luther used for those who don't believe in the word of God.[23] The Erasmian speaker (Hedonius) counters that "there are no people more Epicurean than godly Christians" (538), since no life is more agreeable and more filled with pleasure than the life filled with piety and righteousness. The true Christian, relieved by Christ of the torment of "bad conscience," (Luther's complaint), possesses

---

[22]Erasmus, "An Examination Concerning Faith" in Thompson, ed., *Colloquies*, p. 188.

[23]Erasmus, "The Epicurean" in Thompson, ed., *Colloquies*, pp. 535–51. See Boyle, *Christening Pagan Mysteries*, ch. 3.

"the most enjoyable life of all and the one most full of true pleasure" (549). Since Catholic and Lutheran agree on the essentials of the Christian faith (the point of "The Examination"), their discourse on interesting but secondary matters (like the status of pleasure) can be civil and urbane, unlike the discourse he imagines between Peter and Julius II. The debate with Luther, for Erasmus, was not a matter of defending church doctrine, but—once again—of justifying and advocating the value of non-Christian wisdom for Christian self-understanding.[24]

The Christian theologian who works in the church must converse with significantly different, even opposing, parties. Regardless of the interlocutor, however, all theological discourse in the church pivots around the central distinction between what is essential and what is non-essential in Christian faith and life. In the theologian's dialogue with church officials, this distinction is used as a negative contrast to criticize the official church's failures to measure up to the apostolic ideal. Here the distinction undergirds a posture of dissent and reform. In the dialogue with popular piety and the clerics who service it, the distinction is used again as a negative contrast, first to lampoon popular superstitions for transferring all significance to what is least essential, and second, to call for conversion to the truly significant life of simple faith and virtue. Here the distinction supports a policy of derision mixed with exhortation. Finally, in the dialogue with church reformers, this distinction is used positively, first to affirm the legitimacy of the reformer's dissent, second, to open a forum for reconciling "orthodoxy" and its reformers, and third, to delineate the many points open to debate without causing serious division. Here, the distinction makes possible a conversation which is affirmative, irenic, yet critical. Throughout these conversations, the theologian is called to exercise "discriminating judgement"[25] between essential and nonessential values, criticizing the inversion of value, working for the conversion of these values, and affirming their proper order wherever it may be found.

III. Theology in Society

Theology, finally, has responsibilities to the wider society in which it exists: through moral and political discourse, it seeks to

[24]Boyle, *Christening Pagan Mysteries*, pp. 84–87.
[25]Dewey, *Experience and Nature*, p. 398.

render the tradition's social values practically credible and persuasive. Several of Erasmus's colloquies depict the workings of moral discourse, giving us, in essence, a theatre of moral persuasion and education. Once again, Erasmus proceeds by means of contrasts. The "Old Men's Chat," for instance, portrays a conversation in which four ex-classmates share life-stories after forty-two years of separation, only to discover their enormous differences in character: two men have led virtuous lives filled with moderation and charity, the other two have squandered their talents in "excess and frivolity".[26] In "Pseudocheus and Philetymus," on the other hand, we witness the impossible conversation between a proficient liar and a man of honor: they talk with each other just long enough to discover that their difference in character makes communication altogether impossible.[27] Other colloquies depict conversations where hypocritical discrepancies between a person's outward appearance and his or her real character are exposed, as is the case with the "ignoble knight" who is counseled how to procure the name and honor of knighthood without in fact being one.[28] In each of these dialogues, Erasmus uses contrast satirically, trying "to needle" an interlocutor or reader's moral awareness[29] in order to purge the person of his or her moral delusion and to illuminate the road to a more virtuous life.

Those with political power, however, make a more potent adversary for theological speech. It is, nonetheless, imperative that theologians engage those who wield (and frequently abuse) political power in serious, critical conversation. The best examples of this kind of discourse in Erasmus' colloquies concern the evil of war. The theologian must challenge those who perpetrate the violence and destruction of war: the kings and princes, who "in deadly hatred, clash to their mutual destruction," dragging all of Christendom into "the ravages of war";[30] the popes, like Julius II, who divide the body of Christ by waging "holy war" against the French (and others) in pursuit of worldly glory;[31] the generals, like the one

---

[26]Thompson, *Colloquies*, p. 189.
[27]Erasmus, "Pseudocheus and Philetymus: The Dedicated Liar and the Man of Honor" in Thompson, ed., *Colloquies*, pp. 133–37.
[28]Erasmus, "The Ignoble Knight, or Faked Nobility" in Thompson, ed., *Colloquies*, pp. 424–32.
[29]G. Thompson, *Under Pretext of Praise*, p. 150.
[30]Erasmus, "Charon" in Thompson, ed., *Colloquies*, p. 391.
[31]Erasmus, "Old Men's Chat" in Thompson, ed., *Colloquies*, p. 200. Compare "Julius Excluded from Heaven."

portrayed in the "The Funeral," who grew wealthy "from robberies, sacrileges, and extortions";[32] and finally, the mercenaries, those "reckless, rapacious, and impious adventurers" who bring death and disease to themselves and to all they encounter.[33] The theologian also must expose and denounce the destructive consequences of war, especially for the innocent, as the decidedly Erasmian Carthusian does in "The Soldier and the Carthusian."

> **Carthusian:** What mishap makes you walk so stooped, like a man of ninety, or as though you were some reaper or were crippled by a cudgel? **Soldier:** The disease contracted the joints. **Carth.:** A splendid transformation indeed you've experienced! You were once a cavalryman; now you've become a semicreeping creature instead of a centaur. **Sol.:** The chances of war. **Carth.:** No, it's your own folly. What prizes do you bring home to your wife and children? Leprosy? (Since that pox is nothing but a kind of leprosy.) Unless it's not to be shunned because it's widespread, particularly among the nobility! Yet for this very reason it ought to be shunned all the more. No you'll infect with this disease those who ought to be most precious to you, and you yourself will go through life a rotten corpse.[34]

As Erasmus notes in "Charon," a Lucianic dialogue of the dead, only Charon (who provides passage to the underworld) can benefit from the death caused by war; but even Charon is worried that his boat will be too small to handle the great influx of new shades.[35]

As part of their call for peace, theologians should challenge all those who cause and legitimate warfare. Speaking ironically in "Charon," Erasmus calls attention to the "new epidemic, born of difference of opinion. It has so corrupted everybody's mind that sincere friendship exists nowhere. . . ." No one trusts or listens to anyone else. And to make matters worse, churchmen give religious legitimation to these hostilities:

> **Alastor:** They proclaim in their evangelical sermons that war is just, holy, and right. And—to make you marvel more at the audacity of the fellows—they proclaim the very same thing on both sides. To the French they preach that God is on the French side: he who has God to protect

---

[32]Erasmus, "The Funeral" in Thompson, ed., *Colloquies*, p. 364.

[33]Thompson, *Colloquies*, p. 12.

[34]Erasmus, "The Soldier and the Carthusian" in Thompson, ed., *Colloquies*, ,p. *132–33.*

[35]Erasmus, "Charon," pp. 390–94.

him cannot be conquered! To the English and Spanish they declare this war is not the Emperor's but God's; only let them show themselves valiant men and victory is certain! But if anyone **does** get killed, he doesn't perish utterly but flies straight up to heaven, armed just as he was. **Charon:** And people believe these fellows? **Alastor:** What can a pretense of religion not achieve? Youth, inexperience, thirst for glory, anger, and natural human inclination swallow this whole. People are easily imposed upon. And it's not hard to upset a cart that's ready to collapse of its own accord.[36]

In this little exchange we see an essential step in theology's discourse on war: to expose and question the mechanisms of legitimation which serve to make war seem morally acceptable. In this dialogue, as in "Military Affairs," theological criticism takes aim on just war theory, which, the Erasmian speakers argue, all too easily gives justification for all that is done in war.[37] Through these criticisms and challenges, these speakers hope to move their interlocutors to a better understanding of the evil of war, exhorting them to change "from brute to man," from savagery and violent conflict to concord and more civilized means of settling conflicts.[38]

Theology's role in the public of society involves discourse on two levels: addressing individuals on questions of morality and engaging political agents on questions pertaining to the common good. In both spheres, theologians face adversaries whose characters, policies, and practices diametrically oppose the values cherished by the Christian tradition. Their task, as Erasmus shows us, is educative. Theologians must engage individual moral consciousness in conversation, criticizing moral failure and duplicity, and exhorting individuals to moral conversion. Similarly, in the political sphere, theologians must engage in overt social criticism of the destructive and exploitative use of power, at the same time inviting political agents to adopt more civilized and peaceful forms of conflict resolution. The point of theology's moral and political discourse is the conversion of adversaries through critical and hortative conversation. This is, of course, no easy task, as Erasmus acknowledges when he has characters in his own dialogues mock his efforts to promote peace and concord.[39]

---

[36]Ibid., pp. 391–92.
[37]Erasmus, "Military Affairs" in Thompson, ed., *Colloquies*, p. 14.
[38]Erasmus, "Cyclops, or The Gospel Bearer" in Thompson, ed., *Colloquies*, p. 421.
[39]Erasmus, "Charon," p. 391.

IV. Theologians in Dialogue

Theologians must speak in diverse and heterogeneous social contexts. Every effort to reflect critically on the appropriateness and credibility of Christian faith and life must be articulated in discourse with an array of interlocutors, each with a different set of questions and different kinds of interest, each demanding discourse in terms and under standards proper to their native turf. Erasmus' colloquies and dialogues, I suggest, instruct us about the kind of social reality in which theologians are called to work; they make clear the varied, sometimes conflicting opponents with which theologians must converse; and they elucidate the complex set of communicative strategies necessary to deal rationally with the demands of these different interlocutors. Given the conflicting, sometimes contradictory, demands each public poses, Erasmus counsels theologians to master the art of conversation, engaging its different interlocutors appropriately, alternating argument and ironic laughter, mixing critical dissent with cautious affirmation, and combining moral criticism and rousing exhortation—all for the sake of persuading and transforming their interlocutors to a richer, more nuanced understanding of Christian faith and life. He exhorts theologians, in sum, to initiate and foster conversations which are cultured and evangelical, critical and irenic, and morally and politically educative. The blend of these communicative virtues yields what Margaret Mann Phillips calls that "mellow, balanced sanity" characteristic of the Erasmian ideal for rational theological discourse.[40]

Erasmus brings these ideals into sharp relief in "The Godly Feast," a colloquy of lay, Christian philosophers who gather in a country villa, far removed from the "smoky cities," to enjoy a common meal and "truly enjoyable conversation."[41] In this home, everything speaks: murals, plants, even the wine cups, bear inscriptions with wise counsel for the guests and celebrating "the goodness of God, who gives all these things for our use" (52). Conversation abounds, especially at the banquet, where the guests (all men, unfortunately) join in cooperative interpretation of several biblical passages. Praying that Christ may "deign to attend our feast and rejoice our hearts by his presence" (56), the participants delve into the meaning of scriptural texts, bringing their wisdom alive in open, appreciative, and complementary sharing of interpretations. Moreover, being Er-

---

[40]Phillips, *Erasmus and the Northern Renaissance*, p. 206.
[41]Erasmus, "The Godly Feast" in Thompson, ed., *Colloquies*, pp. 48 and 56.

asmian theologians, they are fully open to the divine revelation in secular literature as well. Eusebius (the host) speaks for all in attendance when he conjectures that "perhaps the spirit of Christ is more widespread than we understand, and the company of saints includes many not in our calendar" (65). Following up on this conjecture, several speakers bring biblical and secular authors into conversation with each other (67), noting the shared wisdom they teach. At the close of the colloquy, Eusebius thanks his guests for their "conversation, which was equally learned and devout" (76). He must leave, he tells them, to visit a sick friend and to settle a conflict between two stubborn men.

This colloquy truly is "a compendium of almost all of Erasmus' theories and preferences."[42] It portrays in miniature the kind of communicative practices which Erasmus took to be essential to theological conversation. The speakers meet in friendship, they work together cooperatively, their inquiry is learned and critical, and together, they build a living community of inquiry. This banquet, as the characters acknowledge, has eucharistic significance, for in amicable and productive conversation, they "recapitulate humanly the economy of Christ, drawing men (sic) together in a bond of charity."[43] Their work together institutes a "microcosm of the Christian commonwealth"[44], a vibrant community which fuses faith and learning together such that both are enhanced, which balances strong criticism (e.g., of ceremonialism) with an irenic spirit, and which weds intellectual inquiry with a passion for justice. Straight to the point and with her characteristically Erasmian flavor, Boyle concludes: "This colloquy is a cameo of the human imitation of Christ, the archetypal conversation, civilizing the commonwealth through language."[45]

"The Godly Feast," it is true, takes place in a quiet retreat, far removed from the divisions and conflicts of public life. This does not mean, however, that the standards of rationality which emerge in this symposium are the exclusive prerogative of a leisured life. On the contrary, this colloquy ends with Eusebius leaving his isle of rich conversation to minister to public needs and conflicts. He turns, in short, from text to life, "from the study to the village."[46] This

---

[42]G. Thompson, *Under Pretext of Praise*, p. 34.
[43]Boyle, *Erasmus on Language and Method in Theology*, p. 136.
[44]Ibid., p. 140.
[45]Ibid., p. 141.
[46]Ibid., p. 140.

colloquy leaves off, in other words, where the rest of Erasmus'
colloquies begin, in the scattered and quarrelsome discourse of
everyday life. This, I take it, is precisely Erasmus' point: the communicative virtues which flower splendidly in Eusebius' country
villa remain the imperatives for theological conversation with all its
many academic, ecclesial, and social adversaries. Theologians are
charged by Erasmus with leaving their godly feast in order to engage
its various opponents in serious conversation, and in so doing, to
open and sustain working ground for amicable but critical dialogue
with these interlocutors, for the purpose of creating and sustaining
living communities of inquiry, faith, and action.

Erasmus' conversational imperative is as pertinent today as it was
in his own day. In our own time, theological discourse is fractured,
broken apart in intellectual disputes, ecclesial quarrels, and social
divisions. It is imperative, therefore, that theologians participate in
conversations shaped by "the habit of amicable cooperation,"[47]
where interlocutors of different stripes and loyalties may communicate intelligently, critically, and responsibly about common truth
and welfare. "Speech," Erasmus tells us, "has been chiefly given to
us by God so that man (sic) might live together more agreeably."[48]
This end is achievable, however, only if theological speech is guided
by that "mellow, balanced sanity" which Erasmus portrays in his
colloquies and dialogues. The many adversative voices facing the
responsible theologian must be dealt with conversationally: they
must be invited to dialogue and turned cooperatively together as an
integrated community of inquiry, faith, and responsibility. The
Erasmian imperative, finally, challenges theologians "to foster and
nurture those forms of communal life in which dialogue [and]
conversation . . . are concretely embodied in our everyday life."[49]
What we today call the university may be an example of such
communal life, but theology will function well in that context only
if it has already become a "university" in its communicative practices, i.e., only if it has learned to turn the many different voices

---

[47]John Dewey, "Creative Democracy—The Task Before Us" in Max H. Fisch, ed.,
Classic American Philosophers (New York: Appleton-Cenury-Crofts), p. 393.

[48]Erasmus, quoted from Boyle, *Erasmus on Language and Method in Theology*, p.
47.

[49]Richard Bernstein, *Beyond Objectivism and Relativism: Science, Hermeneutics,
and Praxis* (Philadelphia: University of Pennsylvania, 1983), p. 229.

(adversaries) toward the one (university) by means of intelligent, critical, and responsible dialogue (conversation). Such dialogue, however, remains an unfinished task for theology, as it was for Erasmus himself. "Saint Socrates, pray for us!"[50]

---

[50]Erasmus, "The Godly Feast," p. 68.

Part Two
CONTEMPORARY MODES OF
THEOLOGICAL REFLECTION

LIVING METAPHORS, LIFE-GIVING SYMBOLS: PERSPECTIVES ON *METAPHORICAL THEOLOGY* AND THE VOICES OF WOMEN

Phyllis H. Kaminski, SSND

Metaphorical Theology

Metaphor is "movement, human movement."[1] The movement of human life vis-a-vis God has long occupied Sallie McFague. Her conviction that imagination is central to the integration of language, belief, and life prompted her to explore metaphor as a radical, dialectic process, "*the* way of human knowing,"[2] and to show how Jesus as "*the* parable of God" calls believers to decision which must be embodied in their lives.[3] McFague, in *Speaking in Parables*, encouraged theology to strengthen its voice in our world by staying close to its primary model, Jesus. She also challenged it to look for ways through metaphoric movement to help people today be encountered by the living word of God.[4]

In *Metaphorical Theology*,[5] McFague took up her own challenge. She used metaphor and scientific models to propose a renewed

---

[1]Sallie McFague TeSelle, *Speaking in Parables: A Study in Metaphor and Theology.* (Philadelphia: Fortress Press, 1975), p. 58.

[2]TeSelle, *Parables*, p. 62 (Italics in text.)

[3]TeSelle, *Parables*, pp. 78–82. (Italics in text.)

[4]TeSelle, *Parables*, pp. 80–88. McFague is aware of the need in theology for conceptual precision but she posits between the primary data of religious experience and the systematic conceptualization of that data, an "intermediary theology," (a term she credits to Michael Novak, p. 3, note). She suggests the following guidelines for such an intermediary theology: 1) the various forms of metaphorical language operative in biblical literature and in the Christian literary tradition need to be looked at as sources for theological reflection; 2) these forms are not secondary embellishments for mainline systematic and doctrinal tradition, but are in fact its nourishment; 3) recognizing the importance of such forms as parable, story, poem, and confession, does not imply substituting these forms for systematic theology, but it does imply a continuum from these forms to systematic theology, p. 64.

[5]Sallie McFague, *Metaphorical Theology: Models of God in Religious Language* (Philadelphia: Fortress Press, 1982).

theological language more inclusive of women and more in keeping
with our pluralistic age. From her standpoint as a "post-Enlightenment feminist" with a Protestant sensibility,[6] she expressed hope
that her efforts would strengthen the voice of women and radically
reform theology.

I share McFague's conviction about the integration of language,
belief, and life. Like McFague, I find the use of metaphor and model
a creative way to approach the revision of theological language. I
also believe that the way we use our imagination is central to our
own transformation, to the paradigm shift taking place in all of
Western culture,[7] and to the survival of our planet. I, too, look to
dialogue with other disciplines as a way of understanding and
enriching our sense of religious tradition. And like McFague, I find
that my growing awareness of feminism challenges me to look
critically at the oppressive structures still operative within Christianity, yet to work for the transformation, not the abandonment, of
that tradition.

From my perspective, however, within the Roman Catholic tradition, I am convinced that the stories of women from diverse classes
and cultures will have staying power only if they are accompanied
by a renewed sense of embodiment and woman-defined symbols.
Moreover, through reading feminist theory within the social and
natural sciences, I have come to believe that these women's voices
in their diversity and richness are moving beyond McFague's original insight about the power of metaphor. It is my thesis that feminist
critiques of scientific metaphors and models as well as woman-
defined symbols must be included with vital metaphors to accomplish the task defined by McFague's thought experiment.

Since *Metaphorical Theology* may be considered the starting point
for this study, a sketch of its major theses is in order. First, McFague
suggests that metaphor as a way of human understanding is aptly
suited for the expression of religious experience. Its indirection and
judgment find the thread of similarity in the midst of dissimilars. It
is and *is not* as we say. Second, for McFague, *Jesus is God* is the
ultimate metaphor. From Jesus' parables we learn what it means to
live in relationship with God. From his life as parable we learn how
to embody that relationship. Third, models are dominant metaphors

[6]McFague, *Metaphorical Theology*, p. x.
[7]See Fritjof Capra, *The Turning Point: Science, Society, and the Rising Culture.*
(New York: Bantam Books, 1983).

which suggest multiple relations as well as emotional associations evoking commitment. Science uses multiple models. Fourth, theology, which needs both primary and secondary language can use models as the bridge from metaphorical to conceptual language. Theology also needs multiple models. Fifth, McFague wants to dislodge the patriarchal model, not to change the root metaphor of Christianity. Her goal is the reformation and transformation of the tradition.

McFague's conviction that metaphorical theology is intrinsically open to other perspectives holds an invitation. It encourages me to continue the conversation she began and to share some of what I hear from the voices of women within the sciences. I propose that their voices help us reframe our theological questions and call forth life-giving metaphors that refine and strengthen McFague's contribution to the renewal of theology. Their stories also lead to woman-interpreted and defined religious symbols. I hope that the presentation of these perspectives furthers our contribution to the theme of theology and the university as it is being shaped by women's voices.

Living Metaphors: The Voices of Women and Feminist Critique of Science

What are women who study the dominant metaphors and models in the sciences telling us? What connection do these women make between women's experience[8] as defined by women and the need of a profound reshaping of all our epistemological categories?

Carolyn Merchant speaks about the use of metaphor in dominant

---

[8] I am aware of how problematic a term this is. For the purposes of this paper, I suggest that women's experience be considered broadly, in its complexity and its variety (the concrete experience of middle class university women is not that of working class women; white women do not have the same experience as women of color, etc.). I also include the recognition that feminist understanding of women's experience is not monolithic. (Radical feminists interpret women's experience differently from liberal or socialist feminists). A careful look at dominant writings and an ear open to the witness of women's stories, however, can build a working definition of women's experience that is helpful to our conversation. As Judith Plaskow proposes, "The construction of such a standpoint, the development of a more rounded view of women's experience, is a matter not of stripping layers of patriarchal falsification from an authentic core of women's experience, but of building a viewpoint from a variety of perspectives, adding layer of complexity to layer of complexity." See Sex, Sin, and Grace: Women's Experience and the Theologies of Reinhold Niebuhr and Paul Tillich, (Lanham, MD: University of America Press, 1980), p. 30. See also Angela Miles, Introduction, in Angela R. Miles and Geraldine Finn, eds. Feminism in Canada: From Pressure to Politics (Montréal: Black Rose Books, 1982).

scientific models. In her critical journey through the history of science from the sixth to the seventeenth century, Merchant recalls the long-standing affiliation of women and nature throughout culture, language, and history.[9] Focusing on the values of egalitarianism and interconnectedness, Merchant traces the patriarchal and sexual root-metaphors around nature as female. She shows how they facilitated broader cultural moves. The earlier organic view, with its normative constraints against anything that would destroy mother earth, was called into question when the agrarian ecosystem of medieval Europe declined. Devastating plagues and the accompanying breakup of the old feudal order heightened fears that nature would interdict her own ways and that chaos and anarchy lay just beneath the sheen of apparent order. Since wild unruly nature was symbolically associated with the dark side of woman, both needed to be ordered in this precarious world.[10]

What we know as the scientific revolution of the seventeenth century climaxed a long developing shift. The resulting mechanized world view increased the oppression of women. Both midwife and witch were "corrected" in the name of scientific advance. Discoveries in the area of reproduction reinforced the cultural biases of male superiority and activity over female inferiority and receptivity in the service of males. The authority of such men as Harvey and Descartes generated "objective scientific evidence" that maintained these ideological assumptions. Accompanying industrialization further restricted women who were now considered not only naturally inferior but who became also economically dependent.[11]

Francis Bacon, one of the celebrated fathers of modern science transformed these growing tendencies into a total program advocating the control of nature for human benefit. Merchant discloses the sexual bias of Bacon's mechanistic utopian program in the *New Atlantis* (1624). It linked mechanics, the trades, middle-class commercial interests, and the domination of nature. Merchant does not imply that Bacon is responsible for all that developed in history subsequent to his writing, but she does credit him with a conscious

[9]Carolyn Merchant. *The Death of Nature: Women, Ecology and the Scientific Revolution* (San Francisco: Harper and Row Publishers, 1983).
[10]See Merchant, *Death of Nature*, especially chapters 1, 4, 5, "Nature as Female," pp. 1–41; "The World as Organism," pp. 99–126; "Nature as Disorder: Women as Witches," pp. 127–148.
[11]Merchant, *Death of Nature*, "Production, Reproduction, and the Female," pp. 149–163.

strategy. Sensitive to the trends and directions of his time, Bacon used his eloquent, suggestive imagery to sanction manipulation and experimental techniques for forcing nature into new forms. He also fostered the control of reproduction for the sake of production in all spheres.[12] Descartes and Newton definitively established the machine metaphor and the world view which repressed an organic view of life and which underlies the will to order and power that have prevailed until our century.[13]

Merchant's documentation of the power of image and symbol in sustaining ideology and in granting ethical sanctions for the oppression of women and the rape of nature strengthens McFague's thesis about the centrality of language to belief and to life. Merchant's critique of the assumptions that science fostered in philosophical and cultural expression has been taken even further by feminist theorists working in the philosophy of science. The voices of these women, who probe to their very roots male-biased imaginative constructs of scientific ways of knowing, can help chart the path to liberating, transformative models.[14]

Aware of the "circular process of mutual reinforcement" that exists in our culture, whereby "what is called scientific receives extra validation from the cultural preference for what is called masculine," while what is called feminine, "be it a branch of knowledge, a way of thinking, or woman herself, becomes further devalued by its exclusion from the special social and intellectual values placed on science." Evelyn Fox Keller explores the images and metaphors that express our assumptions and "beliefs" around science.[15] Besides the implicit sexual metaphor in commonplace usage which dubs the objective sciences as "hard" as opposed to the "softer", i.e., more subjective branches of knowledge, Keller suggests that the sexual metaphor is unconsciously internalized by scientists themselves. The obvious complement to the scientific mind (male)

---

[12]Merchant, *Death of Nature,* "Dominion over Nature," pp. 164–190.

[13]Merchant, *Death of Nature,* "The Mechanical Order," pp. 192–215; and "Mechanism as Power," p. 216–235.

[14]Besides what follows see Margaret Benston, "Feminism and the Critique of Scientific Method," in Miles and Finn, *Feminism in Canada,* pp. 47–66, for a more complete development of the advantages and the limitations of scientific models. See also Sandra Harding, *The Science Question in Feminism* (Ithaca: New York: Cornell University Press, 1986).

[15]Evelyn Fox Keller, "Gender and Science," in Sandra Harding and Merrill B. Hintikka, *Discovering Reality: Feminist Perspectives on Epistemology, Metaphysics, Methodology and Philosophy of Science* (Dordrecht, Holland: D. Reidel Publishing Company, 1983), p. 202.

is, of course, Nature (female), and Keller develops the complex
interrelation of transcendence and power not only in the technolog-
ical abuses of modern science but also in the unbridled ambition of
"pure" research. While the connections she makes are similar to
those made by Merchant, Keller probes the unexamined myths
which affect the very structure of science's drive to dominate nature.

Building on the insights of Freud and Piaget, and from within the
perspective of contemporary physics, which has provided dramatic
evidence for the failure of classical ideals about reality, Keller
discusses the interrelated development of cognitive objectivity and
the emotional conflict surrounding the development of psychic
autonomy. She shows how science itself has been distorted by its
acceptance of false cultural myths about knowledge. Her critique,
which refines the interconnections between affective and cognitive
development, can work for the liberation of women and transformation of science. By disengaging our thinking about science from our
notions of what is masculine, our conception of what is "objective"
can be freed from inappropriate constraints.[16] Keller admits that her
speculations need more investigation, but the model of affective and
cognitive development she invokes may, in time, have consequences
for the changed use of scientific knowledge in our political and
social worlds.

The voice of Hilary Rose advances that hope. From her standpoint
within the natural sciences, Rose suggests that feminist epistemology involves creation of a practice of feeling, thinking, and writing
that opposes the abstraction of male, bourgeois scientific thought.
Feminist methodology stresses shared experience and brings together subjective and objective ways of knowing. Within this theoretical framework, "experience, the living participating 'I,' is seen as a
dimension that must be included in an adequate analysis."[17] Carte-
sian dualisms can be overcome as feminist forces add their voices to
scientific methodology.

Radical marxist critique in the sixties and seventies explored the
political economy of science and then took up the relationship
between scientific production and ideology. Marxist feminists con-
tested the division of mental and manual labor. While this division
partially overcame the mind-body dualism, it still excluded the

---

[16]Keller, "Gender and Science," pp. 192–196, 200–202.
[17]Hilary Rose, "Hand, Brain, and Heart: A Feminist Epistemology for the Natural
Sciences," Signs, vol. 9, no. 1, (1983), p. 87, 88.

third and hidden division of "caring" labor (all the emotional, physical, and mental unpaid labor that goes into the production and maintenance of human beings). A fresh synthesis of both the theoretical and practical significance of such caring labor is critical for the reconstruction of a scientific technology built on life-giving values and harmony with nature. Rose suggests that no less is at stake than the survival of humanity itself.[18] Mary O'Brien's fertile work on the dialectics of reproductive consciousness provides a theoretical basis for moving these practical, strategic questions forward in the socio-political arena.[19] O'Brien too believes that the future calls for transformed social relations around both production and reproduction.

From within the human sciences, Jane Flax substantiates the epistemological transformations still needed to uncover the incompleteness of the all-pervasive dominant patriarchal models.[20] Two of her concluding theses seem particularly relevant to McFague's goal of transformation. First, women's experience is not in itself an adequate ground for a new epistemology:

> As the other pole of the dualities it must be incorporated and transcended. Women, in part because of their own history as daughters, have problems with differentiation and the development of a true self and reciprocal relations. Feminist theory and practice must thus include a therapeutic aspect, with consciousness raising as a model and an emphasis on process as political.[21]

Second, because knowing and being can not be separated, all concepts must be relational and contextual: "Ways of thinking and thinking about thinking must be developed which do justice to the multiplicity of experience, the many layers of any instant in time and space."[22] Thus the movement from model to concept, if it is to

---

[18]Rose, "Hand, Brain, and Heart," pp. 81–90. See also Angela R. Miles, "Ideological Hegemony in Political Discourse: Women's Specificity and Equality," in Miles and Finn, eds. Feminism in Canada, pp. 213–227.

[19]See Mary O'Brien, "Feminist Theory and Dialectical Logic," Signs, vol. 7, no. 1 (1981), 144–157. See also Mary O'Brien, The Politics of Reproduction, (London: Routledge and Kegan Paul Ltd., 1981) for the development of ideas presented in this essay.

[20]Jane Flax, "Political Philosophy and the Patriarchal Unconscious: A Psychoanalytic Perspective on Epistemology and Metaphysics," in Harding and Hintikka, eds. Discovering Reality, pp. 245–281.

[21]Flax, "The Patriarchal Unconscious," Thesis #4, p. 270.

[22]Flax, "The Patriarchal Unconscious," Thesis #7, pp. 270–271.

be than more than simply inclusive of women, will involve continued feminist critique of models themselves and of the very ways we think.

Each of these voices in science, politics, and psychology bears more complete exploration and analysis. Yet as a chorus, our sisters in other academic disciplines remind us that all models have been dominated by patriarchal consciousness. Our ways of conceptualizing, therefore, in all domains must be changed. The radical implications of this transformation emerge when Sandra Harding, a philosopher of science, encourages us to regard as a valuable resource the very instability of feminist analytical categories.[23]

What does she mean? Once feminists understood the destructively mythical character of the essential and universal "man" who was the subject and paradigmatic object of non-feminist theories, they also had to doubt the usefulness of analysis that simply substituted universal woman as its subject or object:

> There are not now and never have been any generic "men" at all—only gendered men and women. Once essential and universal man dissolves, so does his hidden companion, woman. We have, instead, myriads of women living in elaborate historical complexes of class, race, and culture.[24]

Because life itself is in exuberant transformation, because we are aware of our interrelatedness with men and women all over our planet, "feminist analytical categories *should* be unstable—consistent and coherent theories in an unstable and incoherent world are obstacles to both our understanding and our social practices."[25] Faced with ecological disasters, dehumanizing medical technologies, the threat of nuclear destruction, and with the history of sexism, classism, and racism that inhere in our economic, political, and scientific systems, women must resist all dualistic dichotomies as empirically false. We cannot, however, afford to dismiss them as irrelevant as long as they structure our lives and our consciousnesses.[26] The future of humanity (always a domain served by the

---

[23]Sandra Harding, "The Instability of the Analytical Categories of Feminist Theory," *Signs*, vol. 11, no 4, (summer, 1986), pp. 645–664. This article is best understood in conjunction with Harding's larger project *The Science Question in Feminism* mentioned in note 14).

[24]Harding, "Instability," p. 647.

[25]Harding, "Instability," p. 649. Italics in text.

[26]Harding, "Instability," p. 662.

labor of women) demands a commitment to nothing less than a total transformation of our ways of being and doing, a way which is attentive to all that is affected by human actions and relations.

I suggest that these second generation feminist voices invite us to pose our theological questions in a new key. They have moved beyond dichotomous categories. Part of what Canadian feminist Angela Miles calls the "integrative feminist project,"[27] the women mentioned above want to maximize female identity *and* to reject gender as a primary category. It is *not* a question of *either* equality and sameness *or* specificity and difference, but rather of working towards both goals at once. From a variety of perspectives, disciplines, and political commitments, they seek neither simple inclusion nor separation. Rather they are calling for an integrative restructuring of society and human relations which aims ultimately at the transformation of the traditionally known world.

Life-giving Symbols

The perspectives offered by the voices of these feminist scholars can advance the ultimate task McFague accords metaphorical theology, the reformation and transformation of the Christian tradition.[28] Perhaps the most vital energy moving in that direction is found in "relationality", the organizing principle which integrative feminists see as centrally representative of all women's experience and values. Relationality may be called a root metaphor. It refers in all its manifestations to women's "consciousness of the necessary interdependence of human beings, to a sense of connectedness to others, to awareness of one's embeddedness in human, social, and historical contexts, to the maximization of well-being for all persons, and to a commitment to non-violence."[29] Relationality, as used by the feminists cited above, affirms women's specificity. It explains women's

---

[27]For a more expanded description of integrative feminism, see Angela R. Miles, "Integrative Feminism," *Fireweed: A Feminist Quarterly*, Summer/Fall, 1984, pp. 55–81; also A. R. Miles, "Introduction," pp. 9–17 in Angela R. Miles and Geraldine Finn, eds. *Feminism in Canada: From Pressure to Politics*, (Montréal: Black Rose Books, 1982). For a theological perspective that is integrative see Rosemary Radford Ruether, *Sexism and God-talk: toward a feminist theology* (Boston: Beacon Press, 1983), especially pp. 109–115, 232–234.

[28]See McFague, *Met. Theol.*, pp. 28–29, and 145–177.

[29]Jeri Dawn Wine, "Gynocentric, Values, and Feminist Psychology," In Miles and Finn, *Feminism in Canada*, p. 68. While Wine is using the term in contrast to the individuality principle of male-stream psychology, I believe her description is helpful from a broader perspective.

experience in historical terms. It also expresses the perspective that
our social relationships are not determined by nature but are informed by and inform our historical cultural perceptions of the way
things are.

Personally I hold with McFague that the root metaphor of Christianity is "a relationship of a certain kind," the living relationship
between God and human beings, and that Jesus as parable embodies
that relationship.[30] I also hold that relationality, as embodied by
women, has much to contribute to the liberation of our theological
discourse and of our models of God. I find in McFague's minimali-
zation of symbolism[31] and her consequent lack of development of
the embodiment of the God-human relationship a weakness. It is a
weakness that operates against women and limits the success of her
project.

There is adequate demonstration, from such classic theologians as
Tillich and Rahner, that religious symbol is a dialectical reality
which both participates in, yet is distinct from, the reality it expresses.[32] Moreover, Ricoeur, on whom she relies by preference,
makes a connection which McFague reduces to a footnote: "Metaphor occurs in the already purified universe of the logos, while the
symbol hesitates on the dividing line between *bios* and *logos*. It
testifies to the primordial rootedness of Discourse in Life."[33] Bound

---

[30]See McFague, *Met. Theol.*, p. 111, also p. 166.

[31]McFague, *Met. Theol.* pp. 10–14.

[32]Rahner would stress the *is* of the dialectic, while Tillich is stronger on the *is not*.
See Paul Tillich, "Theology and Symbolism," *Religious Symbols*, F. Ernest Johnson,
ed. (New York: Harper & Brothers, 1955), pp. 107–116. Tillich's account of symbols
can be found in the following essays: "The Religious Symbol," trans. J. L. Adams and
E. Fraenkel., *Journal of Liberal Religion*, 2 (1940), 3–13; "The Nature of Religious
Language," *Theology and Culture*, (New York: Oxford University Press, 1959), pp.
53–68; "Existential Analysis and Religious Symbols," in Will Herberg, *Four Existential Theologians*, (Garden City, NY: Doubleday & Co., Inc. 1958), pp. 41–55; "The
Meaning and Justification of Religious Symbols," *Sidney Hook, ed. Religious Experi-
ence and Truth* (New York: University Press, 1961), pp. 3–12; "God as Being the
Knowledge of God," *Systematic Theology*, Vol I, (New York: Harper & Row, 1967), pp.
238–241. For Rahner's classic essay which develops an ontology and theology of
symbolic reality and considers the body as symbol of the human person, see "The
Theology of the Symbol," *Theological Investigations*, IV (London: Darton, Longman,
& Todd, 1966), pp. 221–252.

[33]Ricoeur, "Metaphor and Symbol," in *Interpretation Theory*, p. 59. See McFague,
Met. Theol., p. 202, note 12. For Ricoeur, the distinction between metaphor and
symbol is subtle yet real. When McFague focuses on the extremes of "symbolic
sacramentialism", she seems to overstate the "similarity, connection, and harmony"
that are inherent in religious symbols. Even linguistically, the distinction between
symbol and metaphor seems more a matter of the degree of distance between one
matrix of thought and some further meaning.

in a way that metaphor is not, symbols have roots in the depths of human experience.

Like the metaphors they empower, symbols are tensive and inter-active. It is true that for many that interaction is lost; the symbol is confused with the reality. Thus McFague's reflections on the irrele-vance and idolatry of religious language apply equally to religious symbols.[34] Properly understood, however, the symbol does not ex-press only continuity and harmony. It is ever and always in rela-tional tension, pointing to something beyond itself. "What asks to be brought to language in symbols, but which never passes over completely into language, is always something powerful, efficacious, forceful."[35] Both that force and its expression have been sources of theological reflection.

McFague is right that the metaphoric process, especially in its inventive and constructive origins, holds the key to the kind of revitalization many theologies need in our pluralistic age. Moreover, her parabolic christology invites that kind of change. I want to add that Jesus, as embodied expression, *par excellence* of the meeting of *logos* and *bios*, invites us to claim as women the central Christian symbol as well.[36] As we listen to the voices of integrative feminists, we hear their rootedness in this world and in its history. We may also hear that the matter of relationality, inseparable as it is from human self-consciousness, is, in the theological sense, transcendent. Women in science and feminist theory are calling for a transforma-tion of the world as we know it, a transformation based on the value of life and on the analysis of the actual process that has historically grounded the relations of men, women, and children. Jesus pro-claimed that same kind of transformation.[37] To borrow from Harding,

---

[34]McFague, *Met. Theol.*, pp. 4–10.

[35]Ricoeur, *Interpretation Theory*, p. 63.

[36]See Rahner, "Symbol,"*TI*, IV, p. 236: "The Logos is the 'symbol' of the Father in the very sense we have given the word: the inward symbol which remains distinct from what is symbolized, which is constituted by what is symbolized, where what is symbolized expresses itself and possesses itself." Cf., also David Tracy, *Analogical Imagination* (New York: Crossroad, 1981), pp. 281–7, 306–17, 376–389, for a treat-ment of the event of God's self-manifestation through Jesus Christ, the "tensive" symbols of the "proclaimed *that* and the narrative *who* and *what*" (p. 281); the "adverbial dialectic of an always-already which is yet a not yet" (p. 308).

[37]See Norman Perrin, *Jesus and the Language of the Kingdom: Symbol and Metaphor in New Testament Interpretation* (Philadelphia: Fortress Press, 1976), p. 199. The parables of Jesus "challenge the hearer to explore the manifold possibilities of the experience of God as king, and they do so in ways which constantly remind the hearer that, on the one hand, God is to be experienced in the historicity of the world of everyday, while on the other hand, they claim that God is to be experienced precisely in the shattering of that everyday world."

one might say that his words and his life embodied the instability of
all our traditional categories of knowing and of expressing reality.

Integrative feminists envision a world with embodied connections
very different from the ones that now dominate social relations.
McFague is convinced that it is neither desirable nor possible to
return to a symbolic, sacramental universe "in which all that is, is
connected by a web of being."[38] To the degree that she means turning
back to a static sacramentalism and two-dimensional hierarchical
order, I agree. I disagree, however, with her argument which down-
plays the life-giving power of symbol and the dynamism of incarnation.[39]

Contemporary voices affirm the interrelatedness of reality.[40] The
world of science, to which McFague so readily turned to study
models, maintains that quantum theory points to an "unbroken
wholeness". The classical idea of reality analyzable into indepen-
dently existing parts has given way to the scientific claim that
"inseparable quantum interconnectedness of the whole universe is
the fundamental reality."[41] Political and liberation theologians
around the globe are speaking to the interdependence of one group's
want and oppression and another's abundance and power. Feminist
philosophers, scientists, and theologians are showing that the old
dualisms and dichotomies no longer hold. The euphemisms surrounding nuclear weaponry signal the extent to which man can deny
connections and separate reality. "The baby socks, webs of wool,
photos, and flowers threaded into wire fences by the thousands of
women peace activists ringing Greeham Common" witness to the
profound relationship of the future of humanity and feminist commitment to social transformation.[42]

Because so much of women's experience has been the embodied

---

[38]McFague, *Met. Theol.*, pp. 10. In fairness to McFague, I am aware that she does
accept what she calls the sophisticated revitalizations of the symbolic, sacramental
tradition. She sees in their analogical interpretation a stress on the distance between
image and what it represents and a refusal of easy harmonies. She nonetheless prefers
her metaphorical perspective which sees connections "of a tensive, discontinuous,
and surprising nature." pp. 13–14.

[39]McFague, *Met. Theol.* pp. 10–18.

[40]See for examples Fritjof Capra, *The Turning Point*, (San Francisco, Bantam Books,
1983).

[41]David Bohm, in Einstein, *Principle of Relativity*, as cited in the review by
Mollenkott, "Metaphors of God," *Christianity and Crisis* 42 (1983), 457. See also Gary
Zukav, *The Dancing Wu Li Masters: An Overview of the New Physics* (Toronto:
Bantam Books, 1980).

[42]Rose, "Hand, Brain, and Heart," 90.

internalization of oppression, the use and abuse of her body by others, continued critical reflection by feminist theologians will become bolder in its articulation of the "hint half guessed, the gift half understood" which is Incarnation.[43] McFague seems to fear a too immanent God. Unconscious patriarchal dualisms operate as she suggests a restless, moving, growing human being somehow not centered on the body, the flesh.[44] Rosemary Haughton's poetic theology, in *The Passionate God*, can be cited as a challenge to McFague. Haughton images the flesh-taking of God in Jesus as a "break-through" involving every level of reality. She suggests both metaphors and symbols to express a vital passionate God-human relationship.[45]

Haughton's alternative to a static "incarnationalism," is developed even more radically by Quebec theologian, Monique Dumais. In "Women made flesh," Dumais does a theological reading of the revelatory capacity of woman's body.[46] In light of women's experience of fecundity and sterility in its relationship with menstruation, Dumais reinterprets numerous Scriptural references to sterility and to the flow of blood. Woman's unique experience from within her bodily reality, "to which our faith in an incarnate God gives a very profound meaning," radically shifts traditional interpretations. Our very being enables us to know a participation in God's superabundant creative life as well as our rootedness to mother-earth.[47] Women, Dumais suggests, can have from their experience of birthing and menstruation, a "visceral understanding" of the words "This is my Body; this is my Blood" that is specific to them yet with revelatory possibility for all.[48] By presenting examples of her experience of the body as symbol, by recalling the liberation of the body by Christ and the Christian call to celebrate the redeemed body-person, Dumais provides a life-giving woman-defined significance to the central Christian Eucharistic symbol.

---

[43]T. S. Eliot, "The Dry Salvages," Four Quartets, (London: Faber & Faber Ltd., 1944), p. 37. Eliot's lines are used by Rosemary Haughton, *The Passionate God* (New York: Paulist Press, 1981), on the dedication page, and also by David Tracy, *The Analogical Imagination*, pp. 307–308.

[44]McFague, *Met. Theol.* p. 11.

[45]See Haughton, *The Passionate God*, especially chapters 1, 4, 5, and 6.

[46]Monique Dumais, "Femmes faites chair," in Elisabeth J. Lacelle, *La Femme, son corps, la religion: approches pluridisciplinaires I* (Montréal: Les Editions Bellarmin, 1983), pp. 52–70.

[47]Dumais, "Femmes" p. 60. The translation from the French is my own.

[48]Dumais, "Femmes" p. 66, 70.

Because she remains on the linguistic surface of the metaphoric process, McFague's brief testing of her experiment on the models of God as Father and Friend leaves metaphorical theology short of its final goal.[49] McFague sensitively assesses the *is not* of God the Father. Literalization has "stitched"[50] a divine patriarch into the world of meanings for this dominant and powerful model. The unstitching of the metaphor can happen only by the creation of new living metaphors. Expanding the paternal image with maternal ones is still not sufficient. Therefore, McFague offers "God as Friend" well aware of the limitations of her choice. A non-familial, non-gender related alternative to parental models, God the Friend has the potential to become a model. It does not, however, have the potential to displace the patriarchal model. That deficiency may be a strength, since no single image can express all that is involved in the God human relationship at the heart of Christianity.[51] Still neither model incorporates the uniqueness of Jesus in a way that is liberative of women's equality and specificity.

I suggest that the Sophia-God of Jesus and Christ as Sophia of God proposed by Schüssler-Fiorenza[52] holds more promise of liberation. As metaphor, Sophia engages the perspective and power of the Biblical symbol, *basilea*, God's kingdom. As expressed in the praxis of Jesus, Sophia embodies the decision to work for the wholeness and selfhood of all without exception. Theologians like Haughton and Dumais help us to explore how women embody God's living Wisdom and how our stories express the paradox of God's flesh-taking. Women from all classes and cultures already draw on their experience of Sophia as their folk wisdom smuggled through history empowers them to exchange the life-giving Spirit in, through, across, and beyond confessional lines. The dynamic relationship "between redeemer and redeemed"[53] can and is freeing us as feminist scholars

---

[49]McFague, *Met. Theol.*, pp. 145–192. Cf. Gerhart and Russell, *Metaphorical Process*, p. 117.

[50]I borrow this image from Gerhart and Russell,*Met. Proc.*, p. 116: "This attachment of one part of the surface to another in a direct stitching changes the topological character of the world of meanings. . . . This process is basic to human understanding, and . . . has ontological import as well."

[51]McFague, *Met. Theol.*, pp. 178, 190.

[52]Schüssler-Fiorenza, *In Memory of Her*, Chapters 4, 5, especially pages 118–154. From a different perspective with an entirely different hermeneutic, Haughton also uses Wisdom, Sophia-God, as she establishes the theological implications of Romantic Love. See *The Passionate God*, pp. 53–54, 137–140, 260–266.

[53]Ruether, *Sexism and God-Talk*, p. 138.

and theologians to name our experience and claim our rightful place in the human community and the church.

Dorothée Soelle's suggested symbols fund supporting models for the Sophia-God model. Soelle turns to the language of the mystics and offers "Source of Life and all that is good," "life-giving wind," "water of life," "light," as symbols which do not imply authority as dominating power. The core of our relationship to God is one of union. It is not obedience. When the transcendent is symbolized as radically proximate, and our relationship one of "being at one with what is alive," solidarity replaces obedience as the dominant Christian virtue.[54] Soelle's remarks on the Father image confirm that the least we can do is to relativize that model's dominance. However, her sense of human interdependence and of the contingencies of existence support McFague's appreciation of the model as model:

> If speaking of God as father helps us not simply to face our transcience, as something to overcome, but to affirm our dependency and accept our finite creaturely condition, then there is no reason why we should not do so.[55]

Live metaphors are arising in women's literature[56] and among women gathering to explore their experience of God and church.[57] Even small local groups and women sharing informally find that their stories are shifting the world of meanings and creating something new. We know instinctively that metaphorical discourse "invents" in both senses of the word: "What it creates, it discovers; and what it finds, it invents."[58] We are also growing in conviction at the level of experience. Our metaphors are taking root in woman-defined experience, and the relationality we embody is being narrated with

---

[54]Dorothée Soelle, *The Strength of the Weak: Toward a Christian Feminist Identity* (Philadelphia: Westminster Press, 1984), p. 114. See also her work with Shirley A. Cloyes, *To Work and to Love: a theology of creation* (Philadelphia: Fortress Press, 1984) for a development of this intimacy and solidarity as responsibility for creation.

[55]Soelle, *Strength*, pp. 116–117.

[56]See, for examples, Carol Christ, *Diving Deep and Surfacing: Women Writers on Spiritual Quest* (Boston: Beacon Press, 1980) and Madonna Kolbenschlag, "Women's Fiction: Redefining Religious Experience," *New Catholic World*, 224: 1344 (1981), 252–6. Gayle Graham Yates, "Spirituality and the American Feminist Experience," *Signs*, 9/1 (autumn, 1983), 59–72.

[57]See Linda Clark, Marian Ronan, Eleanor Walker, *Image-breaking/Image-building* (New York: Pilgrim Press, 1981) and Rosemary Radford Ruether, *Women-church: theology and practice of feminist liturgical communities* (San Francisco: Harper & Row, 1985).

[58]Ricoeur, *Rule of Metaphor*, p. 239. Also McFague, *Met. Theol.*, p. 137.

new courage and with new consciousness of women's revelatory capacity.

As we speak and listen to each other, a new phase of theological conversation is beginning.[59] Those of us who believe that the grace of Incarnation is dynamically operative, even as we sense the evil, oppression in our universe, and those like McFague, who are more conscious of the negativities of existence, of the distance between the human and the divine, stand together at a crossroads. The metaphor of Simone Weil still lives:

> There is a God. There is no God. Where is the problem? I am quite sure that there is a God in the sense that my love is no illusion. I am quite sure there is no God in the sense that I am sure there is nothing which resembles what I can conceive with that word.[60]

This brilliant French mystic and activist lived and died in solidarity with the poor. She was convinced that God did not want her in the church. Women who feel called to solidarity, within the church, are also speaking out. These simple words from the journal of a Latin American woman, imprisoned as a revolutionary, echo loudly among us: "I had been taught what God was. I had to decide what God ought to be."[61]

My intention has been to expand McFague's original intuitions. I have suggested two directions for that expansion, the inclusion of feminist critiques of scientific metaphors and models and the appropriation of woman-defined symbols. Further development is needed in both of these areas in order to accomplish the constructive tasks of theological renewal. Our beliefs are shaped by both language and life. All are metaphorical in the fullest sense of the word.

Metaphor is movement, human movement. From her perspective, McFague has prepared a valuable tool to facilitate that movement. Growing numbers of feminist scholars in various disciplines are continuing it. Aware of the particularities of their perspectives, they proclaim a way of seeing, a way of speaking, a way of knowing, embodied in the very matter of our human selves and our history

---

[59]Anne E. Patrick, "Coming of Age: Women's Contribution to Contemporary Theology," *New Catholic World*, 228 (1985), 61–69. Also, Margaret Brennan, "Women and Theology; Singing of God in an Alien Land," *The Way Supplement* 53 (1985), 93–103.

[60]Simone Weil, *Waiting for God* (New York: Harper Torchbooks, 1973), p. 32. Cited in McFague, *Met. Theol.*, pp. 1, 194.

[61]Cited in Kolbenschlag, "Women's Fiction," p. 256.

that will radically transform conventional ways, in science, in politics, in society, and in the church. By gathering the alive metaphors and listening carefully to the insistent ones, those closest to the symbolic depths of our existence, metaphorical theology can shape models that have liberative potential for all. Theology, the academy, and the world have only begun to experience the transformation possible when women's voices are heard.

THE BISHOPS, THE CRITICS, AND THE
KINGDOM OF GOD

Patrick F. O'Connell

A consensus seems to have emerged that the differences between the U.S. Catholic bishops and their critics concerning the pastoral letters on nuclear weapons and on the American economy lie less in the area of general principles than of concrete policy applications.[1] According to this view, it is not the just war theory but the conclusions drawn from it which have prompted opposition to *The Challenge of Peace*.[2] The social philosophy of *Economic Justice for All*[3] has aroused much less disagreement than some of the practical recommendations drawn from that philosophy. A further suggestion is sometimes made that the specifics of the letters owe more to partisan political considerations, a so-called liberal agenda, than to cogent application of principles.[4] Such an analysis fails to take into account the fact that the bishops and their critics differ not only on political and practical questions, but in theological perspective. I believe that a profoundly divergent understanding of the meaning and significance of the doctrine of the Kingdom of God informs the conflicting points of view, and that this factor is more important

[1]See the comment of Avery Dulles in "The Gospel, the Church and Politics," *Origins*, 16:36 (Feb. 19, 1987), 642: "The general principles of social ethics contained in the two pastoral letters aroused only moderate opposition and were to a great extent accepted by the critics. . . . Controversy about the two pastorals has centered less on the principles than on the practical applications, for which the bishops themselves claimed little authority."

[2]All citations from this document will be taken from *The Challenge of Peace: God's Promise and Our Response. A Pastoral Letter on War and Peace* (Washington, D.C.: United States Catholic Conference, 1983), and will be cited by section number in the text.

[3]All citations from this document will be taken from *Economic Justice for All: Catholic Social Teaching and the U.S. Economy* (Washington, D.C.: United States Catholic Conference, 1986), and will be cited by section number in the text.

[4]See the references in Dulles, "The Gospel," pp. 642–43 and notes.

than political considerations for explaining the opposition to the
bishops' positions. The vocation of the Church to be "the instrument
of the kingdom of God in history" (CP, 22) grounds the pastorals'
focus on the distinctive Christian role in social transformation, while
a predominantly historical, transcendent interpretation of the kingdom grounds, or at least supports, the attitudes of those opposing
the pastorals. Different eschatologies give rise to different ecclesiol-
ogies, which lead to different perceptions of social and political
realities and possibilities. To demonstrate this contention, we will
examine the presentation of the doctrine of the Kingdom in the
pastorals and in the critiques of the pastorals by Michael Novak, the
most prominent opponent of the bishops' work.

In a helpful essay on "The Meaning of Faith Considered in Relationship to Justice,"[5] Avery Dulles presents the three basic elements
of faith as a conviction regarding what is supremely important, a
trustful reliance on transcendent power and goodness, and a commitment to what one believes in. The relative importance given to
each of the three elements, Dulles suggests, has a determinative
effect on how the relation between faith and justice is viewed. The
intellectualist approach, favored in Catholic tradition, can be subdi-
vided into illuminative theories, stressing interiority and the presence of the transcendent to the human spirit, and propositional
theories, which view faith as an assent to a body of revealed doctrines; whether the focus be on interior illumination or doctrinal
fidelity, action for justice easily becomes secondary, not strongly
integrated with faith. Fiducial approaches, characteristically but not
exclusively Protestant, which emphasize hope in God's mercy, can
show a tendency toward passivity in the face of sin and iniquity,
and submission to the existing order. Performative approaches emphasize the centrality of praxis, a commitment to the transforming
power of the Word of God to reverse the effects of sin in persons and
in structures. While Dulles stresses the need for retaining a synthesis
of the three elements of conviction, hope and commitment, he
endorses the new awareness of the importance of active engagement
as found in the performative approach, particularly evident in contemporary theologies of liberation.

---

[5]Avery Dulles, "The Meaning of Faith Considered in Relationship to Justice," in
John Haughey, ed., The Faith That Does Justice: Examining the Christian Sources for
Social Change (New York: Paulist, 1977), pp. 10–46.

Building on this typology, I believe the basic approaches to faith can be correlated with different interpretations of the Kingdom of God. For the illumination theories, the Kingdom is above all an interior, spiritual reign of God over the individual human heart: "the Kingdom of God is within you"; for propositionalists, the Kingdom is an historical, transcendent concept, an acceptance of divine sovereignty, and of the Church as the embodiment of that sovereignty in its role of teacher and ruler. Fiducial approaches, as Dulles points out, tend to place the kingdom in the absolute future, beyond history and outside any human participation. For the performative approach, however, it is because the kingdom has definitively entered into human history in Christ that efforts on behalf of justice are expressions of faith. Dulles writes,

> The Kingdom of peace and justice is not simply a remote ideal for which we long. In Jesus Christ the Kingdom of God has entered into history. It is already at work, albeit germinally, transforming the world in which we live. Faith is the Christian's mode of participation in that Kingdom. Insofar as we have faith, the Kingdom takes hold of us and operates in us. This means that through faith we become instruments in the healing and reconciliation of the broken world. We become agents of justice and bearers of the power of the Kingdom.[6]

It is this perspective which I believe characterizes the bishops' pastorals on war and peace and on economic justice, and is absent from or explicitly rejected by the responses of their critics. The major source for the pastorals' presentation on the Kingdom is, I believe, the Second Vatican Council. While much attention has been

---

[6]Dulles, "Meaning of Faith," p. 43. It is worth noting that in his own discussion of the bishops' pastorals in "The Gospel, the Church and Politics," Dulles seems to pull back somewhat from the implications of this position. While he affirms that "the kingdom of God exists not simply in some supercelestial realm, but as a real promise for the future of this earth," and that the "church heralds and anticipates the completion of that which has been inaugurated; it certifies that the kingdom will in fact be realized" ("The Gospel," p. 638), his distinction between faith and experience seems to put the Kingdom outside the realm of concrete human activity: "By faith they belong to the coming eschatological kingdom, but by experience they are involved in the transitory kingdom of this world" (p. 639). He also finds "an almost total lack of eschatological reference" (p. 643) in the pastoral, a statement whose validity depends on defining eschatology in an exclusively final sense. One wonders if Dulles' unease is itself prompted by political considerations, particularly with reference to the peace pastoral, which he seems less comfortable with than with the economic pastoral.

paid, within the letters themselves and by commentators,[7] to the influence on the pastorals of the *Constitution on the Church in the Modern World*, I would suggest that the teaching of *Lumen Gentium*, the *Constitution on the Church*,[8] concerning the nature and significance of the Kingdom of God is also of critical importance for both pastorals. Though the material on the Church and the Kingdom of God in the opening chapter of *Lumen Gentium* was included only in the final stage of the text's development,[9] it emerges as an integral, even central concept for presenting "The Mystery of the Church," as this first chapter is entitled. Rather than including "Kingdom" as one of a number of biblical images, such as sheepfold, field, building and spouse, grouped together in section 6 of the chapter,[10] the drafters of the constitution singled out "kingdom" as having far more than illustrative significance: by associating it with the role of the Son in the initial Trinitarian framework of the document, and then devoting a section entirely to a consideration of the relationship of the Kingdom to Christ and to the Church, they suggest it is basic to a proper appreciation of the Church's identity and mission.

In section 3 of the constitution, following a description of the mission of the Son, in language borrowed from Ephesians, as the re-establishment of all things, the text continues: "To carry out the will of the Father, Christ inaugurated the kingdom of heaven on earth and revealed to us the mystery of that kingdom. By his obedience He brought about redemption. The Church, or, in other words, the kingdom of Christ now present in mystery, grows visibly through the power of God in the world" (*LG*, 3). This presentation of the significance of the kingdom receives further elaboration in section 5:

---

[7]See *CP*, 7–15, and *EJ*, "Pastoral Message" 5–6; 2, and passim; for use of the Pastoral constitution in *The Challenge of Peace*, see especially David Hollenback, "The Challenge of Peace in the context of Recent Church Teachings," and J. Bryan Hehir, "From the Pastoral Constitution of Vatican II to *The Challenge of Peace*," in Philip J. Murnion, ed., *Catholics and Nuclear War: A Commentary on The Challenge of Peace* (New York: Crossroad, 1983), pp. 3–15 and 71–87, respectively.

[8]Unless otherwise noted, all quotations will be taken from the NCWC translation, (Boston: St. Paul Editions, n.d.), and will be cited by section number in the text.

[9]For a thorough discussion of the genesis of this section of the text, see Herwi Rikhof, *The Concept of Church: A Methodological Inquiry into the Use of Metaphors in Ecclesiology* (London: Sheed and Ward, 1981), p. 30 ff.

[10]In the preliminary schema, "kingdom" was included in such a section, and its return was suggested from the floor of the Council; see Rikhof, pp. 17, 23, and Xavier Rynne, *Vatican Council II* (New York: Farrar, Straus, Giroux, 1968), p. 161.

In the word, in the works, and in the presence of Christ, this kingdom was clearly open to the view of men. The Word of the Lord is compared to seed which is sown in a field; those who hear the Word received the kingdom itself. Then, by its own power the seed sprouts and grows until harvest time. The miracles of Jesus also confirm that the Kingdom has already arrived on earth: "If I cast out devils by the finger of God, then the kingdom of God has come upon you." Before all things, however, the kingdom is clearly visible in the very Person of Christ, the Son of God and the Son of man, who came "to serve and to give His life as a ransom for many." . . . The Church, equipped with the gifts of its Founder and faithfully guarding His precepts of charity, humility and self-sacrifice, receives the mission to proclaim and to spread among all peoples the kingdom of Christ and of God and to be, on earth, the initial budding forth of that kingdom. While it slowly grows, the Church strains toward the completed kingdom and, with all its strength, hopes and desires to be united in glory with its King" (LG, 5).

A number of key themes emerge from these passages. First, the Kingdom of God is encountered first and foremost in the mystery of Christ. In his words, his works, his presence, the reign of God has arrived. Jesus establishes and discloses the kingdom in an unsurpassed and unsurpassable way. Second, the constitution therefore emphasizes "realized eschatology": the kingdom is neither exclusively future nor exclusively transcendent; while these dimensions are not excluded, the focus is on the Kingdom as a present, immanent reality, begun on earth by Christ as an integral aspect of his redemptive activity in fulfillment of the Father's will.[11] Third, the Church is defined in terms of the kingdom: it is "the kingdom of Christ now present in mystery"; as the words, works and presence of Jesus revealed the Kingdom, so the mission of the Church is "to proclaim and to spread" the kingdom and "to be" its initial budding forth. In other words the Church is to carry on the mission of the Lord to make the Kingdom present within space and time. Fourth,

---

[11]Friedrich Wulf writes, "God's definitive kingdom, which despite all appearances to the contrary has been set up on earth by Christ's redemptive deed, is henceforth tangible and efficacious in the Church for the believer, whatever age he may be living in. And so the Church, unlike the kingdoms of this world, has no need of temporal power to achieve her ends; like Christ himself, she can renounce external force. Her chief weapon is faith in the power of God dwelling within her, confident expectation of the Lord's return, and self-sacrificing love for all men." *Commentary on the Documents of Vatican II*, Herbert Vorgrimler, gen. ed. (New York: Herder and Herder, 1967), 1:262. The relevance of this perspective for the peace pastoral in particular is evident.

this is a dynamic process, which is not compatible either with a static, juridical identification of the kingdom with the Church as a timeless entity, a perfect society, characteristic of earlier teaching,[12] or with recent theories which divorce the Church, as a human institution, from the kingdom which is a divine reality.[13]

Three further aspects not explicitly dealt with in these passages need to be addressed. First, what is the Kingdom? Despite its central importance, it is never defined by the constitution. I believe the answer can best be found in the description of the Church in the very first section of the document as "a kind of sacrament of intimate union with God, and of the unity of all humankind, that is, . . . a sign and instrument of such union and unity" (LG, 1).[14] The Kingdom is the authentic expression of the community of the whole human race, arising from its union with God as reestablished in Christ: it is the People of God in covenant unity with their Lord and with one another.

Secondly, in what sense is the Church related to, even identified with, the Kingdom? Here again I believe the presentation of the Church as sacrament of union and unity is helpful: the Church is already the Kingdom in the sense that this is the identity given it by Christ, but must actualize that identity in history—a process which may be, but is not necessarily progressive. An analogy with baptism might be helpful here: one who is baptized has already died and risen with Christ, has already assumed, according to Paul, the new identity of one who is "in Christ"—yet this new identity must be claimed, realized, a process that takes a lifetime at least. It is a process of conformation, of becoming who one truly is. Thus depending on one's standpoint, one can say the Christian is already, or should be, or will be, the presence of Christ in the world. So also for

---

[12]For some examples of this teaching in older church documents, see John Haughey, "Church and Kingdom: Ecclesiology in the Light of Eschatology," *Theological Studies*, 29 (1968), 72–74.

[13]A thorough discussion of this issue, which supports an intrinsic relation between Church and Kingdom, is found in "The Church and Eschatology," Chapter 7 of Avery Dulles, *Models of the Church* (Garden City, N.Y.: Doubleday, 1974), pp. 97–114.

[14]The translation here is that found in Walter Abbott, ed., *The Documents of Vatican II* (New York: Guild Press, 1966). The connection between the Church as sacrament and the Kingdom is made explicitly by Aloys Grillmeier in his discussion of this section of *Lumen Gentium:* "Christ establishes on earth the reign of God, in the realization of which the Church is to be the instrument. It is the kingdom of Christ already mysteriously present, that is, in germ and in secret, but also 'sacramentally,' effecting salvation and acting as his instrument." *Commentary on the Documents of Vatican II*, 1:141.

the Church—from one perspective her identity with the Kingdom is already accomplished in the passion and resurrection of Christ; from another, it is still to come. Likewise a failure to embody completely the new identity given by baptism does not vitiate the character of the sacrament, though it alienates a person, to one extent or another, from his or her authentic identity in Christ; so also the Church retains its sacramental identity with the Kingdom despite its failure to incarnate the Kingdom in its fullness, despite its weakness, its sinfulness, even its betrayals. It should also be added that to posit, as *Lumen Gentium* does, an intrinsic relationship between Church and Kingdom does not entail an assertion of exclusivity; the Church's mission to be a sacrament of divine union and human unity does not mean that other signs, other instruments, of this same union and unity are not operating in history, that the Kingdom is not present "in mystery" in other forms, other ways.

Finally, what is the relation of the Church, called to incarnate the Kingdom, to social transformation? As sacrament of the Kingdom, the Church is to be a sign of the new order, the new age brought by Christ, and the instrument for establishing and extending this human communion grounded in divine union. The role of the Church is to witness to a different way of life, what the constitution later calls "a kingdom of truth and life, a kingdom of holiness and grace, a kingdom of justice, love and peace" (*LG*, 36), and to assist the world to conform more closely to that way by encouraging and promoting efforts for greater justice and peace.[15] From this perspective, incidentally, the argument about whether the Kingdom can be furthered by human effort is seen to be fundamentally misconceived.[16] The fullness of the Kingdom is present in Jesus and is given to the Church. The human effort is strictly a matter of living out what God has already done in Christ. The reestablishment of all things has been accomplished once for all by Christ—history is the record of failures and successes of his followers to enflesh that truth in word, action and presence. In the words of Thomas Merton:

> The disciple of Christ, he who has heard the good news, the announcement of the Lord's coming and of His Victory, and is aware of the

---

[15]This passage from *Lumen Gentium* is quoted in *The Pastoral Constitution on the Church in the Modern World* as part of the only substantial use of the Kingdom imagery in the document, at the conclusion of Chapter 3 of Part I (39–40).

[16]For a discussion of this issue in the context of the theological currents of the 1960's and 1970's, see Avery Dulles, *The Resilient Church* (Garden City, N.Y.: Doubleday, 1977), pp. 17–19.

definitive establishment of the Kingdom, proves his faith by the gift of
his whole self to the Lord in order that *all* may enter the Kingdom. This
Christian discipleship entails a certain way of acting, a *politeia*, a
conservatio, which is proper to the Kingdom.

The great historical event, the coming of the Kingdom, is made clear
and is "realized" in proportion as Christians themselves live the life of
the Kingdom in the circumstances of their own place and time. . . . By
their example of a truly Christian understanding of the world, expressed in a living and active application of the Christian faith to the
human problems of their own time, Christians manifest the love of
Christ for men (Jn. 13:35, 17:21), and by that fact make Him visibly
present in the world.[17]

The vision of the Kingdom of God presented in *Lumen Gentium*
provides the fundamental theological orientation for the two recent
pastoral letters of the U.S. bishops as well. The same key elements
which characterized the conciliar document are integral to the
pastorals, though in each case specifically applied to the issue being
considered. The significance of the doctrine of the Kingdom of God
for the issue of peace is first broached in the lengthy introductory
section of the opening chapter, "Peace in the Modern World: Religious Perspectives and Principles." In their initial presentation of
"the religious vision of peace," the bishops state that this "vision
has an objective basis and is capable of progressive realization" (*CP*,
20). The objective basis is the redemptive work of Christ, as set forth
in the second chapter of Ephesians: "Christ is our peace, for he has
'made us both one, and has broken down the dividing wall of
hostility . . . that he might create in himself one new man in place of
the two, so making peace, and might reconcile us both to God' (Eph.
2:14–16)." In this passage the components of peace, reconciliation
with God, the unity of humankind, correspond closely to the "sacramental" characteristics of the Church at the beginning of *Lumen
Gentium*; this peace is not only effected but embodied by Christ: as
an integral dimension of the salvific action of Jesus, it objectively
participates in the definitive, once-for-all nature of that event.

Yet like every aspect of salvation, peace must be claimed, actualized, lived out in the concreteness of space and time, in the history
of individual lives and of the human community: it is "capable of

---

[17]Thomas Merton, "Blessed are the Meek: The Christian Roots of Nonviolence," in
The Nonviolent Alternative, ed. Gordon Zahn (New York: Farrar, Straus, Giroux,
1980), p. 209.

progressive realization." The bishops go on to say that "this peace will be achieved fully only in the kingdom of God." Such a statement seems to set up a framework in which the Kingdom is envisioned as symbolizing the perfect fulfillment of peace, of salvation, beyond history.[18] But the bishops immediately make clear that they are not defining the Kingdom exclusively, or even primarily, in terms of final eschatology. The Kingdom is not simply the future terminus, the absolute completion of the work of peace, but belongs to the same historical process: "The realization of the Kingdom, therefore, is a continuing work, progressively accomplished, precariously maintained, and needing constant effort to preserve the peace achieved and expand its scope in personal and political life."[19] The Kingdom is aligned with peace as having a present as well as a future dimension; the intrinsic relation of the two will be made explicit in art. 22 when peace is described as "one of the signs of the Kingdom present in the world." Thus peace is theologically grounded by the bishops in the objective work of Christ and in the progressive unfolding of the Kingdom, which by implication also has its "objective basis" in that same redemptive work.

It is in the context of this connection between peace and Kingdom that the Church's responsibility for peacemaking is considered:

> The Church is called to be, in a unique way, the instrument of the kingdom of God in history. Since peace is one of the signs of that Kingdom present in the world, the Church fulfills part of her essential mission by making the peace of the kingdom more visible in our time.
>
> Because peace, like the Kingdom of God itself, is both a divine gift and a human work, the Church should continually pray for the gift and share in the work. We are called to be a Church at the service of peace, precisely because peace is one manifestation of God's word and work in our midst (CP, 22–23).

This crucial passage provides the bishops' justification for writing such a pastoral at all, and a rationale for the particular approach to

---

[18]The very first mention of the Kingdom in the letter, part of a summary description of the "biblical vision of the world" as "created and sustained by God, scarred by sin, redeemed by Christ and destined for the Kingdom" (CP, 14), reflects a future interpretation of the Kingdom.

[19]In the second draft of the pastoral, the opening words refer ambiguously to "its realization in the world" (Origins, 12:20 [Oct. 28, 1982], 308), where the antecedent would more naturally be "peace" than "kingdom"; but the clarification, whether expressing the original intent or not, is consistent with the presentation of the Kingdom in the rest of the letter.

the issue which the pastoral takes. Witnessing to and working for peace is located at the center of the Church's mission because peace is understood not primarily in political or even ethical terms, but as a fundamentally religious reality: it is a sign of the reign of God, a manifestation of God's word and work, a divine gift (in Christ) which is also a human work (of "progressive realization"). Moral and political considerations are obviously important, but should not, the bishops maintain, set the terms of the discussion.

This means, as the rest of art. 23 states, that the starting point for theological reflection on peace is not the ethical issue of "limiting the resort to force in human affairs," which has dominated the history of Catholic thought on war and peace, but rather the relation of peace to the person and work of Christ and to his proclamation of the good news of the Kingdom. Christology, soteriology, ecclesiology and eschatology provide the context for discussion of moral issues. The bishops call for a theology of peace which will "ground the task of peacemaking solidly in the biblical vision of the Kingdom of God, then place it centrally in the ministry of the Church" (CP, 25). Thus the bishops reject a disjunctive approach in which transcendent (or interior) peace is on a totally different plane from the "real world"; if the Kingdom is a force within history, then peace as a sign of that Kingdom is relevant to concrete concerns as well, including "the obstacles in the way of peace, as these are understood theologically and in the social and political sciences," and the integration of faith based work for peace with that of "other groups and institutions in society." It is this methodology which the bishops not only recommend but endeavor to employ through the rest of the pastoral. If the results are somewhat problematic and perhaps inconsistent, the insistence on the priority of "the biblical vision of the Kingdom of God" for a Christian understanding of peace is significant in itself, and a principal point of divergence between the bishops and their critics.

The headings for each of the three major sections of Chapter 1 following this introduction reflect this emphasis: "Peace and the Kingdom," "Kingdom and History," "The Moral Choices for the Kingdom." The discussion of the New Testament in "Peace and the Kingdom" provides a detailed summary of the theme of the Kingdom as presented in the gospels, and asserts that "all discussion of war and peace in the New Testament must be seen within the context of the unique revelation of God that is Jesus Christ and of the reign of God which Jesus proclaimed and inaugurated" (CP, 39). The first subsection, on "War," focuses on the exclusively metaphorical use of military imagery in the new Testament, but in the process introduces the central message of Jesus' preaching: "Jesus challenged everyone to recognize in him the presence of the reign of God and to give themselves over to that reign. Such a radical change of allegiance was difficult for many to accept and families found themselves divided, as if by a sword" (CP, 42). Here the present quality of the Kingdom in its relation to Jesus is linked to the demand for a response on the part of his listeners. To accept Jesus is to commit oneself to the Kingdom, not simply as a doctrine requiring intellectual adherence, much less as an exclusively future realm of perfection, but as a concretely different way of life entailing a "radical change of allegiance." Open to all, the reign of God is both gift, received through "faith in Jesus and trust in God's mercy," and task, requiring "living in accord with the demands of the Kingdom" (CP, 43).

This dual focus on the presence of the Kingdom in the person of Jesus and on the response to the Kingdom demanded of the disciple continues through the subsection which follows on "Jesus and the Reign of God." The opening sentence, "Jesus proclaimed the reign of God in his words and made it present in his actions" (CP, 44), echoes the statement in *Lumen Gentium* that "in the word, in the works, and in the presence of Christ, the Kingdom was already open to the view of men" (*LG*, 5); it also establishes the structure for the entire subsection.[21] Among the words of Jesus, particular attention is given to his initial preaching of the good news: "His words begin with a call to conversion and a proclamation of the arrival of the Kingdom. 'The time if fulfilled, and the Kingdom of God is at hand; repent, and believe in the gospel' (Mk. 1:15, Mt. 4:17). The call to conversion was at the same time an invitation to enter God's reign. Jesus went beyond the prophets' cries for conversion when he declared that, in him, the reign of God had begun and was in fact among the people" (CP, 44).[22] Here conversion is identified with the

[20]The subheadings, added in the third draft (*Origins*, 13:1 [May 19, 1983], 6), are somewhat artificial here. Art. 43 has no reference to war at all, and should perhaps have been included as the first paragraph of the following subsection, "Jesus and the Reign of God," though it is clearly linked to the passages quoted from the previous section.

[21]This arrangement is first found in the third draft; though the second draft contains most of the same material, it is less clearly organized, and seems to show less correspondence to *Lumen Gentium*.

[22]The distinction refers back to the final sentence of the Old Testament section,

change in direction required by new allegiance to the Kingdom. The specifics of such a conversion, the concrete "demands of the Kingdom," are revealed by further words of Jesus, particularly the Sermon on the Mount, which "described a new reality in which God's power is manifested and the longing of the people is fulfilled" (*CP,* 45). Central to "the conduct of one who lives under God's reign" is the forgiveness preached by Jesus, a reflection of and participation in "the forgiveness of God, which is the beginning of salvation" (*CP,* 46). The significance of this quality of the Kingdom for peacemaking is clear though implicit; Jesus' description of "God's reign as one in which love is an active, life-giving, inclusive force," which includes love of enemies even "in the face of threat and opposition" (*CP,* 47) is likewise crucial to a theology of peacemaking.

It is quite evident in this presentation that the bishops do not subscribe to the "interim ethic" approach to Jesus' teaching, which presupposes its relevance only if the fullness of the Kingdom were imminent; nor do they follow the typically Lutheran interpretation, whereby the human failure to accomplish these demands reveals one's complete dependence on divine mercy. Though well aware of human sinfulness, the bishops propose that Jesus' teachings be taken seriously as values to be lived in the community of faith. They write, "The words of Jesus would remain an impossible, abstract ideal were it not for two things: the actions of Jesus and his gift of the spirit" (*CP,* 48). The words of Jesus are not abstract ideals because they were embodied in the concrete acts of a real human life: Jesus incarnated the Kingdom in his deeds of forgiveness, reconciliation, mercy and love, and became a sign of contradiction "in a world which knew violence, oppression, and injustice" (*CP,* 48). This confrontation between God's reign and human evil reached a climax on the cross, which is a simultaneous revelation of human "violence and cruelty" and of the reconciling power of suffering live (*CP,* 49). While the crucifixion seems to be evidence of the victory of evil, it actually reveals the ultimate impotence of evil: "The resurrection of Jesus is the sign to the world that God indeed does reign, does give life in death, and that the love of God is stronger even than death" (*CP,* 50).

Only in the context of the resurrection as "the fullest demonstration of the power of God's reign" can the risen Lord's gift of peace to

---

which states that the Israelites "heard the prophets call them to love according to the covenantal vision, to repent, and to be ready for God's reign" (*CP,* 38). Jesus is being presented as the fulfillment of this "Hope for Eschatological Peace," as the subsection is headed.

the disciples be properly understood. This peace is not an interior feeling of personal well-being but "the fullness of salvation, . . . the reconcilation of the world and God, the restoration of the unity and harmony of all creation" (*CP*, 51); it is the conviction of the Kingdom's triumph and thus, as the bishops stated in their introductory discussion, a "sign of that Kingdom present in the world" (*CP*, 22). But of course this conviction, this assurance, is not an invitation to complacency; it is just as much a challenge as Jesus' original call to conversion, for the reality of this peace, this reconciliation, is perceptible only to the eyes of faith, and must be incarnated in the community of believers as it was in their Lord if it is truly to be a sign of the Kingdom to the wider world. As the life of Jesus made the otherwise "abstract, impossible ideal" of the Kingdom come alive in his time, so the life of the community is called to do the same in succeeding ages: such is the task which corresponds to the gift.[23]

Only through a second gift, inseparable from the first, can this mission of peace be carried out. The Spirit of the risen Jesus enables the community to witness to the peace of the Kingdom, despite their own sinfulness and the continued hostility and persecution of the world. The Spirit transforms Christian communities into signs of the Kingdom, "people who would make the peace which God had established visible through the love and unity within their own communities" (*CP*, 54). The bishops' presentation of this final aspect of scriptural teaching on peace and the Kingdom is sober and realistic: they point out that the early Christians were well aware that "reconciliation and peace . . . were not yet fully operative in their world" and that in this sense "the fullness of God's reign" remained a future reality, but they insist that the experience of the Spirit and the memory of Christ were the source not only of hope for the future but of action in the present. Their summation reiterates the paired aspects of sign and instrument, of embodying and extending the peace of God's reign, as the essence of Christian discipleship: "The risen Lord's gift of peace is inextricably bound to the call to follow Jesus and to continue the proclamation of God's reign . . . To follow Jesus Christ implies continual conversion in one's own life as one seeks to act in ways which are consonant with the justice,

---

[23]This phrasing is found explicitly in the second draft: "The gift of peace, made available to us in the Spirit of God who unites us, is also the task of peace" (*Origins*, 12:20, 310).

forgiveness, and love of God's reign. Discipleship reaches out to the ends of the earth and calls for reconciliation among all peoples so that God's purpose, 'a plan for the fullness of time, to unite all things in him' (Eph. 1:10) will be fulfilled" (*CP*, 54).

The ethical stance most consistent with the scriptural evidence provided by the bishops would seem to be a biblically-based pacifism—a commitment to witness to and to work for justice and reconciliation without resort to violence, in conformity with the life and teaching of Jesus, and in reliance on the power of the Spirit. The Church would seek to make the Kingdom inaugurated by Jesus visible in the world by embodying the standards of the Kingdom as Jesus did, mindful that the sinfulness of its members will inevitably obscure and even distort the purity of its witness, so that the Kingdom and its peace remain provisional, tentative, incompletely realized. While the bishops allow for and even commend this response, they do not mandate, or even recommend it, and consider it to be an option for individuals but not, apparently, for the Church as a whole.

The shift in perspective occurs in the section entitled "Kingdom and History," where the emphasis is placed on the extent to which the Kingdom is not present because of the continuing power of sin: "It is precisely because sin is part of history that the realization of the peace of the Kingdom is never permanent or total. . . . Christians are called to live the tension between the vision of the reign of God and its concrete realization in history. The tension is often described in terms of 'already but not yet': i.e., we already live in the grace of the Kingdom, but it is not yet the completed Kingdom" (*CP*, 57–58). Such statements are certainly true to experience, and consistent with the foregoing biblical data, but the conclusions drawn from them are more problematic. Rather than being viewed as a summons to repentance for failing to make the Kingdom visible, and as a call to more faithful dependence on the abiding presence of the Spirit, this tension between vision and actuality is seen as justifying "the complexity of the Catholic teaching on warfare" (*CP*, 60), which permits the use of violence in certain circumstances. That is, because the Kingdom is not completely present, commitment to the values of the Kingdom on the part of Christians need not be absolute: "In the Kingdom of God, justice and peace will be fully realized" (*CP*, 60), but in the arena of history, the demands of justice will at times conflict with, and take precedence over, dedication to peace. Here the meaning of peace has been shifted from its theological sense as a sign of the Kingdom instituted by Christ to the more empirical sense of absence of conflict, as the Kingdom itself recedes into the absolute future, to the point that the tension between "already" and "not yet" with respect to the Kingdom gives way at one point to a polarity between "history" and "kingdom" as between time and eternity: "It is within this tension of kingdom and history that Catholic teaching has addressed the problem of war" (*CP*, 61). While the bishops continue to assert that Christ's "command of love and his call to reconciliation are not purely future ideals but call us to obedience today" (*CP*, 58), and revert to a less polarized phrasing when they state, "In the 'already but not yet' of Christian existence, members of the Church choose different paths to move toward the realization of the Kingdom in history" (*CP*, 62), the conclusion reached is that in so far as the Kingdom is not yet actualized, the methods for moving toward the Kingdom will not necessarily be those of the Kingdom itself. The end (the peace of the Kingdom) need not be already present in the means to that end. Hence the acceptance of the theory of the just war, which will actually provide the set of criteria to be used in the second chapter of the pastoral to evaluate the morality of the use and possession of nuclear weapons.

The biblical perspective is further deemphasized in the last section of the chapter, "The Moral Choices for the Kingdom." In the second draft of the letter,[24] the two subsections, "Non-violence" and "Just War," described the alternative "moral choices"; the second received somewhat more detailed attention than the first, but not to a disproportionate extent. In the final version, the section on non-violence, though strengthened by the addition of important patristic quotations, has been retitled "The Value of Non-violence" and shifted to the end; the section on "The Just War Criteria" has been greatly expanded to include a total of thirty-one paragraphs (as compared with eleven, two of which summarize both positions, under non-violence); two additional subsections, on "The Nature of Peace" and "The Presumption against War and the Principle of Legitimate Self-Defense," have been added, principally to provide a framework for the just war principles which now follow them. Not only has the priority of the nonviolent position, corresponding to the priority of the biblical material as well as to the historical development of Christian thought, been reversed, but the balance of the two choices has completely disappeared, to the point that the

---

[24]See *Origins*, 12:20, 311–12.

rationale for the title of the subsection is obscured. In fact, the Kingdom is not mentioned at all in "The Moral Choices for the Kingdom." It will not be referred to again until a section on contemplative prayer in the last chapter,[25] and then for a final time in the last paragraph of the letter, which returns to a focus on faith in Christ, who "does not solve our problems but sustains us as we take responsibility for his work of creation and try to shape it in the ways of the Kingdom" (CP, 330).[26]

Given the direction in which their argument develops, it could be concluded that the initial discussion of the Kingdom has minimal significance for the bishops' moral judgments and policy recommendations in the central chapters of the pastoral. However, I believe such an assumption is oversimplified: though the logic of the letter relies on natural law principles, the underlying moral passion of the letter, which remains powerful even in somewhat diluted form, draws on the religious vision with which it opens. The vision of peace as a sign of the Kingdom remains a sign of contradiction to any easy accommodation to the use of force, any comfortable acceptance of violence. The "strong presumption against war which is binding on all" (CP, 70) in the Church's teaching arises not from the just war theory, a series of objective criteria, but from the teaching of the Gospels. For the bishops, rejection of violence is not an absolute, but it is a norm to be suspended only in exceptional circumstances governed by stringent conditions, a concession to the provisional character of the Kingdom but at the same time an acknowledgement that the Kingdom remains the ultimate standard of judgment. It could be maintained that the greater length of the sections on the just war, and on the application of just-war criteria to the possession and use of nuclear weapons, are not evidence of greater importance, but of the degree of difficulty which exists in any effort to determine when the presumption against the use of force may be overriden. It is true that there is no evidence that Christ either sought such exceptions for himself in time of crisis, or made provision for such exceptions for his disciples, and that in doing so the bishops and the tradition they are following are inconsistent with the Gospel. Even granting this does not put the just war theory in direct opposition to the Kingdom: though the bishops' prohibition of violence is

---

[25]The bishops state that "silent, interior prayer bridges temporarily the 'already' and 'not yet,' this world and God's kingdom of peace" (CP, 294).

[26]The final quotation from Rev. 21:1–5 which concludes the letter is also described as envisioning "the beautiful final kingdom" (CP, 339).

not absolute it is strong and firm. Not only is there a presumption in favor of peace but a clear statement that non-violent resistance to injustice is more consonant with the teaching of Christ: "We believe work to develop non-violent means of fending off aggression and resolving conflict best reflects the call of Jesus both to love and to justice. Indeed, each increase in the potential destructiveness of weapons and therefore of war serves to underline the rightness of the way Jesus mandated to his followers" (CP, 78). If force is to be preferred to passivity and acquiescence in the face of injustice, non-violent resistance and suffering love, the "mandate," the command, of Jesus to his followers, is to be preferred to violence. Thus the initial presentation of the Kingdom of peace continues to exert a kind of pressure, occasionally articulated, as here, but largely implicit, which serves to keep the presumption against violence taut rather than flabby and easily evaded. As unsatisfying, logically and theologically, as this combination of scriptural vision and natural law may be, it does serve to distinguish the position of the bishops from those for whom the Kingdom represents a future reality discontinuous with the sinful present, a transcendent realm which has no practical impact on social or political policy.

The vision of the Kingdom of God in *Economic Justice for All* is complementary to and remarkably consistent with the presentation found in *The Challenge of Peace*; but the tension between biblical teaching and natural law formulations which marked the discussion there is largely absent in the second pastoral, because there is a basic congruence between the scriptural and more philosophical elements, rather than the somewhat strained and not completely persuasive effort in the peace pastoral to demonstrate a convergence between non-violence and the just war approach. Consequently the material on the Kingdom in the economic pastoral, while somewhat less extensive, seems better integrated into the overall structure of the document, though perhaps less significant, paradoxically, as it does not have to function as a counterweight to a contrary tendency.

In the "Pastoral Message" which introduces *Economic Justice for All,* the Kingdom is successively linked to the poor, the Church and Christ himself, three principal themes to be developed in greater detail in the body of the document.[27] The first mention of the

---

[27]This Pastoral Message, added to the final version of the document, is different enough in language and structure from the body of the text it summarizes to warrant its own comment.

Kingdom appears under the heading, "All members of society have a special obligation to the poor and vulnerable" (EJ/PM, 16), and emphasizes the special association of the Kingdom with the marginalized: "The Kingdom that Jesus proclaimed in his word and ministry excludes no one," and is preached especially as "glad tidings to the poor" (LK. 4:18), as in Jesus' inaugural discourse at Nazareth. As Jesus identifies himself with those most in need, so the disciple is called "to speak for the voiceless, to defend the defenseless, to assess life styles, policies, and social institutions in terms of their impact on the poor." Here the basic pattern of proclamation of the Kingdom and challenge to conversion, based on Mark 1:15 and found also in the peace pastoral (CP, 42, 44), is given specific application to "the least of these." As a summons to make a "fundamental 'option for the poor'," the demands of the Kingdom correspond to a key theme of the entire letter, justice for the poor as the main criterion for economic and political activity: "Decisions must be judged in light of what they do *for* the poor, what they do *to* the poor, and what they enable the poor to do *for themselves*. The fundamental moral criterion for all economic decisions, policies, and institutions is this: They must be at the service of *all people, especially the poor*" (EJ, 24).

The Kingdom next appears in the context of a description of the Christian community: "As a Church, we must be people after God's own heart, bonded by the Spirit, sustaining one another in love, setting our hearts on God's Kingdom, committing ourselves to solidarity with those who suffer, working for peace and justice, acting as a sign of Christ's love and justice in the world" (EJ/PM, 24). What is meant by "setting our hearts on the Kingdom"? In this series of parallel phrases, it is related on the one hand to being "people after God's own heart," a community of faith sharing intimately the divine will and purpose for creation, God's own heart set on the full manifestation of the Kingdom, and on the other to action in solidarity with and on behalf of those who suffer injustice. The double focus on "working for justice and peace" and being "a sign of Christ's love and justice" reflects and concretizes the basic sacramental understanding of the Church in *Lumen Gentium*. Embodying and extending justice and peace is central to the Church's identity and vocation.

The third passage, near the conclusion of the "Pastoral Message," gives the Kingdom of God the same Christological grounding as that found in *Lumen Gentium* and in *The Challenge of Peace*: "Jesus has entered our history as God's anointed son who announces the coming of God's Kingdom, a Kingdom of justice and peace and freedom. And, what Jesus proclaims, he embodies in his actions. His ministry reveals that the reign of God is something more powerful than evil, injustice, and the hardness of hearts. Through his crucifixion and resurrection, he reveals that God's love is ultimately victorious over all suffering, all horror, all meaninglessness, and even over the mystery of death" (*EJ/PM*, 28). The Kingdom, and the justice which is an essential dimension of it, is thus a fundamentally paschal reality, an expression of the salvation wrought by God in Christ. In the resurrection, the end of history, the fullness of God's reign, is reached, in order that the energy of the victory, the power of the Kingdom, might inform the ongoing struggle against evil within history. Thus the vision of the Kingdom is a source of true hope: it leads not to passive resignation in the face of injustice but to active engagement in the process of personal and social transformation.

These same basic elements, Christ, the Church, the poor, provide the framework for discussion of the Kingdom of God in the letter proper, though the rhetorically effective arrangement leading to the Christological climax in the "Pastoral Message" is reversed in the more logical development of "The Christian Vision of Economic Life," the second chapter of the pastoral. Here discussion of Old Testament themes of creation, covenant and community is followed by "The Reign of God and Justice." As in *The Challenge of Peace*, the Kingdom is the master image which organizes the presentation of Jesus' life and message and the call to discipleship. Though more concise than the corresponding sections of the peace pastoral,[28] the biblical material here conveys the same vision.

Thus the opening paragraph of the New Testament material combines the expected Christological focus and a stress on realized eschatology with a challenge to the followers of Christ to make the Kingdom present today:

> Jesus enters human history as God's anointed son who announces the nearness of the reign of God (Mk. 1:9–14). This proclamation summons us to acknowledge God as creator and covenant partner and challenges

---

[28]The biblical section was actually considerably longer in the first draft of the pastoral, 39 paragraphs to the present 26 paragraphs (see *Origins*, 14:22–23 [Nov. 15, 1984], 343–48). It was evidently shortened in the general interests of space in what proved to be a lengthy document.

us to seek ways in which God's revelation of the dignity and destiny of all creation might become incarnate in history. It is not simply the promise of the future victory of God over sin and evil, but that this victory has already begun—in the life and teachings of Jesus (EJ, 41).

One noteworthy feature here is the way in which the proclamation of the Kingdom is seen to be in continuity with the Old Testament themes of creation and covenant, and consequently the more cosmic dimension of the Kingdom is highlighted, encompassing not only humanity but all created reality. This will of course be important for later discussion of stewardship of the earth and its resources as an integral dimension of work for justice.

As in *Lumen Gentium* and *The Challenge of Peace*, the reign of God is made present by the word and work of Jesus: "What Jesus proclaims by word, he enacts in his ministry" (EJ, 42); here word and deed are interwoven into a single presentation, rather than being arranged in successive blocs of material as in the peace pastoral. The focus is of course on issues of justice, simplicity of life, compassion for the oppressed and marginalized. The centerpiece is Jesus' exhortation "not to be anxious about material goods but rather to seek first God's reign and God's justice" (Mt 6:25–33) (EJ, 42): here the search for justice is seen to be intrinsic to the "incarnation" of the Kingdom in history identified above with the call to conversion. The climax of this section, and extended reflection on the last judgement scene in Matthew 25, emphasizes that the failure to act in love and justice, to care for "the poor, the outcast, and the oppressed," is in fact a rejection of Jesus himself, who "is hidden in those most in need" (EJ, 44). Those who perform works of mercy and compassion "are welcomed into God's Kingdom" and those who fail to do so are excluded, for the Kingdom which is embodied by Jesus can be found, must be found, among those with whom Jesus has identified himself.

In the section "Called to Be Disciples in Community" which follows, the essential mission of the Church is expressed in terms of the Kingdom: "Jesus summoned his first followers to a change of heart and to take on the yoke of God's reign (Mk 1:14–15; Mt 11:29). They are to be the nucleus of that community which will continue the work of proclaiming and building God's kingdom through the centuries" (EJ, 45). Like Jesus, the Church is called to the double expression of word and action in work for the Kingdom. In particular, Jesus' example of selfless service and of suffering love even in the face of persecution become models for the process of building the Kingdom. As in *The Challenge of Peace,* though more briefly, the paschal pattern of death, resurrection and gift of the Spirit is seen as the source of the Church's mission to spread the Kingdom, and of the empowerment to carry out that mission:

> Jesus' death is an example of that greater love which lays down one's life for others (cf. Jn 15:12–18). It is a model for those who suffer persecution for the sake of justice (Mt 5:10). The death of Jesus was not the end of his power and presence, for he was raised up by the power of God. Nor did it mark the end of the disciples' union with him. After Jesus had appeared to them and when they received the gift of the Spirit (Acts 2:1–12), they became apostles of the good news to the ends of the earth *(EJ,* 47).

Once again the understanding of Church is essentially sacramental, as the "power and presence" of Jesus, manifested in his life and confirmed in his resurrection, are experienced in the life and work of Christian disciples: "In the face of poverty and persecution they transformed human lives and formed communities which became signs of the power and presence of God" *(EJ,* 47).

It is particularly towards the poor that the Church is called to be a sign of God's power and presence in the world, a sacrament of the Kingdom. In the section headed "Poverty, Riches, and the Challenge of Discipleship," the bishops emphasize the special relationship between the poor and the Kingdom as expressed in the first beatitude:

> When Jesus calls the poor "blessed," he is not praising their condition of poverty, but their openness to God. When he restates that the reign of God is theirs, he voices God's special concern for them, and promises that they are to be the beneficiaries of God's mercy and justice *(EJ,* 50).

The Church is to be a sign of the Kingdom to the poor by its "proper use of possessions to alleviate need and suffering" and its development of "structures to support and sustain the weak and powerless" *(EJ,* 51); it is to be a sign of the Kingdom of the poor by "an emptying of self, both individually and corporately, that allows the church to experience the power of God in the midst of poverty and powerlessness" *(EJ,* 52); it is also to be an instrument of the Kingdom for the poor, "an instrument in assisting people to experience the liberating power of God in their own lives so that they may respond to the Gospel in freedom and dignity" *(EJ,* 52). Thus the basic perception

of Church found in *Lumen Gentium* makes clear the reasons why
the "concerns of this pastoral letter are not at all peripheral to the
central mystery at the heart of the Church," but are in fact "integral
to the proclamation of the Gospel and part of the vocation of every
Christian today" (*EJ*, 60).

As in the peace pastoral, a recognition of "the tension between
promise and fulfillment" (*EJ*, 53) modifies the emphasis on realized
eschatology, but here the tension does not lead to a dilemma of
means and ends, as in the issue of the use of violence in *The
Challenge of Peace*. (The question of a possible conflict between the
demands of justice and of peace is never raised here, despite the
primary focus of justice.) The provisional character of the Kingdom
is fundamentally perceived as encouraging deeper commitment to
the vocation of actualizing the Kingdom, while guarding against
discouragement at the continued evidence of injustice and disunity:

> Our action on behalf of justice in our world proceeds from the convic-
> tion that, despite the power of injustice and violence, life has been
> fundamentally changed by the entry of the Word made flesh into human
> history. Christian communities . . . will embody in their lives the
> values of the new creation while they labor under the old. The quest
> for economic and social justice will always combine hope and realism,
> and must be renewed by every generation (*EJ*, 54–55).

Thus a remarkable feature of the economic pastoral is that references
to the Kingdom do not cease with the shift to the material on
"Ethical Norms for Economic Life," as they did when the criteria for
the just war were considered. The comparable material in this letter,
the discussion of the three dimensions of basic justice, commutative,
distributive, and social justice, is introduced by placing these concepts in the framework of biblical teaching: "On their path through
history, . . . sinful human beings need more specific guidance on
how to move toward the realization of this great vision of God's
Kingdom. This guidance is contained in the norms of basic or
minimal justice" (*EJ*, 68). The philosophical, "natural law" principles are not an alternative to the scriptural vision of a just society,
but tools for actualizing that vision in the concrete circumstances of
each varied social setting. While the bishops are aware that the
Kingdom is not present in its fullness and that "knowledge of how
to achieve the goal of social unity is limited" (*EJ*, 67) and subject to
disagreement, their basic outlook is one of hope and motivation

rooted in faith. As they express this vision in the section on prayer later in the letter.

> For the Eucharist to be a living promise of the fullness of God's Kingdom, the faithful must commit themselves to living as redeemed people with the same care and love for all people that Jesus showed. The body of Christ . . . empowers them to work to heal the brokenness of society and human relationships and to grow in a spirit of self-giving to others (*EJ*, 330).

It is this sense of empowerment, rooted in the dynamic understanding of the Kingdom, manifested in the vitality of the Christian community, which characterizes this pastoral as well as *The Challenge of Peace*. As summarized at the conclusion of this section, this vision is explicitly seen as a concrete expression of the doctrine of the Church formulated at the Second Vatican Council: "In worship and in deeds for justice, the Church becomes a 'sacrament,' a visible sign of that unity in justice and peace that God wills for the whole of humanity" (*EJ*, 331).[29]

Both pastorals, bear eloquent witness, then, to the importance of the Kingdom of God for social transformation. By emphasizing the crucial significance of the Kingdom for Christology, ecclesiology and ethics, the bishops have located action on behalf of justice and peace at the center of the Church's ministry (cf. *CP*, 25; *EJ*, 60). It can be argued that the teaching of the pastorals is not completely consistent: the continuing presence of sin is allowed to relativize somewhat the normative status of the Kingdom as an expression of fidelity to the inseparable commitment of justice, reconciliation and nonviolence shown by Jesus in the face of the very same forces of sin. Nevertheless in both pastorals it is clearly the awareness of the Kingdom of God as a dynamic process within history which serves as the primary justification and motivation for the Church's teaching and action on the issues of justice and peace. This is just as evidently not the case with the principal critics of the pastorals, of whom Michael Novak is perhaps the most visible and persistent.

Resident scholar at the American Enterprise Institute, a conservative think-tank in Washington, D.C., Novak wrote his own "alternative pastoral," *Moral Clarity in the Nuclear Age*,[30] in response to *The*

---

[29]The notes on this sentence refer to *Lumen Gentium*, 1, as well as other passages from Council documents which talk about the sacramentality of the Church.

[30]First published in *National Review*, 35:6 (April 1, 1983), 354–92; it is thus a response to the third draft of the bishops' text, not to the final version. All references in the text will be cited by page number to this edition.

Challenge of Peace, and was vice-chairman and principal author for the "Lay Commission on Catholic Social Teaching and the U.S. Economy" which produced *Toward the Future: Catholic Social Thought and the U.S. Economy.*[31] Before considering the theological vision, and particularly the perspective on the Kingdom of God, which informs these works, it will be helpful to examine Novak's theological presuppositions as they are presented in his 1982 work, *The Spirit of Democratic Capitalism.*[32]

Novak places himself in the tradition of Christian realism which he sees running from Augustine to Reinhold Niebuhr. It is not unfair to say that the central theological category for Novak is clearly sin: "At the heart of Judaism and Christianity is the recognition of sin" (p. 353). Salvation, redemption in Christ, is not viewed as having any practical social consequences. In his discussion of the Incarnation, he maintains that this doctrine teaches the believer to face facts and be realistic, which for Novak means to relinquish any form of utopian hope for a better world. He writes, "The point of the Incarnation is to respect the world as it is, to acknowledge its limits, to recognize its weaknesses, irrationalities, and evil forces, and to disbelieve any promises that the world is now or ever will be transformed into the City of God. If Jesus could not effect this, how shall we? . . . The world is not going to become—*ever*—a Kingdom of justice and love" (p. 341). Such a statement avoids at least two questions central to *Lumen Gentium* and the two pastorals: Is it not the role of the Church to be a sign of such a Kingdom even in a world which is not marked by justice and love? Are not efforts to extend the realm of justice and love, even if not completely success-ful, preferable to settling for the status quo? The issue, as Novak himself recognizes, is fundamentally soteriological: "The single greatest temptation for Christians is to imagine that the salvation won by Christ has altered the human condition. Many attempt to judge the world by the standards of the gospels, as though the world were ready to live according to them. Sin is not so easily overcome.

---

[31]New York: American Catholic Committee, 1984; unlike *Moral Clarity,* this is not a direct response to the bishops' pastoral, which had not yet been issued even in a first draft, but an independent effort. References in the text will be cited by page number to this edition.

[32]Michael Novak, *The Spirit of Democratic Capitalism* (New York: American Enter-prise Institute/Simon & Schuster, 1982); all references in the text will be cited by page number to this edition.

A political economy for sinners, even Christian sinners (however well intentioned), is consistent with the story of Jesus. A political economy based on love and justice is to be found beyond, never to be wholly incarnated within, human history. The Incarnation obliges us to reduce our noblest expectations, so to love the world as to fit a political economy to it, nourishing all that is best in it" (pp. 343–44).

Here is certainly the crux of the matter: whatever Paul meant by "If anyone is in Christ, he is a new creation" (2 Cor. 5:17), he did not mean, according to Novak, that redemption, or grace, or the presence of the Holy Spirit, alters the human condition—no distinction is made between pagan and Christian in this regard. Salvation is reduced to a juridical transaction or an exclusively interior transformation. One does not have to believe in human perfectability, or that a polity of love and justice will be wholly incarnated within human history, to hold the Christian community can and must live according to the standards of the Gospels, to be a sign and instrument of the world's salvation, whether the response of the world is favorable or not. Novak sets up a dualistic world-view consisting of two and only two options, realism, which accepts the human condition as it is and works within its limitations, and utopianism, which imagines a society in which these limitations can be eradicated. No allowance is made for a third view, which holds that these limitations have been overcome in the victory of Christ, and that the vocation of the Christian community is to enflesh, model and extend, albeit in a contingent and imperfect fashion, the reign of God already established by Christ. Such a perspective is based not on a utopian dream of some indefinite future, but on a sacramental understanding of the Church as "the Kingdom of Christ now present in mystery." Novak's refusal to allow for such a position suggests that his disagreements with the bishops' pastorals are not only political and tactical but theological. Such a perspective is based not on a utopian dream of some indefinite future, but on a sacramental understanding of the Church as "the Kingdom of Christ now present in mystery." Such a supposition is borne out by an examination of the two documents in which these disagreements are directly expressed.

In explaining the approach of *Moral Clarity in the Nuclear Age*, Novak writes, that "We are certain only that we have tried to be faithful to biblical realism" (p. 358),[33] a term which is not defined

---

[33]It should be noted that Novak presents himself as writing on behalf of an

but presumably is connected with the predominance of sin. It is noteworthy that his starting point is the fact that humanity has been consistently warned that God might will or permit its destruction, a perspective buttressed by reference to Cain, Noah, Sodom and Gomorrah, the destruction of the Temple, as well as the levelling of Carthage and attacks on Greece and Rome, culminating in the barbarian invasions which inspired Augustine's *City of God*. This is evidently the "biblical realism" to which he strives to be faithful. The nuclear threat should be considered from this standpoint:

> The ruin of civilization is not a theme new to our time, nor is the theme of the destruction of all things living. Since Jewish and Christian conscience has long been steeled by contemplation of the fragility of this world and the overpowering sovereignty of God, our generation should not separate itself too dramatically from all others. The prophecies of the Book of Revelation exceed even the horrors of the twentieth century (p. 356).

The point, centered on the divine sovereignty and the fragility of creation, is presumably that if God has permitted or even willed destruction before, He may well do it again, for sin still governs human life.

For Novak, this pervasiveness of sin is imperfectly balanced by the divine image in the human person: "The perennial sinfulness of human beings makes the threat of war perennial, their longing to be true to the image of God within them makes perennial the longing for peace" (p. 359). There is no indication that the coming of Christ has any relevance to the satisfaction of that longing. Quite the contrary: Novak interprets the death of Christ as being in tension with his proclamation of peace:

> Although Jesus comes as the Prince of Peace, inaugurating a Kingdom of peace, He was a man of sorrows, bloodily slain on the cross. He called His disciples to share in self-sacrifice. His vision of this world was no vision of the easy triumph of justice and light. On the contrary, the vision of Jesus is a divisive force in history, dividing even families . . . (p. 360).

Thus the teaching and the fate of Jesus are invoked as further evidence of the sinfulness of the world. The notion that Christian

---

unidentified group of people; cf. "Among ourselves, we also have differences" (p. 358).

discipleship involves fidelity to Jesus' Kingdom of peace even in, especially in, a world beset by sin is simply dismissed. Despite his use of the heading "Peace and the Kingdom," "Kingdom and History," and "Moral Choices for the Kingdom" (borrowed from the bishops' pastoral), Novak's only substantive discussion of the concept of the Kingdom comes in a single sentence in the context of Augustine's endorsement of the just-war theory: "St. Augustine understood that the world of history is in part evil, and that action to restrain evil is an essential component of justice. While some Christians stress the fact that the 'New Kingdom' has already come with Jesus, others, like Augustine, stress the continuing power of sin and the complex texture of social ambiguity" (p. 364). Here it is clear that Novak recognizes the significance of a doctrine of the Kingdom for formulating a teaching on the role of the Church in the world. The rest of Novak's text demonstrates that he identifies with the second group; but he does not deal any further with the first position, beyond implying that it depends upon a naive optimism about "the continuing power of sin." For Novak the "New Kingdom" has not come with Jesus in any meaningful sense, despite the perspective of *Lumen Gentium*.[34]

However, a reference to the Kingdom does find its way into the final paragraph of *Moral Clarity*, in which the "biblical realism" of the document is allowed to end on a somewhat hopeful note:

> It is the vocation of Christians and Jews not only to reflect on the world but to change it, bringing it closer to the outline of the Kingdom promised in the Old and New Testaments. It is the vocation of American citizens, civilian and military, called by the Seal of the United States to evoke *Novus Ordo Seclorum*,[35] a new order of liberty and justice by peaceful means, through the consent of the governed. Although not

---

[34]In *Tranquillitas Ordinis: The Present Failure and Future Promise of American Catholic Thought on War and Peace* (New York: Oxford University Press, 1987), George Weigel is particularly critical of the use of Kingdom terminology by the bishops, which he identifies with "a tendency to temporalize the eschatological peace of *shalom*: to teach that the Kingdom in which conflict is no more can be constructed by human hands. Here, seeds planted by the vulgar Marxism of the Vietnam-era New Left have come to flower" (p. 394). Weigel's entire book is a sustained attack on the approach to peace taken by the bishops in their letter, and particularly on their understanding of the Kingdom.

[35]Novak cites this motto again on p. 3 of *Toward the Future*, as well as in *Freedom with Justice: Catholic Social Thought and Liberal Institutions* (San Francisco: Harper and Row, 1984), p. 35; its connotations of a secularized eschatology realized in America are suggestive.

without failures and flaws, the United States' foreign and military
policy since World War II has had as its purpose to defend and extend
such liberties, on which alone true peace can rest (p. 392).

Two points in this peroration deserve mention. First, no distinction
is made between the outline of the Kingdom in the Old and New
Testaments; the distinctive, definitive role of Christ in relation to the
Kingdom is ignored: true peace depends on civil liberties, not on
Jesus. Secondly, the Judeo-Christian vision of the Kingdom is paral-
leled, if not assimilated, to American political and military policy.
Though failures and flaws are admitted, it is evident here as throughout the document that the "continuing power of sin" is to be
perceived, and opposed, almost exclusively in the adversary. The
author finally invites his audience not, as his emphasis on pervasive
sinfulness might suggest, to a healthy suspicion of the motives and
actions of any large institution whose power is threatened, but to a
nationalistic act of faith in the virtuous intentions and policies of
their own government. There seems to be, at very least, a profound
inconsistency here.

The so-called "lay economic pastoral," *Toward the Future*, begins
with a Preamble dealing exclusively with the Kingdom of God. It is
interesting that the approach taken is that of the conclusion, rather
than the body, of *Moral Clarity*. The symbolism of the Kingdom is
presented in a positive way, and in the context of the American
experience: "The brave settlers who first brought Christianity to
America took seriously these words of the Lord's prayer, 'Thy
Kingdom come . . . on earth as it is in heaven' " (p. ix). It seems as
though Novak and his colleagues are also taking them more seriously
than he did previously, when references to the Kingdom coming on
earth received disparaging if not contemptuous treatment. The writers are careful to state that they "do not identify American society
with the Kingdom of God," and cite Lincoln's second Inaugural to
the effect that "our system stands now, and ever, under the judgement of the Almighty" (p. ix). But that judgement consists, if I read
their argument correctly, in an evaluation of the system's success in
putting into practice "three further passages about the nature of this
Kingdom which is to 'come on earth'—remarkable passages which
established a framework, then and now, for reflecting on the U.S.
economy (p. ix). All three passages are taken from Matthew 25. The
first, on the wise and foolish virgins, is interpreted to mean that
"good intentions are not enough," that "God cherishes watchfulness

and practicality," and that the foolish virgins were excluded "because of their improvidence" (p. x). The relevance, or even the
identity, of the Bridegroom for whom the virgins are waiting is not
mentioned. The second passage, the parable of the talents, "details
the terrible punishments which lie in store for those who do not
produce new wealth from the talents God has placed in their stewardship" (p. x). Later in the letter, the authors return to this parable
and find its lesson to be that "preserving capital is not enough—it
must be made to grow" (pp. 30–31). It can be safely said of these
interpretations that they are not representative of contemporary
biblical scholarship. Perhaps Novak intends to take the contention
of liberation theologians that the Bible can be read properly only
from the perspective of the poor and turn it on its head, for his
attempt to show that Jesus was a proto-capitalist is definitely exege-
sis which would occur only to the rich.

The discussion of the third text, the last judgement scene, is even
more revealing of the perspective of the document. The basic point
is unexceptionable: the passage "instructs those who seek to build
the Kingdom on earth to care for the poor and needy, lest they forfeit
their own salvation" (p. x). But this gives rise, according to the
authors, to two ambiguities: "Should care for the needy be personal—or systemic? our answer is 'Both.' Is the 'Kingdom on earth'
to be built in the soul or in society? Again our answer is 'Both.'—
although no society in history ever fully embodies the kingdom"
(pp. x–xi). For those readers who are surprised, perhaps even dis-
mayed, at the authors' response here, an explanation is provided.
Personal care for the needy implies a minimalist interpretation of
governmental responsibility: "Individuals cannot shirk their personal responsibilities to help the poor, by 'letting the system do it' "
(p. xi). Dorothy Day is even invoked here (along with Mother Teresa)
as an example—apparently a rather cynical effort to coopt a revered
figure who would almost certainly agree with little else in the
document.

But what of the structural element in the passage? It is satisfied,
the authors tell us, by the establishment of "an order of political
economy in which the poor and needy might routinely raise themselves out of poverty by methods economically wise and conducive
to unparalleled economic activity" (p. xi). In other words, to be
numbered among the sheep, one should rely on private charity and
the operation of the free enterprise system. In the body of the text
itself, the passage receives further elaboration: "Feeding the hungry,

giving drink to the thirsty, and clothing the naked means, in the long run, ceasing to frustrate the talents given every people of the planet by their creator" (p. 50).[36] This means, practically, keeping "the heavy hand of politics" (p. 50) from inhibiting the invisible hand of the free market. It is in this way that "such passages as Matthew 25 have not only personal but systematic application" (p. xi). The second ambiguity, about the "Kingdom on earth," unfortunately receives no further elucidation, but it is perhaps not illegitimate to suppose that as private charity will establish the Kingdom in the soul, so "democratic capitalism" will build the Kingdom, imperfectly of course, in society. Of this Preamble it can accurately be said, I believe, that it does not engage the issues raised by the vision of the Kingdom already present in Christ as found in *Lumen Gentium* and the two pastorals.

Novak himself is well aware of the challenge of that vision. In his recent book on liberation theology, he writes, "it is here that the early drafts of the U.S. Catholic bishops' pastoral on the U.S. economy erred, precisely in the section on the Bible. The early drafts summarized what contemporary biblical scholars find of interest in the Bible. But the current interest of the biblical scholars of this generation, whose wisdom will wither as the grass of the field, is not decisive. To accommodate biblical texts, written for a pre-democratic, pre-capitalist, pre-growth period of history, and then to leap from *that* context to today is a kind of fundamentalism."[37] It is for each reader to determine whether the bishops and the biblical scholars or Novak and his lay commission are more accurately characterized by "a kind of fundamentalism" which accommodates scriptural passages from a "pre-capitalist" period of history to the present day, and perhaps for succeeding generations to determine whose wisdom will wither as the grass of the field more quickly. It should be clear to all, however, that there are fundamental theological differences, not simply divergences on politics and policy applications, which separate the bishops and their most prominent critic.

---

[36]See also the passage on pp. 45–46: "If the words of Christ in Mt. 25 apply to systems, then they demand systems which actually do help the poor, not systems which so suppress economic activism as to frustrate the poor systematically."

[37]*Will It Liberate? Questions about Liberation Theology* (New York: Paulist, 1986), p. 37. The reference to "early drafts" is evidently because Novak was writing before the final version of the pastoral was completed: though this material was rewritten throughout the drafting process, the major points, and presumably Novak's objections, remain the same. An interesting comparison can be made with a statement found in *Toward the Future:* "Even though the classic Catholic teaching on the social virtues was developed in and for a pre-capitalist, pre-democratic era, much of it has perennial and universal validity" (p. 7).

"WHAT IF JESUS . . .?" NARRATIVE NAMING AND THEOLOGICAL REFLECTION

John McCarthy

With the mention of the name "Sherlock Holmes" I can be assured that there is enough shared ground between us that a conversation could ensue, probably even for those who have never read this character's adventures. The name suggests uncanny deductive abilities, level-headed control in even the most dangerous situations, success at solutions for which lesser minds are no match: at times, it may even suggest a voice: "Come, Watson, come! The game is afoot!" or "Elementary, my dear Watson!" It almost makes no difference that in fact Conan Doyle's texts never have Holmes say precisely, "Elementary, my dear Watson." It almost seems as if it is what Holmes could have said, or even should have said, and often times has said. Christopher Morley, in his Preface to the authoritative collection of the Holmes stories (composed, in fact, as a eulogy entitled "In Memoriam Sherlock Holmes") writes:

> The whole Sherlock Holmes saga is a triumphant illustration of art's supremacy over life. Perhaps no fiction character ever created has become so charmingly real to his readers. It is not that we take our blessed Sherlock too seriously; if we really want the painful oddities of criminology let us go to Bataille or Roughead. But Holmes is pure anesthesia. We read the stories again and again; perhaps most of all for the little introductory interiors which give a glimpse of 221B Baker Street.[1]

Morley's comments are suggestive in several ways: the assertion of art's supremacy over life; the almost divine stature of this character

---

[1]Sir Author Conan Doyle, *The Complete Sherlock Holmes* with a preface by Christopher Morley (New York: Double Day and Company, Inc., various copyrights), pp. 5–6.

designated as "blessed"; the phenomenon of repetition; the anesthetic effect of these stories. But here I want to focus on the recognition of the "reality" of the fictional character.

It is a point of historical fact that there never was an individual
who fulfilled the description of the narrated Holmes. Conan Doyle
indicated the influence of his student memories of one Dr. Joseph
Bell of the Edinburgh Infirmary. But it is not the case that the death
of this Dr. Bell raised the international consternation which the
seeming death of Sherlock Holmes did at the end of the Memoirs.
Doyle wrote:

> A few words may suffice to tell the little that remains. An examination
> by experts leaves little doubt that a personal contest between the two
> men ended, as it could hardly fail to end in such a situation, in their
> reeling over, locked in each other's arms. Any attempt at recovering the
> bodies was absolutely hopeless, and there, deep down in that dreadful
> cauldron of swirling water and seething foam, will lie for all time the
> most dangerous criminal and the foremost champion of law of their
> generation.[2]

But turning Holmes into a corpse was not acceptable even though
the author had tired of writing of him. There was such an outrage
that "the examination by experts which left little doubt" had to be
reinterpreted to leave enough doubt to bring back Holmes for another
700 pages. It generated not only the further adventures penned by
Doyle himself, but also those later written by his son, Adrian, and
by countless others in a variety of mediums: written texts, films,
phonograph records, tapes, plays, etc. The December, 1986, issue of
the Smithsonian[3] ran a feature length article on the contemporary
Holmsians who have constructed a series of first class relics—the
Persian slipper, the Calabash pipe, the gasogen lamps, the violin,
various letters—and enshrined them in replica rooms which host
regular meetings of Holmes clubs around the world who delight in
re-reading the stories, speculating on new adventures hinted at but
never recounted in the original texts, and delving into the trivia of
Sherlock. The character has been too real to die for the reader.
Indeed it seems as if the reality of the fictional character outside of
the texts of his adventures could even overcome the textual narrative

---

[2]Ibid., p. 480.
[3]Fred Strebeigh, "To His Modern Fans, Sherlock Is Still Worth A Close Look,"
Smithsonian 17 (December, 1986): 60–68.

of his death. Such is the potential power of the reality of the fictional character—that it cannot even be narrated to death.

The example of the character of Sherlock Holmes is a particularly strong one to illustrate the sense of reality generated in fictional characterization. Certainly not all characters are consigned to an endless life. Characters are narrated to death all the time, but even in the narration there is always the possibility of rereading the story from the start, of having the character back to life again. Almost as permanent as nuclear fuels, characters die in half lives of lack of reading and rereading much more quickly than in narrations. Even if Holmes had not had his death reversed in a narration which took advantage of the gap left by the expert's doubt, there were already countless other gaps in which Holmes could have been squeezed back into life. The Holmes' stories are filled with hints of unsolved cases, named, but quickly dismissed because, like the silenced story of The Giant Rat of Sumatra, "the world is not yet prepared." In the textual spaces Holmes can go on forever. Once named characters like this can be endlessly reinvoked—a phenomenon which suggests what might be called a reality beyond the text.

Let us call a halt to these remarks on Sherlock Holmes for the moment and make an abrupt shift to matters more Christian, if not necessarily—Morley's point in mind here—more divine. The matter more Christian is the figure of Jesus as a figure within, and without, a set of texts. While it may not be exhaustively true to say that the Christian understanding of the figure of Jesus is the understanding of the name of Jesus within the canonical and interpretive texts of the Christian tradition, it is at least largely the case. As the term "Christian" implies, this interpretation of human existence makes at least implicit claims to draw from the figure of Jesus as Christ a set of norms, a particular perspective, a way of being—however it may be put—which is both appropriate to these canonical textual materials and adequate to human being in the world. It is not far-fetched to suggest that within the term "Christian" there is embedded an extension of the figure of Jesus as Christ outside of the text, interpreted in the actions of those who claim to be followers of Jesus. It has been claimed that the second most circulated text after the bible is Thomas à Kempis' The Imitation of Christ.[4] This notion of the imitation of Christ as the core of Christian existence is one

---

[4]Jaroslav Pelikan, Jesus Through the Centuries: His Place in the History of Culture (New Haven: Yale University Press, 1985), p. 141.

traditional way of extending the character of the figure of Jesus beyond the canonical texts in new situations. Likewise the closure of the canon is a way of suggesting that there are limits to these extensions. To have, for example, Jesus be the small child who, when pushed by a playmate, responds by striking the child down, as is done in the Gospel of Thomas, has been deemed unacceptable. To understand the Christ-ian as a follower of Jesus, or Christian existence as an imitation of Christ, or the church as the body of Christ, or Christian life as a dying and rising with Christ, are various ways of suggesting that the character of Jesus as Christ extends beyond the texts in significant ways.

This abrupt turn from matters Holmsian to matters Christian may not be quite as abrupt as it first seems. What ties these two together for this analysis is the issue of the reality of the character outside of the text. Gaps have been opened within the canon of Sherlock Holmes literature precisely by the textual suggestions of unaccounted adventures which allow for the modal existence of the named character to be situated in new adventures. "What if Sherlock Holmes were to . . .?" If the Holmes literature subsequent to Conan Doyle's writing is any indication, the response to the question suggests that the gaps lie in the plot, while the character of Holmes remains largely reiterated. Holmes might be brought back to existence in a new situation of adventure but precisely as the reserved, rational and crafty Victorian gentleman that he always has been. The anesthesia of Holmes is the repetition of the character in the gap of a tense, new circumstance which calls for the almost certain resolution only a character as reliable as Holmes could provide.

The Christian claim is that in the colossal textual gap opened between the resurrection and the time in which Jesus is to be seen again (variously in Galilee, in Jerusalem, in the eucharist, in the age of the spirit, at the end of time, etc.) the presence of the figure of Jesus "outside of the text" is of fundamental, indeed salvific, importance for those who claim to be faithful readers and re-readers of these texts. The question arises in this gap: "What if Jesus were to . . .?" Again, if the Christian literature subsequent to the canonical literature, especially that of the gospel narratives, is any indication, the response is both similar and different from that observed with the Holmes stories. Certainly Christian literature has often responded as if the character of Jesus were monumentally stable, generating a body of written and oral responses parallel to the model of the Holmes material: reiterate the character in the gap of a new situation in order to generate a stable resolution to a tensive situation. But as opposed to the Holmes literature the gap extends beyond that of the unrecounted situation (although certainly that is there, eg. Jn 21:25) to that of the instability of the character itself. The character acts and speaks so often to question, to set at odds, to overturn assumptions, to destabilize, that reiteration leading to resolution would simply betray the textual character. There are surely vast differences in genre, in narrative conflict, in plot, in styles of characterization, etc., between the mysteries of Holmes and the Gospel narrative. Yet beyond these differences of literary convention, the gaps[5] of the text differ in interpretively important ways, ways which shape the reality of the character outside of the text.

Lest I cause needless offense by suggesting a similarity between the existence of Sherlock Holmes and Jesus (despite Morley's ascription of divinity to the former), let it be clear that the issue is the understanding of the reality of a character narratively portrayed beyond the original narrative. The investigation of the extra-textual reality of fictional characters is used as a heuristic device with the wager that clarification of this literary/philosophical issue may contribute to theological reflection.

From Sherlock Holmes and the Christian canonical texts, let us make another abrupt shift, this time to a more theoretical investigation of character in narrative texts. The goal of this investigation is to situate fictional characters and their names within the interlocking spheres of textual composition and reading. I will argue that narrated fictional character is not interpretively bound to the text to begin with.

To open this investigation I want to suggest that fictional character be placed within two dialectics. The first dialectic focuses on character, the terms of the dialectic being character as mark and character as unique person. Semantically the term "character" easily bears this distribution. On the one hand "character" designates distinct marks used on the written page. In this sense character is associated closely with inscription. To say that fictional characters are simply marks on a page is thus not wholly false. But the mark does not

---

[5]The category of the gap is grounded in the discussion of the role of "the blank" and "negation" developed by Wolfgang Iser, particularly in *The Act of Reading* (Baltimore: Johns Hopkins University Press, 1978), pp. 180–231. Briefly, I use gap to refer here to any structure of textual indeterminacy which calls for the reader's interactive involvement with the text to create some relatively adequate interpretive response.

exhaust the semantic field of "character." It is likewise appropriate
to designate an individual as "quite a character," which is to say
that the one so referred to is both a human person (or has characteristics conventionally associated with human persons) and a distinctive, possibly peculiar personality. Character here has its anchorage
in speech used to refer to real persons. By locating "fictional character" between "mark" and "person," we locate a major struggle in
fictional character: namely the struggle of saying that such characters
are simply marks on a page, and that such characters refer to human
persons. Both statements seem intuitively, but not exhaustively,
true. Fictional characters seem to be something like "word-per-
sons."[6]

With a second dialectic I want to place the term "fiction" between
"pretense" and "fabrication." In speaking of fiction within legal
structures, Lon Fuller underscores the element of pretense or false-
ness, but carefully distinguishes it from the deceit or the lie or the
inadvertency of the mistake.[7] He summarily notes:

> A fiction is either (1) a statement propounded with a complete or
> partial consciousness of its falsity, or (2) a false statement recognized
> as having utility.[8]

A fiction suggests that some statement or series of statements does
not reproduce—as report—a person, object, or situation. Given our
shared assumptions of reality, fictions are false, a pretense, played
either playfully or maliciously, provocatively or trivially, but none
the less involving the elements of acknowledged and accepted
feigned representation. Yet fictions are not intellectual fraud for
fictions seem to act as agreements not to judge the pretense on
positivistic canons. Thus fictional worlds can have talking bears that
are other than Teddy Ruxpin.

At the same time however fictions use language which commonly
makes reference to a human world or at least to a world which is
capable of being understood by humans. In this sense fictions—at
least developed ones—fabricate a world on the other side of the

---

[6]These are not the only locations which the term "character" can generate. For
instance, nothing has been said about character as possession, stature or role—eg.,
"she has character;" "his character is good;" "she is playing a seamy character;"—
but these are not as pertinent to this investigation.
    [7]Lon Fuller, *Legal Fictions* (Stanford: Stanford University Press, 1967), pp. 5–9.
    [8]Fuller, p. 9.

agreement not to judge them by these positivistic canons. Fictions can include the obvious pretense of talking bears, playing on the assumption that we know what bears and talking are, and are willing, at least on Saturday mornings, to grant the pretense that video bears can talk. But fabrication can go further than this trivial suspension of commonly accepted limits; it can create contexts in which the suspension of limits has gone to such an extent that the text itself seems to create its own world. The fabrication associated with the fictional name is a prime example. While I may be able to assume an almost immediate recognition for a talking animal like Smokey the Bear, the introduction of "Bluptuous Blifuls" (the pretense extended to incoherence) depends upon the fabrication[9] which occurs in a possible narrative. Bluptuous Blifuls can be fabricated, either as a class or as a proper name—the state here is ambiguous—but the fashioning needs the elements of characterization that the narrative provides.

We can return at this point to "fictional character," keeping in mind the double dialectics of mark/person and pretense/fabrication. A fictional character is fabricated within a narrative, not simply with the introduction of the name of the character, but at the level of the text. It is this process of fictional characterization, or narrative naming, which at once draws together the mark and the person in the space of the pretense through the fabrication brought about by narrative strategies. The name as the mark of the person is continuously reiterated, or adjusted, or developed through various forms of dialog, action, allusion, conflict, etc. Thus narrative naming is the process in which the dialectical elements of the fictional character achieve some degree of relative coherence. More than simply the title or word, the name is a "semantic gap"[10] opened in the narrative with the suggestion that this gap may be filled to varying degrees with all that is associated with personality. As the narration progresses the characterization takes place in a series of ways. If this process of narrative naming is consistent then the reiteration of the nominal marks suggests a complex source of action, speech, desire,

---

[9]The reason why I have chosen the term "fabrication" rather than "fashioning" or "construction" is because fabrication has within its semantic field the notions both of making and weaving together, as in a fabric. It is this combination which I would suggest adequately addresses the construction of characters within extended fictions.

[10]Relying on Philippe Hamon, Thomas Docherty presents a well crafted analysis of the name in fiction in *Reading (Absent) Character: Towards a Theory of Characterization in Fiction* (Oxford: Clarendon Press, 1983), pp. 43–86; for the reference to the "semantic blank" see p. 47.

history, urges, goals, impulses, etc., which we come to associate with person. If it so happens that Bluptuous Blifuls becomes a proper name (as does Sherlock Holmes and Jesus) it is so as a process of characterization which includes all these narrative strategies. The narrative name is thus the trace of a process of narrative naming, the sometimes tense, sometimes stable, coherence of the double dialectics.

Thus far our approach to fictional character and name has been implicitly from the side of composition. The character as mark creates a distance from the non-narrated world, a distance which separates the narrative character from person and, in the fabrication of the story, suggests simultaneously a realistic world and realistic characters. The mark is a breach which suspends this everyday world and its characters between the pretense and the report. At this point in the narrative production, largely at the point of inscription[11], the fictional characters are posited in the text as the world which supports their characterization. The narration of this world sets in motion a series of actions, words, description, motives, goals and the like which create the gravity needed for any world with realistic characters. The centripetal movement created in this process of narration moves the co-developing fictional world and character ever further from the need to be report like, and ever more toward an independence which allows fictional characters to seem to speak real words, to have real motives, to work from real histories, to walk real roads. The marks which make the characters tend to become transparent while the characters become more dense.

And yet the consideration of fictional characterization and naming solely from the side of composition is partial. Character is inscribed in the narrative, but it is likewise rendered in the process of reading, announcement, dramatization and the like. To realize this is to realize that the world engendered by the fashioning process is less an alien world to be stormed in the violence of reading than an invitation to co-fabricate, for which reading is the appropriate response. The fashioning of fictional character is the work of at least inscription and rendering, each of which suggests differing authori-

---

[11]There is a great deal of material on the "death of the author" and the effect of writing in severing the text from the author. See for instance, Roland Barthes, "The Death of the Author" in *Image Music Text*, trans. Stephen Heath (New York: Hill and Wang, 1977), pp. 142–149; Paul Ricoeur, *Interpretation Theory: Discourse and the Surplus of Meaning* (Fort Worth: The Texas Christian University Press, 1976), pp. 25–44.

ties and consequently the possibility for plural readings of characters from the same text. The inscribed character is not the fictional
character, precisely because it has been fabricated only by inscription. In the reading process a disruption of the privacy of inscribed
character takes place which renders the fictional character as real,
not only "in the world of the text"—the world whose gravity is
narration—but also on the other side of the text, in the world "in
front of the text." The fictional character as the private property of
the author or the text, as the private holdings of a particular historical period, cultural tradition or language, as existing in the private
and unbreechable space of a print world enclosed between two
covers—these assumed privacies accorded the inscribed character
are disrupted, not as an intrusion, but in the textually invited
process of reading. Thus narrative naming as a process of achieving
a relative coherence of the dialectical terms is simultaneously the
invitation to co-fashion the fictional character as the newly public
character drawn out from inscribed privacies. The text as the invitation to reading spells the first disruption of fictional character—the
disruption of the privacy of inscribed character.

This first disruption offsets both the sole authority of authorship
and the tendency to construe the fictional work as aesthetically self-
contained. But this disruption if taken to an extreme opens the
possibility of severing the rendered character from the inscribed
character. In such a situation the text is construed less as invitation
and more as the raw material of the reader. The nominal marks then
marginally intertwine with the textual characterization; the gap
opened up by these marks becomes the colony of the reader rather
than the meeting of text and reader. This colonization of the gaps of
the text by the fashioning of the reader alone is itself a fascist
reading. Such a reading begs the corrective of the text as invitation
with reading as response to the structured mark. Whether understood as script, score, code, norm or form, the text is deposited for
the reader as that which is to be neither simply reiterated, nor
simply discarded, nor simply pirated, but rather rendered.

A second disruption of fictional character is possible, however.
Just as reading disrupts the privacy of fictional character "in" the
text, so the fashioning of character as the deposit for reading can
disrupt the privacy of subjectivity in the fashioning of the reader.
With the gap opened by the nominal mark, and with the text inviting
response, the reader is all too willing to fill the gap quickly with the
understandings of subjectivity that the conventional use of name

suggests. To say "Sherlock Holmes" or "Jesus Christ" is to suggest a person. From the side of the reader the tendency to characterization is most often the tendency to personification, the tendency to construe the gap of the nominal mark as a person. But if the placement of fictional character between mark and person, between pretense and fabrication is appropriate, the tension cannot be resolved too quickly on the side of person, just as above the dialectic could not be resolved on the side of mark and pretense. In the fashioning of fictional character from the side of composition the mark makes its presence known. The fictional character need not simply confirm the subjectivity of the reader, either as idealistic, political, psychological, economic, or in any other socially conditioned way. Narrative characterization bears the possibility of disrupting the private subjectivity of the reader precisely in the textual fabrication of character.

Where does this all too incomplete reflection on fictional character and narrative naming leave us? I would suggest that it leaves us primarily with fictional character as narratively named. This naming is a fabrication which takes place in both the inscription and the rendering of the nominal marks of the text. As a textual process it is a process which makes character public both in the disruption of the privacy of inscribed character through reading and the disruption of the reader's subjectivity through the processes of narrative characterization. Such fictional characterization is suspended between the report of personalities and the feigning of the person by the marks inscribed on the page. In this gap opened by the nominal marks, the text exercises the process of characterization which results in the potentially disruptive inscribed character. In the gap taken up in the reading process invited by the text, the process of characterization is co-completed by the disruption of the seeming stability of the nominal marks inscribed in the text. Fictional character exists necessarily outside of the text as the disruption of the character as mark, and yet is rooted in the text as the disruption of the subjective renderings of various readers. Such is the process of narrative naming, a process distributed over both the text and the reader in the rendering of inscribed character, in the relative coherence of the dialectical terms.

The comments which began this paper dealt with the reality of the fictional character of Sherlock Holmes outside of the texts of his adventures, a reality which, as was noted, overcame the narrative of the character's own death. A turn was made to the extension of the character of Jesus as Christ outside of the canonical texts of the Christian tradition with suggestions of how this existence outside of the text might be understood in the themes of imitation, ecclesiology, canonical criticism, sacramentology, etc. A final turn was made toward a more theoretical account of fictional character and narrative naming which located more clearly the fashioning which goes into the creation of character in the narrative text. I suggested that this investigation involved a wager, namely that this kind of thinking might contribute to theological reflection. I will end by anteing up on this wager with a brief instance of interpretation.

The Gospel texts as narratives involve various processes of characterization: actions, speech, geneologies, announcements, contrast, conflicts, analogous characters, etc. The reader is certainly invited to understand the name of Jesus as one which suggests a human person. But likewise in the text the reader's understanding of this person is disrupted in several ways: the character of Jesus does unusual deeds, the character denies his family, the character disrupts an accepted set of institutions. He narratively describes himself as a road, a vine, a corner stone, water. Even more abruptly the character redescribes himself as bread and wine, and is narrated beyond the narration of his own death. In these latter two instances particularly (alongside the instances of teaching and the stories of healing, etc. which may be better encompassed as the character beyond the text in the reiteration of these stories) the narrative makes claims that the central character exists outside of the text, beyond the world of the text, in ways which persons cannot conventionally claim to. The narrative asks the reader to do more than to remember a story. It narrates a claim to extend beyond the narrative itself. But in this textual extension beyond the text it is important to note that there is a certain disruption of the expectations of subjectivity in the metaphors. Bread, wine and resurrection on the other side of death are more than a simple protraction of the character narrated earlier. The character outside of the text is a transformation of the expectations for personality. The reality beyond the text is the reality of bread and wine, of the instances of encounter in which recognition is not clear, of the promise of meetings in lands which are distant or times that are unspecified. The reader/listener of these texts is left with a disrupted description of the person engendered by the marks of the text itself. The proper name, Jesus, provides the semantic gap which is partially filled by narrative characterization confirming the expectations of a reader for the report of a person.

But likewise the narrative, precisely when it narrates the character beyond the text, disrupts these expectations: bread and wine are not reflexive subjects or centers of cognition and will; subjectivity cannot survive death.

Contemporary literary critics have made us aware of the subtle and varied ways in which a character may be referred to within a text. The relation of the name to the reflexive pronoun is one point of concern. Our standard reading is one in which the assumption is made that the pronoun acts as substitute, pure and simple, for the noun. If I write "Jesus" in one sentence and "He" in the next, then the pronoun seems to succeed in so far as it reiterates the name without remainder. If it does not do this then some uncertainty, some confusion, some lack of definition, seems to slip into the text. But it may be that this very possibility of uncertainty built into the pronoun, precisely as the non-repetition of the name, discloses the possibility of something other than a continuation of the expectation of the person alone. If the name itself cannot be governed by the assumptions of personification, then surely the pronoun can be even less so. In this regard it is particularly interesting to note that in the eucharistic and the resurrection accounts in Mark, for instance, the name recedes and the pronoun, a much more indefinite form, takes precedence.[12]

> Take; this is *my* body. And *he* took a cup, and when *he* had given thanks *he* gave it to them and they all drank of it. And *he* said to them, "This is the blood of the covenant which is poured out for many. Truly *I* say to you, *I* shall not drink again of the fruit of the vine until the day when *I* drink it new in the kingdom of God. (Mk. 14:22–25)
>   And he said to them, "Do not be amazed; you seek Jesus of Nazareth who was crucified. *He* has risen, *he* is not here; see the place where they laid *him*. But tell his disciples and Peter that *he* is going before you to Galilee; there you will see *him* as *he* told you. (Mk 16:6–7)

The texts in their marks restructure the character of Jesus in unexpected ways, indeed ways which are saturated with gaps, with untold appearances, with pronouns rather than proper names, with promises of return and presence, with a narrative of departure. At the same time there is the narrative demand of presence: Jesus is not the dead character, the corpse, at best present in the reiteration of teachings or in memory alone. The text invites reading and in the

---

[12]See the analysis of Docherty, esp. pp. 68–71; 80–86.

invitation invites the structured interpretations of these puzzling gaps. The fictional character is present in these gaps. But this presence is a transformed presence, a presence which disrupts the expectations of personality. It is a presence where that which congeals around the nominal mark of "Jesus," if it is appropriate to the text, is not a return to the relics of a person enshrined in rooms for anesthetic readings, but in bread and wine rendered in new readings, readings which may disrupt, even dislodge, readings which rely heavily on subjectivity.

CAN VIRTUE BE TAUGHT? EDUCATION, CHARACTER, AND THE SOUL

David Tracy

However difficult the question of character and theological education in our period, it may still be helpful at times to distance
ourselves from them by returning to the origins of both education
and character for Western culture itself. This may seem a luxury if
not a distraction from the perplexities of the present. And yet, it is
not. The more I reflected on this question, the more it seemed to me
fruitful to return to reflection on the origins of Western education
itself; the Athens of Socrates, the great tragedians, and Plato. For
here one may find not only the origins of the problems of education
and character formation in our culture but also a cultural and
political situation uncannily like our own.

The intellectual situation of Socrates was parlous: the great threat
of the Sophists, for Socrates-Plato, was as much moral and religious
as it was intellectual. For the sophists (especially Protagoras)
claimed that virtue could be taught—but taught not as a *praxis* but
as a *techne,* a technique of success in any particular community the
sophists happened upon. Even the great moral exemplars of Greek
culture (Homer, Hesiod, and the great tragedians—in sum, "the
poets") could not function, in such a corrupt situation, as transformative of character towards virtue and the good.

Moreover, as such analyses as Thucydides' (and, by implication,
Plato's himself) make clear, the earlier heroic age was in shambles
as a result of the degradation of political life in an Athens turned
into an imperialist power. The political disaster of Sicily, as much
as the moral disaster of the treatment of Melos, and the intellectual
disaster of Plato's own failed educational experiments in Sicily
united to expose a situation where education must be rethought *if*
both character and virtue as well as intellectual inquiry were to

transform the community and not merely technically inform or merely entertain it. Contemporary social scientific analyses of ancient Athens, moreover, have correctly increased our sense of the full extent of the moral and intellectual dilemma faced by those first educators of virtue: the economic reality of a slave-population; the systematic distortion of the role (more accurately, non-role) of women in that society; the understanding of the "others" as "barbaric."

As liberation, political, and feminist theologies have persuasively argued, a Christian theologian should already be alert to these latter distortions in all their systemic and, yes, sinful actuality. As all classical theology (as *theologia*) can also note, the cultural, intellectual, moral, and religious systemic distortion of sophistic beliefs and political imperialism render a new model of education for character (a *paideia* in Werner Jaeger's sense) crucial. It is exactly this need, I believe, which gave birth to the Western notions of liberal education—both the oral practice of Socrates and the written dialogues of Plato, as well as his founding of the first "academy."

I have argued elsewhere that our own "post-modern age" is best characterized as one of increasing plurality and a heightened sense of the radical ambiguity of all our traditions. All the "grand narratives," including the Christian narrative, are far more plural, even heterogeneous, than we realized. I have also argued against dropping a concern with "character" altogether and contenting ourselves with Baktin-like or Derrida-like notions of our history as a multi-voiced test. And yet I admit to a certain hesitation here. On the one hand, the notion of character can function to introduce the notion of "personal identity" too soon by assuming, too easily, that our communal narratives are more like the "grand narratives" of the great nineteenth century realists and less like the modernist "epiphanic" narratives of Woolf, Proust, and Joyce, or even the anti-coherence, heterogeneous, post-modern experiments in the anti-narratives of Borges, Nabokov, or Marquez. The word "character" and its communal and narrative demands are, I believe, at once imminently retrievable in its classical senses from Aristotle through Jane Austen. At the very same time, "character," if not also subjected to suspicion, can too easily align itself with precisely the problem most of us now admit to be *the* problem of our culture: that distinctive form of "individualism" so well portrayed by Bellah *et al.* and so well characterized as the central temptation of the European and North American churches and seminaries by Cobb and Hough.

For those reasons, I have, in these reflections, returned to another largely forgotten word to try to understand our dilemma better: the word "soul" (or *psyche*). It is this word which is at the heart of the enterprise of inquiry, dialogue, and education for Socrates and Plato. It is this reality of soul, transformed by Paul into a new Christian anthropology and transformed in myriad new ways by Christian educators from Clement and Origen and Augustine through Bernard, Thomas Aquinas, Eckhart, Teresa of Avila, and John of the Cross which seems to me more promising for reflection on education and character. The historical-theological category of "soul," to be sure, needs its own suspicions (especially on soul-body relationships). But thanks to such post-modern thinkers as Julia Kristeva and others (especially feminists), the category "soul" has a better chance, I believe, of freeing us from the individualism which plagues us. Thereby, reflection on education and the soul may also free us for the notion of "a subject-in-process" which theological education as both identifiably Christian and genuinely open to our present global context may well need. Why that may be so is a longer story than the one I attempt here. For the moment, it seems imperative to return to this Western journey of education as a training of the soul in Socrates and Plato. For there, I have come to believe, is where education as we know it at its best was first conceived and there is where the unbreakable link between education, properly conceived, and character (reconceived as a training of the soul) was first forged.

Education and the Soul in Socrates-Plato:
Dialectic, Dialogue, Myth, Theology

The first candidate for education in Plato is dialectic. But what is that? Indeed, I agree with David Smigelskis that rather than trying to define a specific set of characteristics that we can then name "dialectic" in Plato, it is better to begin with a very general definition, viz. dialectics is any mode of reflective inquiry on a fundamental issue. Dialectics, on this reading, is not another "specialty"—it is, rather, a mode of inquiry that functions in every specialized form of inquiry.

This general description can be further specified in several ways. First, any mode of inquiry (whether in mathematics, in ethics, or in theology) that begins from some assumption and then inquires into the grounds for that assumption (rather than simply the consequences of that assumption) is dialectical. There is no specific subject-matter for dialectics in Plato (here the difference from Aristotle is startling); there is only the mode of inquiry which, as reflective, demands a constant examining of all our assumptions, opinions, beliefs.

There are, therefore, dialectical scientists (now named "philosophers of science") and non-dialectical scientists. There are dialectical understandings of piety (Euthrypho), justice (Republic), love (Symposium and Phaedrus), courage (Laches) and all the other virtues, beliefs, and practices, as well as non-dialectical understandings. There are dialectical understandings of the Good, the Forms, the Beautiful, and non-dialectical ones. There are dialectical understandings of the traditional myths, gods, rites, and beliefs and non-dialectical ones. To repeat, any mode of inquiry that involves a sustained and rigorous reflective analysis of the basic assumptions of any given belief or practice is dialectical. Any that does not, is not.

But what "signs" can we find to indicate whether a particular mode of inquiry is or is not dialectical? A modern thinker (or, for that matter, an ancient or medieval Aristotelian) would be likely to suggest "argument" (in both its formal and substantive modes) and modern theories and methods as the principal "signs" of reflective thought. Yet what is interesting in Plato is that he does not make this characteristically Aristotelian-modern move.

To be sure, the demand for argument is present in Plato throughout his work: both the formal demands for internal consistency of concepts, and, above all, the formal and substantive demands for self-consistency in the inquirer (negatively self-contradiction). The latter demand is most prominent in Plato's use of the dialogue form itself to communicate indirectly with the reader the direct demands of face-to-face conversation: viz. the elenchus method of inquiry characteristic of Plato's Socrates.

It is not what a particular person says that determines whether she or he is dialectical. It is only what persons mean by what they say and whether they can give reasons for that meaning that is the sign of the dialectical. And that functions best (for Plato) through that sustained and rigorous mode of question and answer which is the main thrust of the "early" and "middle" dialogues in which Socrates is the main dramatic figure.

In the early aporetic dialogues, the open-endedness occasioned by the aporias functions well to indicate three central Platonic presuppositions for all inquiry and all education: the fact that the question prevails over the answer in all true inquiry; the fact that true inquiry always provokes further inquiry; the fact that true inquiry, like true education, is always directed to the horizons—the interests, experience, and character—of the actual inquirers. The sophists, for Plato, give speeches—Socrates engages in conversation. Even in the great "middle" dialogues, especially the *Republic*, where more "constructive" results are presented, the open-endedness of the dialogue form reasserts itself to forbid dogmatism and to assure further inquiry. The loss of the dialogue in modern thought is a loss, I believe, not merely of the unexampled artistry of that form as exemplifying genuine inquiry in Plato, Cicero, Augustine, Berkeley, and Hume. It is also a loss of one crucial way to remind all genuine inquirers that the formal treatise or essay comprised of written arguments may be less faithful to the substantive and self-revelatory demands of all face-to-face encounters.

The *elenchus,* as the cross-examination of the inquirer in face-to-face conversation, is, for Plato-Socrates, the manifestation of whether one means what one says and can give reasons defending that meaning. In more explicit terms, the *elenchus* reveals whether or not *logos* is present in the inquirer's soul. It is always the "soul" of the inquirer, as we shall see below, that is ultimately at stake in all dialectical inquiry. In genre terms, a dialogue can exemplify this substantive existential struggle better than a formal treatise can. In terms of inquiry, the "dramatic" character of any face-to-face dialogue allows for both a wider range of probing inquiry and a greater manifestation to all participants of the state of their character, the presence or absence of "logos" in their souls, their commitment or lack of such for the "examined life," and the relationship between the formal and substantive elements in all their arguments.

I have defended elsewhere the claim that the more encompassing term "conversation" rather than "argument" should be the principal example of inquiry demanding analysis by all contemporary inquirers—including those proponents of "communication-theory" like Habermas and Apel who sometimes seem to narrow too quickly the demands of "rational communication" to the sole demands of the "better argument." Arguments are a necessary moment in a properly dialectical conversation. But the dialogue form is more comprehensive as a revelation of the state of the "soul" (or, alternatively, of the existential self-understanding) of the dialectical inquirer as a subject-in-process of education. I wish we possessed more than the fragments we presently do of Aristotle's lost dialogues. I am thankful that we do possess Plato's—for there one can find dialectical inquiry in all its complexity, ambiguity, openendedness, and sometimes confusion. I do not regret the loss, if they ever existed, of the "unwritten doctrines" of Plato, for I believe that his dialogues function better than a formal treatist as an indirect communication of a life of genuinely dialectical inquiry.

To describe the *elenchus* method as *the* sign of dialectical inquiry in Plato is not to disparage the other signs also there: including the later signs for strict argument which Aristotle, with finer logical skills and his extraordinary clarifying genius, later refined. In Plato himself, one can find the procedures of generalization, definition, and division in his early and middle dialogues; these same procedures are both used and reflected upon in his later, relatively non-dialogical dialogues, like the *Sophist,* the *Theatetus* and, above all, the *Parmenides.*

It is notorious that Plato, however much he praises dialectic and the philosophic life, nowhere actually defines dialectic with the precision he brings to bear on all his other fundamental questions. Even in the famous section on "dialectic" in Book VII of the *Republic,* the reader is made to understand the importance of dialectic— even, it can be said, to feel its import through Plato's artistically wondrous and philosophically dialectical way of relating his parable of the cave, his simile of light, and his image of the "divided line." But even here, we are not given a definition of dialectic analogous to the definition of justice.

This, to be sure, is a puzzle, but one worth dwelling upon. For if all dialectic is reflective inquiry on fundamental issues, if dialectic shows its reflectiveness by addressing assumptions and grounds for any practice or belief, if dialectic functions best in person-to-person sustained cross-examination via the *elenchus* method and second-best in written dialogues which exemplify not only the arguments but the interests and characters of the inquirers (the *logos* in their souls or its absence), if even attempts at definition, generalization, and division are genuine but not the sole exemplifications of all dialectical inquiry, then it follows that explicit arguments are also important but not the sole exemplifications of dialectical inquiry. Another exemplification (and one to which such communcation-theorists as Habermas and Apel would do well to give further reflection via Plato) is one that no theologian can avoid: the question of myth. Is myth ever an exemplification of dialectics? If so, how? If not, why not? This central issue, which has haunted contemporary theology like a guilty romance, haunted Plato as well—especially whenever he turned dialectical inquiry to the most fundamental question of all: the nature of the whole as that whole can be understood by the dialectical thinker attempting to educate her or his "soul."

The dialogue form, to repeat, seems uniquely qualified to manifest dialectic-in-action in written form. This is the case, not merely through the artistry which is clearly Plato's. Indeed, whether Plato's model of dialogue is fashioned principally on the model of the mime or the drama is a moot point. In either case, Plato's discovery of this form allows him to show the true drama he observed in Socrates: the drama of the philosophic soul in conflict with others and, often, with the other in himself.

On this reading, therefore, it is a matter of philosophical and educational and not merely artistic import for Plato to have fashioned the dialogue form. For dialogue not only nicely exemplifies the the question-and-answer method of face-to-face Socratic cross-examination. Dialogue also exemplifies dialectic-at-work in the *elenchus* method and in such refinements of that mode of inquiry as arguments on definition, generalization, and division. Dialogue is also a form capable of revealing the souls of the characters in the inquiry. In more familiar contemporary terms, dialogue is geared to reveal the existential self-understanding of the inquirers, or, more exactly, the emergence of a subject-in-process, a soul. It is this latter search that is at the heart of Plato's entire work and that makes him so clearly a contemporary of all those late twentieth-century inquirers concerned to continue the tradition of dialectical reason in Plato's sense as well as in Aristotle's clarified modes of argument. In dialogue one can show inquiry at work while also relating that inquiry directly to our primordial existential self-understanding of the self as intrinsically relational: related to itself, to society, nature, and the whole.

Plato's principal word for such existential self-understanding is *psyche* or soul. Amidst all the scholarly debates on Plato's understanding in different contexts in different dialogues on "soul," this much, I believe, is clear: besides its other functions (e.g. on self-movement), the term "soul" is a direct analogue of what a modern like Bultmann or Ogden means by existential self-understanding or a post-modern like Kristeva means by "subject-in-process." To be sure, like Ogden (or in their distinct ways, Voegelin and Lonergan), Plato's interest in this existential self-understanding is deeply informed by his belief in the differentiation of consciousness that occurs to a philosophic soul engaged in dialectical inquiry. For Plato, as his famous attack on the mimetic "poets" shows, once the philosophic drama of the soul occurs (as it did, for him, in Socrates), then even "dear Homer" and the great tragedians (even Aeschylus to whom he otherwise seems so similar) become inadequate as accounts of our "souls."

The emergence of Socrates, the emergence of dialectical inquiry, has transformed the soul from its internal conflicts so well portrayed by the "poets," especially the great tragedians, Aeschylus and Sophocles. To understand "soul" properly, we must replace their mimesis of those conflicts with the new drama of the soul—the mimesis of the idea in the emergence of Socrates. But before one assumes that this is proof of the "rationalism" so often charged to the Greek Socratic Enlightenment one needs to reflect further on the drama of the "soul" in the Platonic dialogues.

The most convincing case for the charge of rationalism could be made if one examined only the *Phaedo* where the *rational* character of the soul is sternly portrayed. But even there the figure of Socrates, the presence of myth, and the open-ended nature of the inquiry-in-dialogue form are far more complex than this familiar reading suggests. But the matter of the "soul" for Plato is complicated by several factors in other dialogues: for example, the tripartite "division" of the soul into rational, spirited, and appetitive "parts" in the *Republic* and the *Phaedrus* and, above all, the microcosm-macrocosm analogue that dominates Plato's dialogues in the *Republic* (soul and polis) and the *Timaeus* (soul and cosmos).

The tripartite view of the soul can be read as a challenge to any purely rationalist understanding of the "soul." For it is one thing to claim (as Plato clearly does) that the "rational" is the spark of the divine in the human and, once differentiated as philosophic reason employing dialectics, the rational part of the soul should justly rule the other parts which cause the inner conflicts of the soul. It is quite another matter to claim, as traditional rationalists do, that conscious reason alone is sufficient for existential self-understanding. This latter position, however familiar to many readings of Western notions of enlightenment and however devastating in its effects upon modern individualism, is not Plato's.

Reason is the great hope; but only a reason that can faithfully (i.e. dialectically) acknowledge its own possibilities, complexities, and limits. However unsettled some forms of Platonism may be by the discovery of the reality of the unconscious in Freud and Lacan, by the "dialectic of enlightenment" of Adorno and Horkheimer, or by the fragile character of "reason" in post-modern thought, these discoveries, on my reading, complicate but hardly devastate Plato's own account of the soul.

Reason acknowledges its own possibilities by engaging in genuinely dialectical inquiry—this surely, as our prior analysis urged, is at the heart of the Platonic corpus, early, middle, and late, and at the heart of all of Plato's successors in Western educational theory—from Aristotle on argument to modern communication theorists. But reason—as dialectical reason—can and must, as rational, also acknowledge its own limits. This is the case not so much because reason, although the "ruling element" in the soul, is only one of three elements. This is the case, rather, because reason-in-the-soul is the spark of the divine in the human: the way in which reason can recognize both its extraordinary possibilities and its own finite, limited status. Thereby can the soul be led to acknowledge all genuine manifestations of the whole and of the divine including those not arrived at by strictly dialectical procedures. For example, before dialectical inquiry, as the use of myth in some of the early dialogues indicates, myth is a dubious aid to the soul. In the midst of dialectical inquiry, however (here the several uses of myth in the *Republic* and the *Phaedrus* are exemplary), myth is a genuine aid to the soul.

The central clue here remains Plato's much disputed reading of art and myth. There can be no doubt that Plato is the great demythologizer of the traditional myths (even the Olympian gods) and the poets (from Hesiod through the great tragedians). For Plato, in Socrates the differentiation of dialectical reason has occurred and the drama of the philosophic soul must dialectically challenge the anthropomorphism of the traditional myths of the gods and the heroes and the mimetic disclosure of the inner conflicts of the pre-philosophic soul and the pre-Socratic polis of the great tragedians. Neither Homer, nor the traditional myths in Hesiod, nor the great characters and actions of the tragedians can "give a rational account"—a dialectical account—of themselves.

The poets for Plato can only mimetically describe the confusions of the soul in the individual and the polis while also "projecting" this confusion on their anthropomorphic portraits of the gods. To be sure, the traditional myths and the "poets" contain great truths worth retrieving. But, for Plato, we must demythologize them where we find ourselves in a situation of political decadence (which Plato

clearly considers the Athens of his day or even the earlier Periclean
period) or in a situation of intellectual decadence where even the
great *peitho* or persuasion theme of Aeschylus can become a travesty
of true persuasion (viz. persuasion-without-inquiry into the truth of
things) of the new rhetorical persuaders, the sophists.

There can be little doubt that Plato, like every dialectical theologian, does not hesitate to demythologize when either the situation
(Athenian political and intellectual decadence) or the tradition (anthropomorphic portraits of the Olympian gods acting as badly as
decadent humans, blasphemous portrayals of the gods demanding
bribes, materialistic accounts of the whole and the divine) demands
it. Plato needed to write his famous "Dear Homer" passage as much
as any dialectical Christian theologian today needs to write her or
his "Dear Paul" passage for authentic theological inquiry. But to see
Plato as only the great rational demythologizer of traditional myth
and art is, I believe, seriously to misunderstand him.

It is not only the case that Plato is a great remythologizer—
although that is indeed true, as his apparently original creation of
such great myths as the Myth of Er in the *Republic* and the myths of
creation and Atlantis in the *Timaeus* and the *Critias* shows. It is,
rather, that Plato is also the great rational-dialectical defender of the
truth of both myth and art.

The dialectical soul, i.e. the truly educated soul, unlike other
souls, finds it necessary to give a rational account of itself. As that
account proceeds, the soul, for Plato (here the descent-ascent theme
throughout the *Republic* seems paradigmatic), finds itself "pulled"
to a depth both grounding and beyond itself which it cannot account
for dialectically but can and must acknowledge through its own
dialectical experience.

In modern language, authentic "existence" demands the acknowledgement of "transcendence"—and recognizes that transcendence
in the "traces" or "ciphers" of transcendence of the great myths.
That experience of a depth where the soul somehow "participates"
in or "imitates" the whole and the divine can come in several ways:
through reflection on *eros* as a divine gift (as in the *Symposium* and
the *Phaedrus*); through reflection on *thanatos* as providing the clue
to the truth of the philosophic life (as in the *Phaedo* or the Myth of
Er in the *Republic*); through the manifestations of new works of art
disclosive of the soul and its kinship with the whole (as in the
mimesis of the philosophic soul which is the central drama of the
dialogue form); or through new, "true" myths which disclose the

soul as participating in or imitating the cosmos itself (as in the great philosophy of myth in the *Timaeus* wherein cosmos and soul can only be understood together).

True inquiry (dialectics), as true persuasion, is driven by the divine power of *eros* that manifests the soul's participation in the divine and the whole. Inquiry and persuasion without love are as helpless for Plato as *eros* without true inquiry, and true persuasion is inevitably decadent. That the philosophic life is the erotic life *par excellence* is, for Plato, the central clue not only to the *eros* which drives every soul in myriad forms. It is also the central clue to that mode of inquiry which drives the philosophic soul to its own depth where it recognizes that it participates in the whole and the divine through all its *eros* from physical passion to the "divine madness" which is a gift of the gods to the poets and seers, the *daimon* which drove Socrates to his calling, and the faithful, *eros*-driven inquiry of the dialecticians.

The dialectical soul, thus impelled by love and differentiated by true reason, eventually finds itself compelled to acknowledge the truth of myth and art. Even without the backing of Plato's controversial interpretation of *anamnesis*, this position can be warranted on Platonic grounds. The warrant is this: in the great myths and the great works of art, the soul discovers itself by discovering—acknowledging its own participation in and imitation of the whole and the divine. At the same time, the cosmos and the divine are the central clue to the psyche. Whether Plato invented or discovered the great myth of creation of the *Timaeus* remains a moot point. But that Plato accords some truth status to that myth seems incontrovertible. One can either dismiss the myth of the creation in the *Timaeus* as the strange fantasy of an old and disillusioned philosopher or accord it the kind of truth Plato did: the truth of any great myth or any great work of art that manifest the truth of the intrinsic kinship of soul and cosmos. This truth the dialectician was already led to acknowledge in her or his inquiry upon love and persuasion. This truth the dialectician turned dialectical mythologizer and artist can now acknowledge anew by recounting the myth as a "likely story"—its likeliness is not in its details but in its central insight: the kinship of soul and cosmos.

Dialectics can acknowledge even when it cannot dialectically ground this ultimate truth. Dialectics can turn to the traditional myths and poets and retrieve this truth from their confused (because anthropomorphic and philosophically differentiated) mimetic accounts. Dialectics can lead the inquirer to find persuasive any "likely account" of what dialectical inquiry rationally acknowledges but never grounds: the reality of the divine, the reality of cosmos and soul, as jointly participating in the divine. A dialectician who is also a great artist (here Plato is alone) may also risk the development of a work of art (a dialogue) that can portray the new myth in the context of genuinely dialectical inquiry: the myth of Er in the *Republic,* the myth of creation in the *Timaeus,* the myth of Atlantis in the *Critias.*

Plato, I believe, continues to persuade because there is a whole in his texts which we later "footnotes" can only glimpse: a commitment to that singular differentiation of consciousness that is Western philosophic reason; a rendering of the Socratic oral performance of cross-examination into the written texts of the dialogues; the refinement, within the encompassing genre of the dialogue, of the need for argument, for *elenchus,* for definition, generalization, division and subdivision—even, potentially, for those refinements of argument and its conditions of possibility elaborated by Aristotle in one way and by Toulmin, Habermas, and Ogden in modern terms; the insistence on the need for theological inquiry on the fundamental question of the whole and our existential relationship to that whole as the mode of inquiry demanded by dialectical reason itself; the ability to provide an artistic-philosophic rendering of existential self-consciousness in its full complexity from rational differentiation to its acknowledgment of the *eros* driving all true inquiry; the defense of the truth of art and myth as evoking commitment without romanticism and with an insistence on much necessary demythologizing, provoked by all true inquiry.

The educational conclusion is sound: commitment and action not open to inquiry is blind; inquiry not open to commitment and action is empty. Inquiry and action, like education and the soul, rise or fall together.

The *Timaeus* remains, I believe, not only the most influential Platonic text in the history of Christian theology but the clearest example of one of Plato's many uses of myth. More exactly, "myth" is no longer only the work of the poets and sophists who functioned prior to the emergence of dialectical inquiry—as it often is in the "aporetic" early dialogues (e.g. the use of myth by Protagoras in the *Protagoras*). Moreover, myth, for the *Timaeus,* is not only in the middle or at the end of dialogues when dialectical thinking has already begun (e.g. in the *Republic*). Rather, in the *Timaeus,* myth pervades the dialogue as a whole so that one could almost name this relatively non-dialogical dialogue by the genre "myth" rather than dialogue.

And yet such a "naming" would not be accurate either—despite the delight that later Christian neo-Platonists found in this great myth of creation which seemed to them so resonant with the Hebraic-Christian myth of a Creator-God in *Genesis*. Rather the *Timaeus* remains a dialogue, however atypical, insofar as here myth and dialectic, dialectic and myth, interpenetrate throughout the whole text-as-Platonic-dialogue. Even in the main body of the text, where Timaeus is almost the sole speaker and the other interlocutors listen but do not question in the familiar Socratic way, the dialectical character of the whole reading of the myth assures that we find here not merely a formal treatise nor a pure myth, but an odd form of dialogue where myth and dialectics seem always-already together to assure the movement of inquiry. This is especially the case in the great "new start" of the entire inquiry of Part II (47E–49A) where the errant cause or necessity *(ananke)* enters to complicate the portrait and where reason *(nous)* must learn to persuade *(peitho)* necessity to bring about order. On the one hand, this new theme, as Cornford observes, is resonant to the great *peitho* theme of the conclusion of the *Oresteia*. On the other hand, the introduction of this new and dialectically necessary component of "necessity" is a dialectical advance in the inquiry (similar moves occur in the mythic-dialectical notion of the "receptacle" and the more strictly dialectical but mytically contextualized notions of the "same" and the "different"). Above all, the great persuasion theme recalls not only the extraordinary poetic-mythic vision of Aeschylus but the crucial Platonic dialectical theme of "true persuasion" in the *Gorgias* and the *Phaedrus*.

I believe that such a curious but ingenious interpretation of myth and dialectic pervades the whole text of the *Timaeus* to the point where familiar debates on whether Plato's cosmology is "myth" or "science" seem beside the point for understanding the kind of educated inquiry into the cosmos which the *Timaeus* is. Only a full treatment of the whole text, with this model in mind, could verify my hypothesis. For the moment, the examples in the text cited above may serve to provoke reflection on the plausibility or implausibility of the hypothesis.

Some further evidence, however, is clearly needed. I will, therefore, end by citing some examples from the very beginning of the

Timaeus where this curious genre is formed—a dialogue that is at once mythical and dialectical all the way through.

(1) The characters of the dialogue do not bear the lively traits to which the early dialogues have accustomed the reader. And yet they do seem mythically resonant: Socrates merely summarizes a part of the *Republic* and, uncharacteristically, wishes now simply to listen; Timaeus of Locri (probably a fictional invention) does recall the Pythagoreans whose combination of mathematics and something like a mystery-cult does lend itself to the kind of dialectical mythic discourse which shall be his in the dialogue; Critias clearly recalls the ancient aristocracy of Athens which will free him both to remember Solon's Egyptian tale and prepare him to tell the story of Atlantis and Athens; Hemocrates (an historical figure) may serve as a warning to the Athenians—as the general who will one day (in the time of the dialogue) crush the Athenians in their most humiliating defeat at Syracuse—he reveals, by his mere presence, a warning to the *hybris* of contemporary Athens.

(2) 17C–19: Socrates' "summary" of the discourse of the *Republic* is notorious for all it leaves out from that great dialogue. My own reading of why this is so is less speculative than most commentators: first, Socrates has already given the discourse "yesterday" and finds no need to repeat its dialectical subtleties here: he is here to listen, not to speak further; second, the mere recall of the discourse can remind the reader that dialectics is necessary for a proper under-standing of any myth—including the highly dialectical myth of Timaeus which shall encompass the whole text.

(3) 19B–20B: Socrates' request: the city Socrates has earlier de-scribed is a city of the idea. How could it function in reality—especially the reality of war? For that one needs to turn not to philosophers like Socrates (much less to the "poets" and "soph-ists"), but to philosopher-statesmen like Timaeus, Critias, and Hem-ocrates.

(4) 20–24C: The initial responses of first Hemocrates, and then Critias to Socrates' request seem strange: Critias, as a result of an effort of (Platonic?) recollection of a story he heard in his youth (25E–26C) tells the Egyptian tale of Solon. This amazing myth, of an Athens which once was great and indeed seems to be the Athens in actuality of Socrates' city-in-idea, functions well to recall two salient facts about the *Timaeus* as a whole: first, dialectics (resulting in the city of the idea), and myth (disguised as history) can work together to train the soul; second, the true epic, greater even than Homer's,

would be the epic of that polis—the epic of the idea which could show how, in the past, the city of the idea actually existed. A true artist—one formed by the philosophic soul—could write that epic. Socrates (ironically?) cannot. But, as the great dialectician, he can listen and learn without the kind of further questioning which he ordinarily felt obliged to give to all the earlier pre-philosophic "poets." He can, more precisely, on one condition: that the poet-mythologizer is also a philosopher-dialectician who, in a sense, can do Socrates' new work for him: produce an epic of the idea which unites cosmos, soul, and polis in a dialectical-mythical tale. In the persons of Timaeus and Critias (and presumably in Hemocrates) Socrates finds these dialectical tellers of tales to whom he can listen and be silent without the fear that he is hearing "only" myth or "only" a dialectics which will disclose the idea but not the idea-in-action.

(5) 27C–29D: In Timaeus Socrates has finally found his teller of tales, a mythologizer, to whom he can listen. It is important, I believe, to see how Timaeus first engages in dialectical inquiry of a very Socratic-Platonic sort (on knowledge and opinion, on being and becoming) *before* he sets forth his mythical-dialectical creation narrative. It is almost as if the last books of Augustine's *Confessions* were required reading for all Christians about to read the Book of Genesis! Timaeus, we are shown, is indeed a fine dialectician—for he knows (29D) that to tell the story of the cosmos we can only hope for a likely story: likely, because the story is an *eikon*, the incarnation of the idea, which the *cosmos* as *eikon* is. Dialectics can lead us to glimpse the idea. Only a *likely* story can lead us further: to render the idea (of cosmos, of polis, of soul) actual in the state of incarnate becoming modelled in the ideas which we are and where we discover ourselves to be in kinship with the cosmos. At that point, the likely story can begin.

It is, I think, a good beginning to a good mythical-dialectical creation story. Such a curious combination of myth and dialectic in mutually critical correlation is an odd genre, to be sure: it is sometimes called theology.

Education of the Soul:
Action and Theological Education

In a sense, the community of inquiry in the West lives through the power of the great Socratic ideal for true education—classically

expressed in the saying "The unreflective life is not worth living."
All communities of commitment and faith add to that classic Socratic ideal of the Western community of inquiry the equally important though: "And the unlived life is not worth reflecting upon."

This addition is, of course, no minor one. For all thought, I repeat,
exists ultimately for the sake of action and commitment. It is true
that mere action without thought is blind. It is equally true that all
thought not ultimately directed to action, concern, commitment is
empty.

Of all the educational institutions, the ministry programs in
schools of Theology are those singular institutions where action and
thought, academy and church, faith and reason, the community of
inquiry and the community of commitment and faith are most
explicitly and systematically brought together. For anyone who
enters a seminary enters primarily with the goal of action, the goal
of the practice of ministry in and for the community of the church
and people. One enters to be educated—in the hope of finding a
community that unites both thought and action to help us find our
way to both the "reflective life" suggested by Socrates and the "lived
life" proclaimed by Jesus.

As Plato taught us, a life of inquiry has its own demands—the
demands of what Bernard Lonergan nicely called the pure, detached,
disinterested, unrestricted desire to know. But there is a further
insight which the community of faith has to teach. For the *eros* of
inquiry, as Augustine reminded the Platonists of his day, is itself
driven by our commitments, our faiths, our loves. To know the truth
of Augustine's great insight—*amor meus, pondus meum*—is to know
what ultimately drives the life of reflection in a community of
inquiry rooted in a community of commitment and faith: our ideals,
our hopes, our loves.

For the community of faith—the church—is that community
where despite its faults, even sins, God's word is yet preached, God's
story of redemption and creation is yet reflected upon and appropri-
ated by the "souls" of all Christians who have joined themselves to
that multi-voiced narrative; God's sacraments are made present
anew; God's people attempt to live out in action and commitment a
life of faith working through love and justice in a global context. In
the community of faith each person individually and the whole
people as a community attempt, now well, now poorly, to make
God's own story—the story of God's pure unbounded love for all

creation disclosed in the story of the people of Israel and that Jesus who is the Christ—become their story as well.

The life of the mind cannot live alone. As Aristotle insisted, only gods and beasts can do that. Rather to think is to converse with the classics; to converse with the classics is to join the community of inquiry of the living and the dead. It is to recognize that we too can and must become part of that conversation. In truth, we are that conversation.

Nor does the life of faith live alone. We live that life because past communities of faith passed it on to us. Christians know the decisive narrative of Jesus Christ because our tradition has seen fit to pass along, to hand over this healing, transforming, gracious possibility to us. As my historical colleague Martin Marty has written, "Christianity is always one generation away from extinction." We too must recognize that what conversation is to the life of the mind, solidarity is to the life of action.

The Christian community of faith is a tradition which has lived by shared disclosive and transformative meanings for almost two thousand years. Christians find that those shared meanings have expressed themselves through the centuries in an explosively pluralistic way as each generation attempted to think and live them as its own. And in retrieving that reality each generation added some new classic possibility, some new insight, some new retrieval or suspicion of this extraordinary story.

As we experience more deeply the pluralism of our Christian community, we are likely in the future to turn yet more fully to those who are the privileged ones of the ancient prophets and of Jesus Christ—the poor, the oppressed, the marginalized, the forgotten ones. They are the ones whose present and future voice the Christian gospel calls us to hear. This truth of the Christian faith seems to me more powerfully realized in the modern seminary than in the seminary of my day. And their voice, if listened to, can become our voice as well.

Some have suggested, with a sense of resignation, perhaps even quiet despair, that even the future is not what it used to be. Yet the truth is, it never was. For at the heart of the Christian revolution of consciousness is the insistence that the future cannot be a mere *telos*—a working out of what already is. The future, for the Christian gospel is *adventum*—that which is to come, the new, the unexpected, judgment and threat, gift and promise from God and God's disclosure in history and nature.

A theological education, grounded in continuous searching of the Christian classics, especially the Bible, open to the demands of inquiry become the demands of retrieval, critique, and suspicion, can become again a school for the training of the soul. That is how theological education began. That is how, I believe, it needs to see itself again. Otherwise even our noble contemporary attempts to teach "values" and "character-formation" may become trapped again in a mere individualism. To rethink theological education in our increasingly pluralistic and ambiguous global context is to rethink as well, not the "individualist" model of the purely autonomous self of Enlightenment modernity, not even, primarily, the classic notions of identity-formation through character of Aristotle and his successors. It is also to retrieve—critically, even at times suspiciously—the Christian soul as the subject-in-process of the Christian identity.

Part Three

THE PLACE OF THEOLOGY IN THE UNIVERSITY

DOES THEOLOGY BELONG IN THE UNIVERSITY? THE NINETEENTH-CENTURY CASE IN IRELAND AND GERMANY

William Madges

Introduction

Can an educational institution be both "Catholic" and a "university?" If it can, why *should* it be? These questions have been pondered before. Most recently, they have been discussed in the context created by the publication of a Schema for a Pontifical Document on Catholic Universities (November 1985) and the censuring of Rev. Charles Curran of the Catholic University of America. Both events have raised once again questions about the limits of academic freedom, the rights of the theologian vis-à-vis the rights of the official magisterium, and the possibility of truly Catholic *universities*.

The primary purpose of this paper is to examine the context and describe some of the important discussions that attended the nineteenth-century proposals for establishing Catholic universities in Ireland and in Germany. The paper's correlative, yet indirect, purpose is to stimulate thought about the nature of Catholic universities in general and about the proper role of theology in a university education in particular. After identifying certain important aspects of the Irish and the German contexts, I will highlight, on the one hand, the ideas of John Henry Newman with regard to the goals of university education and the place of religious studies within that hierarchy of goals; on the other, I will outline the ideas of Ignaz von Döllinger and Johannes Kuhn on the value of teaching theology in a civil rather than in an ecclesiastical institution, or—to state the matter conversely—why they thought it was *not* a good idea to establish a free Catholic university in Germany.

My thesis is that whereas Newman ably highlights some of the values in having theology or religious studies as part of the university curriculum, Kuhn and Döllinger identify precisely the dangers, both for the church in general and for theology in particular, that loom when universities are in the control of ecclesiastical authorities. The issue of control is emphasized more in my exposition of the German situation since it appears to have been a more fundamental stumbling block to the founding of a Catholic university in Germany than it was in Ireland. I do not mean to suggest, however, that the question of lay versus ecclesiastical control was not an issue in the Irish situation.[1]

Ireland
The Founding of the University

The Catholic University of Ireland was founded by the Irish hierarchy in 1852. It began its active educational work two years later with John H. Newman as its rector. The most important forces behind the idea of establishing this university were a majority of the Irish bishops and Pope Pius IX, who wanted to provide Irish Catholics with an alternative to the "secular" colleges on the island.

At the midpoint of the nineteenth century, there were few Catholic educational institutions in Ireland. St. Patrick's College (Maynooth) had been founded in 1794, but it was a college for those who were studying for the priesthood. Its faculties consisted solely of philosophy, theology, and canon law. On the secondary level, the Jesuits had begun two residential schools in 1814 and 1818. And a beginning had also been made with a system of Catholic secondary schools. As Aubrey Gwynn has observed, that indeed was "a weak foundation on which to erect the scaffolding of a Catholic University."[2] The introduction of an English bill for the establishment of three secular colleges in Cork, Galway, and Belfast, however, militated against the more sensible course of action, namely, the full expansion of Catholic secondary education before attempting the

---

[1]Newman apparently wished the School of Philosophy and Letters to be run by lay people. See Paul Misner, "Newmanian Reflections on Religious Literacy," in *Foundations of Religious Literacy*, ed. by John V. Apczynski (Chico: Scholars Press, 1982) 131. But, as the ninth discourse of his *Idea* makes clear, he was emphatic that the church exercise some kind of direct jurisdiction over the Catholic University. John Henry Newman, *The Idea of a University*, ed. with Introduction and Notes by I. T. Ker (Oxford: Clarendon Press, 1976) 184 and 193.

[2]Aubrey Gwynn, "Newman as the First Rector of the Catholic University of Ireland," *Newman Studien* (1957): 101.

more ambitious task of founding a Catholic university. Sir Robert Peel's proposed legislation of 1845 was seen by some as a serious threat to Catholicism because it offered the growing Catholic professional and middle class "an education that was essentially secular in outlook, and which was carefully planned to eliminate any form of clerical or ecclesiastical influence."[3] Lambert McKenna has argued that, although the desire to establish a Catholic university was not simply a political reaction against the Queen's Colleges, it is "probable that, if the Queen's Colleges had not been founded, there would have been no question of any Catholic University; but when they were *de facto* founded, the Bishops considered it an imperative duty to establish a parallel institution which would provide the same type of education, but one in harmony with Catholic ideals."[4]

Pope Pius IX played a significant role in the founding of the Irish Catholic University by condemning the Queen's Colleges and, in a Rescript of October 9, 1847, by suggesting to Dr. Paul Cullen, the Rector of the Irish College in Rome, the idea of founding a Catholic University in Ireland on the model of the Catholic University of Louvain.[5] Pius's fourth and final condemnation of the Queen's Colleges in May, 1851 "effectually deprived them of all episcopal and clerical favour, and seemed to promise the blessing of success on their projected Catholic rival."[6]

The Irish hierarchy, however, was not of one mind with regard to the university question. On the one side were men such as Archbishop MacHale of Tuam and Dr. Cullen (1803–1878), who saw the Queen's Colleges either as possible proselytizing agents for the

---

[3]Concerning the "ascendancy of the Catholics," see Robert Ornsby's letter to Newman, 16 April 1852, in : Fergal McGrath, *Newman's University: Idea and Reality* (New York: Longmans, Green and Co., 1951) 143.

[4]L[ambert] McKenna, "The Catholic University of Ireland," *The Irish Ecclesiastical Record* 31 (Jan.–June, 1928): 225. That the issue was not simply political is underlined by the case of Denis Caulfield Heron (1843–1845), described by Roger J. McHugh, ed., *Newman on University Education* (Clonskeagh: Brown and Nolan Limited, The Richview Press, 1944) viii–ix. This case indicates that, although they were admitted since 1793 to Ireland's one university (Trinity College), Catholics were denied proper educational advancement.

[5]McHugh xi; McKenna 226.

[6]McKenna 228. Although some think that Pope Gregory XVI, under whose auspices Louvain was founded, was thinking of a similar institution for Ireland, it was Pius IX's advocacy that made the idea a reality. See 226, note 1. Cf. McHugh, who says, xiii: "It is doubtful whether without great pressure from Rome the Catholic University of Ireland would have taken definite shape at all; but the need of combating the Queen's Colleges was urged on Pius IX by his advisers. These included the Rector of the Irish College in Rome, Doctor Paul Cullen . . ."

Church of England or (worse) as institutes for promulgating skepticism, anti-clericalism, and revolution. Archbishop MacHale expressed this fear in a letter to Lord John Russell:

> Is it not hazardous to erect infidel colleges for the propagation of infidel and revolutionary mania, which, should it succeed in overthrowing the altar, will not spare the throne?

And to Cullen, rigid control of the laity, especially in educational matters, appeared to be the best remedy against the dangerous foes that besieged the church, especially against the new critics of religion in the fields of philosophy and science.[8]

On the other side were church leaders such as Archbishop Daniel Murray (1768–1852) of Dublin and Archbishop William Crolly (1780–1849) of Armagh. These men were willing to allow Catholics to attend the Queen's Colleges, "if certain 'safeguards' were provided and if a fair proportion of Catholics was admitted to the Senate and staffs of the colleges." These bishops apparently thought that "mixed" or undenominational education would not undermine the faith of Catholic students.[9] In fact, a few thought that mixed education was the most appropriate form for their country. As one bishop remarked:

---

[7]Cited in McHugh x.

[8]"He [i.e., Cullen] embodied the typical Conservative ecclesiastic of his day, filled on the one hand with a sense of the hereditary spiritual patrimony of the Church, and on the other with a deep distrust of all who seemed in any way aligned with the new critics of religion who were presenting themselves daily in the fields of physical science, philosophy and sociology. Such men would naturally tend to extreme caution in intellectual research, and to the constant invocation of ecclesiastical discipline in their dealings with both their own body and the laity. In their minds this attitude was justified by the conviction—which they shared with more broad-minded Catholics—that they were guided by an unerring authority in the midst of a world of shifting values." McGrath 96. Cullen shared the attitude of Pope Pius IX. As McHugh presents it, the pope's expulsion from Italy by Mazzini's young Italians taught the pope conservatism. "Henceforth, he held, centralized ecclesiastical jurisdiction must be restored to Rome at all costs, while all elements identified with liberalism and revolution, such as mixed education, must be ruthlessly fought." McHugh xiv–xv.

[9]Although it rejected the bishops' demands for the appointment of a fair proportion of Catholic professors, the establishment of dual chairs in certain subjects, and episcopal representation of the appointing board, the British government "was prepared to establish Catholic halls under Catholic deans, to assign lecture-rooms for religious instruction, and to take disciplinary measures against teachers who attacked revealed religion or students who failed to attend their religious duties." McHugh x–xi.

> How can separate education be carried out completely? If it is to be carried out completely, Catholic lawyers and medical men must be kept separate in their professional education from others and then the Catholic professions are ruined and extinguished.

And Frederick Lucas, founder of the *Tablet* and one of Newman's advisers concerning Ireland, summarized the feeling of some with the phrase that in Ireland, "where people are mixed, and society is mixed, education must be so."[10]

The side in favor of an independent Catholic university, however, was given decisive aid from Rome. In December, 1849 Dr. Cullen was appointed to the See of Armagh—vacated by the death of his opponent on the university issue, Archbishop Crolly (April, 1849); in April, 1850 he was named Apostolic Delegate. The new status conferred upon Cullen made him such a power that "for many years he practically nominated bishop after bishop to Irish sees."[11] With regard to the university question, his appointment meant that the pope was determined to have the party in favor of a Catholic university triumph.

> By this step, the most determined member of the minority, Dr. Crolly, was replaced by an uncompromising enemy of mixed education, and the minority representation amongst the archbishops was reduced to Dr. Murray, now nearing the end of his long life.[12]

Cullen took charge at the national, episcopal synod at Thurles. He got the other bishops, by a narrow majority, to approve the measure that any priest who engaged in administrative or academic work in the Queen's Colleges be liable to ecclesiastical censure and suspension. And immediately after the Thurles Synod, the bishops published their *Address to the People of Ireland* (September 9, 1850), in which they announced their intention to establish a Catholic university. The Address explained the need for the university this way:

---

[10]Both statements are made in Lucas's letter to Newman, 9 October 1851, in McGrath 131. Cf. McHugh xx.

[11]McHugh xv.

[12]McGrath 90. The various public addresses concerning the Catholic University constantly invoked the pope's authority for the project. One of them declared that "the Holy Father suggested the founding of a Catholic University," and the *Address to the People of Ireland* (September 9, 1850) stated: "The resolution of your Prelates . . . has been taken in conformity with the expressed wishes of our most Holy Father Pius IX." McGrath 84–85.

> Without undervaluing secular learning or over-rating the importance
> of religion, is it not of the utmost consequence that the education of
> our youth be Catholic? One of the greatest calamities of modern times
> is the separation of religion from science, whereas the perfection of
> knowledge is the union of both, which produces the most perfect form
> of civilized society by making men not only learned but also good
> Christians.[13]

If science were to be taught without religion, "a spurious philosophy" would result in the intellectual sphere, whereas "anarchy will
be the result" in the civil sphere. The Address remarked that in the
recent European revolutions, the "standard-bearers of anarchy" were
"students of colleges and universities in which, according to the
modern fashion, everything is taught but religion."

The Address also responded to the objection that the establishment of a Catholic university would encourage religious bigotry and
hinder the cultivation of good feeling between Protestants and Catholics. The bishops replied that education from within a particular
religious tradition would produce better people and better citizens
than its undenominational or secular alternative.

> We fear that any attempt to fuse down all religions into one mass would
> result in an indifferentism more fatal to the interests of true religion,
> and more dangerous to society, than the most violent religious conten-
> tions. And then, as to the cultivation of kindly feeling between man
> and man, we believe that the Catholic who is brought up strictly
> according to the tenets of his own Church will, in all the relations of
> life, be incomparably a better man than one who is not so brought up—
> more obedient as a subject—more useful as a citizen—more exact in
> observing all the charities of life towards those who profess a different
> religion.[14]

By the Spring of 1851 things seemed to be well underway.

Newman's Role

Newman's actual involvement in the creation of the Catholic
University in Ireland began in mid-April, 1851 when he was asked
by Bishop Cullen for his advice about establishing the university

---

[13]Cited by McGrath 100–01.
[14]McGrath 101–02.

and was invited to "deliver a set of lectures in Dublin against Mixed Education."[15] Newman accepted the invitation for the following May (1852). A few months later, Cullen offered him the rectorship (July 18, 1851) of the new university.

Cullen invited Newman to become involved in the Catholic university cause because he thought Newman could disarm the remaining opposition to founding a Catholic university.[16] Newman accepted the post of rector (November 14, 1851), even though he knew little of Ireland and would be managing a university in the diocese of its chief opponent (Dr. Murray), because he thought he "saw a fair opportunity of doing for the Church a work for which his talents were well suited," i.e., describing how Catholics should respond to the modern world in the face of the rising tide of scientific and critical research.[17] Or, as Newman put it in his own words:

> I contemplated making provision for both the liberal and professional education of the various classes of the community, but I added other objects still larger as well as various in their nature, those for instance of providing philosophical defences of Catholicity and Revelation, of creating a Catholic Literature, of influencing the general education of the country, of giving a Catholic tone to society, and of meeting the growing geographical importance of Ireland.[18]

The Dublin lectures, originally entitled *Discourses on the Scope and Nature of University Education*,[19] set out Newman's ideals for

---

[15]J. H. Newman, *Memorandum*, sec. 1. This manuscript memorandum, entitled by Newman *My Connection with the Catholic University*, includes a series of transcripts Newman made of letters, etc., that he thought important for the history of the university. See McGrath 104.

[16]"It is true that Newman's intellectual pre-eminence and the dramatic events connected with his entry into the Church had drawn the eyes of the Catholic world upon him, and that his lectures on Anglican Difficulties, delivered in London during the year 1850, had revealed him as a powerful and persuasive controversialist, well equipped to assist Dr. Cullen in his contemplated campaign against mixed education." McGrath 103. Although opposition to the idea after the Synod of 1850 was more cautious, it was still considerable. "Many bishops refrained from open resistance only because of Archbishop Cullen's power; as it was, twelve petitioned Rome in the same year against the experiment." McHugh xvi.

[17]Gwynn 102. Cf. McKenna 228.

[18]Newman, *My Campaign in Ireland* (1896) 9. Cf. McHugh xliii. The defensive tone is comprehensible in the context of the considerable anti-Catholic sentiment current in Great Britain. The outcry against the re-establishment of the Catholic hierarchy in 1850 was so great that on August 19, 1851, the Catholic Defence Association of Great Britain and Ireland was formed. McGrath 126.

[19]For the changes in title and content of the various editions of this work, see McGrath 154–55, note 1, and the Editor's Introduction of Newman, *The Idea of a University*, ed. with Introduction and Notes by I. T. Ker (Oxford: Clarendon Press, 1976) xxix–xli.

the Catholic university. Their principal themes were the necessity
of including theology in any scheme of university studies and the
idea that the primary end of a university is the cultivation of the
mind, not the immediate preparation for professional occupations.
Both claims continue to merit serious consideration today.

Before setting out his substantive claims concerning the place of
theology in university education, Newman endeavored to make clear
the basis of his argumentation and his procedure. He asserted that
the principles upon which his inquiry into the nature of a liberal
education was based were principles derived from "the mere experience of life." They were derived neither from theology nor from
revelation. Rather, they wre dictated by human wisdom and recognized by common sense. Insofar as the principles were true, just,
and good in themselves, they "may be held by Protestants as well as
by Catholics."[20] Common sense and reason provided at least two
reasons for the inclusion of theology within a university curriculum.

Newman set forth the first reason or argument in his second
discourse, entitled "Theology a Branch of Knowledge". Theology,
he said, ought to be included because a university "by its very name
professes to teach universal knowledge," and theology "is surely a
branch of knowledge."[21] To exclude theology was "intellectually
absurd" and "logically inconsistent." Newman stated his thesis
more precisely:

> I say, then, that if a University be, from the nature of the case, a place
> of instruction, where universal knowledge is professed, and if in a
> certain University, so called, the subject of Religion is excluded, one of
> two conclusions is inevitable,—either, on the one hand, that the prov-
> ince of Religion is very barren of real knowledge, or, on the other hand,
> that in such University one special and important branch of knowledge
> is omitted. I say, the advocate of such an institution must say *this*, or
> he must say *that*; he must own, either that little or nothing is known
> about the Supreme Being, or that his seat of learning calls itself what it
> is not.[22]

In the course of his lecture, Newman formulated his thesis even
more provocatively: If nothing is taught about God in an institution
that professes all knowledge, then "it is fair to infer that every

[20]Newman, *Idea* 22. [Discourse 1,2]
[21]Newman, *Idea* 33. [Discourse 2,1]
[22]Newman, *Idea* 34–35. [Discourse 2,1]

individual in the number of those who advocate that Institution, supposing him consistent, distinctly holds that nothing is known for certain about the Supreme Being." In short, "it is very plain, that a Divine Being and a University so circumstanced cannot co-exist."[23] Newman, of course, thought that knowledge of God was not only possible, but also actual.

The modern objection to Newman's argument that immediately comes to mind is that theology does not offer knowledge in the same way that the natural sciences offer knowledge. Newman responded to this objection by seeking to undercut its validity and by identifying its source. On the first point, he asked his critics what criteria they proposed to use for determining which disciplines ought to be included in the university. If sense experience was the criterion, then ethics and metaphysics were excluded; if abstract reasoning was the criterion, then physics was excluded.[24] Newman's point was that theology, although different from other types of knowledge, has as much right to be included in a university curriculum as did ethics, history, metaphysics, or physics. On the second point, Newman identified the current Protestant conception of religion as responsible for making of religion a private matter and, hence, providing grounds for the exclusion of theology from the university. Insofar as religion was reduced to feeling and faith to emotion or affection, the connection of faith and theology with truth was "more and more either forgotten or denied."[25] Newman staunchly opposed such a trend, because he thought that if one did not resist it, one would end up either in Humean skepticism or atheism.[26]

Newman insisted that theology had a valid cognitive content. Moreover, he asserted that theology was neither provincial in character nor narrow in scope. "Theology" did not mean *Catholic* theology, familiarity with Scripture, "Christianity," or polemics. Rather, it meant "the Science of God, or the truths we know about God put into system."[27] Such knowledge about the deity could be formulated

[23]Newman, *Idea* 37. [Discourse 2,2]

[24]Newman, *Idea* 38. [Discourse 2,3]

[25]Newman, *Idea* 40. [Discourse 2,4]

[26]". . . and when I find Religious Education treated as the cultivation of sentiment, and Religious Belief as the accidental hue or posture of the mind, I am reluctantly but forcibly reminded of a very unpleasant page of Metaphysics, viz., of the relations between God and Nature insinuated by such philosophers as Hume." Newman, *Idea* 49. [Discourse 2,8]

[27]Newman, *Idea* 65. [Discourse 3,7] Cf. Newman's ninth discourse, where he contrasts the inductive method of the physical sciences with the deductive method of theology, 190–91. For further elaboration of what Newman means by "theology," see Misner, 131–33.

and studied "scientifically," i.e., in a manner that was "precise and consistent in its intellectual structure." Newman thought theology so conceived had a prima facie claim to our attention because it had a place in the intellectual world and in culture from time immemorial.[28] To use our current idiom, Newman was arguing for the public character of theology and its claims to truth.[29]

Newman introduced his second argument in support of the inclusion of theology within the university curriculum in his third lecture, entitled "Bearing of Theology on Other Branches of Knowledge." There he proposed a conception of knowledge as "one large system or complex fact," of which each science treated a particular aspect.[30] Newman's argument was that, insofar as each science could offer no more than a partial, albeit important, view of the whole, each science needed to be complemented or completed by the perspectives of the other sciences. Conversely, the omission of any one science prejudiced "the accuracy and completeness of our knowledge together, and that, in proportion to its importance."[31] According to Newman, a discipline was important to the degree that it enlightened the mind in the true knowledge of things. Insofar as theology dealt with ultimate knowledge and ultimate reality, it could be excluded from a university education the least of all. Theology so impinged on the whole system of what could be known that Newman concluded:

---

[28]Newman, *Idea* 70. [Discourse 3,9]

[29]Newman, however, is not a prototype of David Tracy or other revisionist theologians. His conception of God as well as his conception of art as making claims to truth are different from Tracy's. For Newman's conception of God, see *Idea* 46, 65–70; for his thoughts about art, see 42, 80–81, 239. In his third discourse, Newman defined truth this way: "Truth is the object of Knowledge of whatever kind; and when we inquire what is meant by Truth, I suppose it is right to answer that Truth means facts and their relations, which stand towards each other pretty much as subjects and predicates in logic." *Idea* 52.

[30]Newman, *Idea* 52. [Discourse 3,2]

[31]Newman, *Idea* 57. [Discourse 3,4] Although each science might be true in the abstract, independent of the other sciences, it was not true in the concrete. Newman used the notion of human agency and volition to illustrate his point. If there really is human agency (however limited), then it would be wrong, argued Newman, for a person to attempt to explain all of civilization in terms of physical causes, making no mention of human causes. Newman then extended this analogy to God: "Moreover, supposing man can will and act of himself in spite of physics, to shut up this great truth, though one, is to put our whole encyclopaedia of knowledge out of joint; and supposing God can will and act of Himself in this world which He had made, and we deny or slur it over, then we are throwing the circle of universal science into a like, or a far worse confusion." *Idea* 63.

Religious Truth is not only a portion, but a condition of general knowledge. To blot it out is nothing short, if I may so speak, of unravelling the web of University Teaching. It is, according to the Greek proverb, to take the Spring from out of the year; it is to imitate the preposterous proceeding of those tragedians who represented a drama with the omission of its principal part.[32]

Newman, however, did not advocate the study of theology to the detriment of the sciences. He wanted to promote a university education that integrated all the disciplines that promote cultivation of the mind. To claim that one's partial perspective of the truth was the whole truth was bigotry.[33] This was no less true of theology than of the other academic disciplines.

Not even Theology itself, . . . so far as it is relative to us, or is the Science of Religion, do I exclude from the law to which every mental exercise is subject, viz., from that imperfection, which ever must attend the abstract, when it would determine the concrete. Nor do I speak only of Natural Religion; for even the teaching of the Catholic Church, in certain of its aspects, that is, its religious teaching, is variously influenced by the other sciences.[34]

Despite his advocacy of a place for theology in the university, Newman disappointed some of his listeners. Archbishop Cullen, on the one hand, wanted Newman to "insist on the necessity of all learning being guided strictly by the principles of faith; and to point out the importance of all college training and discipline being in the hands of the Church."[35] Newman did not do that. What he did do was to demand a place for theology in the university on the basis of its scientific character and cognitive content, while rejecting "the notion . . . that Theology stands to other knowledge as the soul to the body; or that the other sciences are but its instruments or appendages." Although he conceived of theology as the highest science, Newman did not want to allow it to interfere with the "real freedom of any secular science in its own particular department."[36]

---

[32]Newman, Idea 71. [Discourse 3,10]

[33]Newman, Idea 62–64. [Discourse 3,6]

[34]Newman, Idea 57–58. [Discourse 3,4]

[35]McKenna 230.

[36]Newman made these statements in the original fifth discourse of 1852, entitled "General Knowledge Viewed as One Philosophy," which is reprinted in Ker's edition of Newman's Idea, 427–28. Newman suppressed its publication, however, in the 1859 and 1873 editions of Idea, where its place was taken by the sixth discourse, "Knowl-

Other critics, on the other hand, thought that Newman should have described the inculcation of virtue as one of the tasks of teaching theology. Newman, however, distinguished between the teaching of theology as a speculative science and the fostering of virtues. To make people better was not the aim of teaching theology. And although it was reasonable to expect that one who was liberally educated might indeed become a good, fair, and compassionate person, it was important to Newman to distinguish between the "theoretical" task of university education (i.e., imparting knowledge in the broad sense) and the "practical" task of religious formation.

> Knowledge is one thing, virtue is another; good sense is not conscience, refinement is not humility, nor is largeness and justness of view faith. . . . Liberal Education makes not the Christian, not the Catholic, but the gentleman. It is well to be a gentleman, it is well to have a cultivated intellect, a delicate taste, a candid, equitable, dispassionate mind, a noble and courteous bearing in the conduct of life;—these are the connatural qualities of large knowledge; they are the objects of a University; . . . but still, I repeat, they are no guarantee for sanctity or even for conscientiousness . . .[37]

With regard to theology, Newman added:

> If, for instance, Theology, instead of being cultivated as a contemplation, be limited to the purposes of the pulpit or be represented by the catechism, it loses,—not its usefulness, not its divine character, not its meritoriousness (rather it gains a claim upon these titles by such charitable condescension),—but it does lose the particular attribute which I am illustrating . . . for Theology thus exercised is not simple knowledge, but rather is an art or a business making use of Theology.[38]

---

edge Its Own End." Concerning the reasons Newman had for suppressing the original fifth discourse, see Ker's Introduction, xxxiv–xxxvii. One reason was Newman's apparent dismay over the discrepancy between the argument of his original fifth discourse and the papal brief of 1854, which stated that all disciplines of the university ought to assume Catholic doctrine in their intrinsic treatment of their subject matter and that professors ought to mold the youth to piety and virtue in conformity with the church's teaching. It is important to note that although Newman held theology, considered as a branch of knowledge, to be the "highest and widest" science, he did not think it was the course of study best suited for the cultivation of liberal knowledge. See Misner, 128 and 130; Ker's Introduction to Newman's *Idea*, xlvii and lxiii.

[37]Newman, *Idea* 110. [Discourse 5,9]
[38]Newman, *Idea* 101. [Discourse 5,4]

The criticism of Newman's first few Dublin lectures was apparently serious enough to cause him to insert a temporary introduction (July, 1852) at the beginning of his sixth discourse. In this Introduction, he noted that his lectures did not elucidate the *indirect* effects of university education, which effects included the religious. Rather, he was addressing the direct end of such education, viz., the "cultivation of mind." Newman's statements under heading 11–14 of the introduction are particularly illuminating:

> 11. A University is not *ipso facto* a Church Institution, and a good, even though it teaches Catholic Theology, as the Spanish Inquisition was an Institution of the State, not of the Church, yet had Catholic theologians at its head.
> 12. A University has no direct call to *make* men Catholics or religious, for that is the previous and contemporaneous office of the Church.
> 13. Men are Catholics *before* they are students of a University.
> 14. As the Church uses Hospitals religiously, so she uses Universities, viz., that, having given her children faith, she may *add* mental culture.[39]

Newman's lectures offer a clear rationale for the inclusion of theology within university studies. They argue for that inclusion not out of a desire to promote parochial propaganda or out of a desire to have universities responsible for religious formation of their students, but out of the desire to have university students educated well and "liberally." Religion has been an integral part of human culture. That is the historical argument in favor of studying religion and even theology. But Newman also provides a theoretical argument: Insofar as theology deals with the questions of ultimate reality and of ultimate meaning, not to ponder critically these questions would be to neglect essential questions of human existence, which

---

[39]Reprinted in Ker's edition of *Idea*, xxxii–xxxiii, note 5. This sixth discourse became the fifth in the 1859 and 1873 editions of *Idea*. What may be considered the official view of the hierarchy concerning the end of a Catholic university was expressed by Bishop Moriarty, who, in a letter to Newman after his lectures in Dublin, wrote:
". . . I made up my mind that the colleges were condemned at Rome because, being systematically mixed, Catholic exposition, Catholic feeling, Catholic fact should all be suppressed. While in a University such as the Church would wish, all instruction should be leavened with Catholicism, or at least, it should be freely used, . . . I thought . . . that a University was charged with the morals as well as the mind of a youth—that she was bound *in solidum* for him, that she was bound to see the work done in some way or other, and either *per se* or *per alium*." Bishop Moriarty to Newman, 21 July 1852, in McGrath 171–72.

is the domain of a liberal education. This is the legacy of Newman's lectures which we ought to consider seriously today.

Newman, however, did not address in detail the problems that can beset a university which includes theology within its curriculum and which is administered by ecclesiastical officials. The German theologians, Johannes Kuhn and Ignaz von Döllinger, were much more aware of those problems because of their occupation and the situation in Germany in the latter half of the nineteenth century.

The Situation in Germany
The Context

There was a variety of forces active from the 1840s to the 1860s in promoting the idea of establishing a "free, Catholic university" in Germany. There was also a variety of motivations. Among the higher clergy, a principal motivation was to insulate seminarians from the innovative and sometimes heterodox theology that was being taught in the state universities. Among the laity, a principal motivation was the desire to shield Catholics from the secular influences of modernity and to equip them to repel the attacks, both subtle and overt, upon Catholic culture that culminated in the *Kulturkampf*. The desire to establish a Catholic university, wherein these aims could be achieved, became focused first in the 1840s and was renewed in the 1860s. Although clerics and lay people could be found in both of these decades to support the university project, the two most vocal and visible advocates were lay men: Franz Josef Buss, who inaugurated the discussion in the 1840s, and Heinrich von Andlaw, who tried to renew the momentum in the 1860s. In order to understand and appreciate the opposition of Kuhn and Döllinger to the university plan, it is necessary to examine not only Buss's and Andlaw's advocacy of the project, but also to attend to the context in which the discussions took place.

Representatives of the thinking of many members of the clergy in the 1830s and 1840s concerning Catholic education in general and the education of priests in particular are Augustin Theiner (1804–1874), a member of the Roman Oratory and later adviser in the Curia, and Clemens August Droste zu Vischering (1773–1845), archbishop of Cologne. In his 1835 publication, *History of Institutions for the Education of the Clergy*, Theiner argued that the entire system of higher education needed to return to the close supervision of the church, by which Theiner meant the supervision of the bishops. He claimed that it was necessary to transfer the faculties of theology from the state universities to the seminaries so that future priests could be protected from "the influence of the immoral and irreligious age."[40] Archbishop Droste zu Vischering, who gained notoriety from his clashes with the Prussian government, similarly opposed the idea of mixed education. Since he thought it promoted indifferentism, he gave serious thought to the idea of setting up in Cologne something like the Catholic University of Louvain. Such a move seemed to him desirable because the purity of Catholic thought was threatened not only by the secular influence of the state, but also by the innovative theology propounded at the University of Bonn. Georg Hermes's (1775–1831) followers at Bonn gave, in the bishop's estimation, ample evidence of how easily theology strays from Catholic truth when it is taught in state universities.[41] In February, 1837 Droste zu Vischering forbade all but two of the theology professors at Bonn to hold any more lectures.[42] In the same summer, he removed two instructors from their posts in the Cologne seminary, and he closed down the entire operation in November in order to establish a replacement under his watchful eye in the episcopal palace.[43] Droste zu Vischering thought that the bishops needed to exert more control over the teaching of theology and philosophy; and episcopal institutes free of all state influence seemed to be the appropriate solution.

Although not a cleric, Franz Josef Ritter von Buss (1803–1878), professor of law at the University of Freiburg, supported the idea of liberating education from the total control of the state. In 1846 he published *The Difference Between Catholic and Protestant Universities of Germany*, in which he called for the restoration of those universities that were formerly Catholic and for the elevation of the University of Freiburg to become the "great, purely Catholic Univer-

---

[40]Augustin Theiner, *Geschichte der geistlichen Bildungsanstalten* (Mainz: Florian Kupferberg, 1835) 384–85.

[41]In 1835 Pope Gregory XVI condemned the rationalism believed to be implicit in Hermes's thought. The condemnation, however, only intensified debate about his orthodoxy. And the Prussian government did not permit the publication of his condemnation at Bonn.

[42]Hans-Jürgen Brandt, *Eine katholische Universität in Deutschland? Das Ringen der Katholiken in Deutschland um eine Universitätsbildung im 19. Jahrhundert* (Cologne: Böhlau Verlag, 1981), 105–06. I am deeply indebted to Brandt for the exposition of the German context that follows.

[43]Johann Heinrich Schrörs, *Die Kölner Wirren (1837). Studien zu ihrer Geschichte* (Berlin: F. Dummler, 1927) 379, 622–23.

sity of the German nation."[44] Buss thought that such a move was necessary if Catholic culture were to survive in Germany. Two years later, at the Bishops' Conference in Würzburg, he actively launched his ardent campaign for a Catholic university. The episcopal conference, which met from October 22 to November 16, 1848, was the first general German bishops' conference since 1786. It met at a time when the exact relationship between church and state in Germany had not yet been worked out. The school question was one of the major concerns of the bishops, and among the propositions they passed at the Conference was the right of the Catholic Church to establish the appropriate private schools if an un-Christian spirit ever permeated the existing public schools.[45] Although the question of a "private" Catholic university was not discussed at any of the official sessions of the Conference, the participants still present toward the end of the Conference were invited to attend a presentation by Buss on this issue in the bishop's residence.

In his lecture, Buss proposed concrete steps for the founding of a Catholic university. His recommendations were in line with what he had published in his 1846 book, with one exception. In light of the changed political context of 1848, Buss no longer proposed to make Freiburg the central Catholic university. Instead, he recommended that a new university be founded in the spirit of the University in Louvain. Buss made clear what he understood by a "Catholic" university a few years later in his book, The Reform of Catholic Scholarly Education in Germany at Secondary Schools and Universities (1852). Only Catholics were to be allowed as professors, and all prospective professors would first have to be recommended by the appropriate faculty, then evaluated by the chancellor and an episcopal committee. At the beginning of each academic year, the instructors would be required to profess the Tridentine Confession of Faith and to promise to conduct their instruction in a "direction that was in accord with Catholic principles." Although only theology lectures were to begin and end with prayer, all members of the university were expected to participate in the liturgical celebrations of the academic community.[46] In short, the university

---

[44]See Brandt 119.

[45]See Ernst Rudolf Huber and Wolfgang Huber, Staat und Kirche im 19. und 20. Jahrhundert. Dokumente zur Geschichte des deutschen Staatskirchenrechts, 2 vols. (Berlin: Duncker and Humblot, 1973–1976), 2: 16–18.

[46]Franz Ritter von Buss, Die Reform der katholischen Gelehrtenbildung in Teutschland an Gymnasien und Universitäten; ihr Hauptmittel, die Gründung einer freien

was to be Tridentine in spirit and opposed to the new insights of science and philosophy wherever they challenged traditional orthodoxy.

Insofar as Buss's proposal would severely limit the creativity and critical rigor of their discipline, theology professors were legitimately concerned about the future quality of their work in such a system. This concern was deepened by the activity of Bishop Wilhelm Emmanuel Ketteler (1811–1877) and his Mainz Circle of theologians, who became the vanguard of neoscholasticism in Germany.

One of Ketteler's first official acts after being consecrated bishop of Mainz (1850) was to make the Mainz seminary, not the University of Giessen, the proper place for priests to study philosophy and theology. Ketteler was of the opinion that academic theology possessed only secondary importance in the education of priests, and he was convinced that the university was not a beneficial environment in which to form loyal and good servants of the Church.[47] The bishop responded to a papal letter (December, 1850), in which he was exhorted to attend to the proper education of priests, by reestablishing the study of philosophy and theology in the Mainz seminary on May 1, 1851.[48] This was in reaction to the current practice of attendance first at a university for theology studies, and then at a seminary for the completion of one's priestly formation. The effect of Ketteler's decision on the theology faculty at the University of Giessen was disastrous. By summer the faculty had no more students. And the theology professors either switched to pastoral work in parishes or waited for retirement. With the retirement

---

katholischen Universität teutscher Nation (Schaffhausen: Hurter, 1852) 508–09. With regard to the education of the clergy, Buss followed the program of Theiner. That is, he thought it imperative that speculative German theology be moderated by the more practical Roman theology. Moreover, he thought more time in a priest's education should be devoted to the study of canon law: "Allein wie die verhältnisse der katholischen Kirche . . . [es] notwending machen so bedarf die mehr speculative Theologie Roms, durch die kanonistische Geschäftskunde der römischen Curie. Wie es daher wünschenswerth wäre, dass Rom alljährlich einige Theologen an die theologischen Facultäten und an die bischöflichen Curien Teutchlands entsändte, so sollen der teutsche Episkopat das Collegium Germanicum in Rom alljährlich mit Theologen zum Behuf dieser praktischen, kanonistischen Ausbildung besenden." Buss, Die notwendige Reform des Unterrichts und der Erziehung der katholischen Weltgeistlichkeit Teutschlands (Schaffhausen: Hurter, 1852) 469.

[47]See Brandt 182–83. Cf. Wilhelm Emmanuel Ketteler, Public Schools or Denominational Schools? Pastoral Letter on "The Separation of the School from the Church" (Cincinnati: Benziger Bros., 1892).

[48]See J. M. Raich, ed., Briefe von und an Wilhelm Emmanuel Freiherr von Ketteler, Bishof von Mainz (Mainz: F. Kirchheim, 1879) 222–24.

of the last theology professor in 1859, the Catholic faculty of theology at Giessen died out.[49] Ketteler had achieved with Giessen what Droste zu Vischering was unable to achieve with the Catholic faculty at Bonn.

Despite some powerful, vocal advocates, such as Ketteler, for bringing higher education under closer episcopal supervision, not much progress was made in the 1840s or 1850s for the realization of a Catholic university under church control. One reason for this failure, Hans Jürgen Brandt suggests, was Buss's mistake in planning. In the 1840s Buss believed that he only needed to get the bishops excited about the idea in order for it to become a reality. Although some bishops expressed particular interest in the project, they did not provide uniform, definite, and consistent direction. The 1848 episcopal conference established a commission of ten bishops and two university professors (viz., Buss and Döllinger) to examine the issue more closely.[50] The commission never got beyond the stage of initial considerations. If the Catholic university were ever to become a reality, a new initiative would have to be made.

At the 1862 meeting of the Catholic Association (*Katholischer Verein*) in Aachen, the new initiative was made. Since the bishops seemed unable to move the project forward in the 1850s, the laity would now have a go at it. The first proposal made on the first day of the convention was to consider anew the idea of founding a Catholic university. The proposal received a warm reception. The form which the university was to take, however, was not explained in detail. The Catholic University of Louvain seemed to many to be a noble model. Hence, on the second day of the convention Johannes Möller (1806–1862), a German and professor of history at Louvain, was invited to address the group concerning the desirability of establishing in Germany a university similar to Louvain. Möller underlined two characteristics that distinguished the University of Louvain from other universities in Belgium: the Catholic orthodoxy of its teaching in all disciplines of knowledge and its vigilant discipline over the

---

[49]Otto Pfülf, *Bischof von Ketteler (1811–1877). Eine geschichtliche Darstellung*, 3 vols. (Mainz: F. Kirchheim, 1899) 1: 239–44.

[50]See Brandt 146–48, 242. The bishops on the commission were Cardinal Friedrich Schwarzenberg (1809–1885), the primate of Germany and prince-archbishop of Salzburg, Archbishop Count Reisach of Munich, Archbishop Vicari (1773–1868) from Freiburg, Georg Oettl (1794–1866) of Eichstätt, Peter Joseph Blum (1808–1884) of Limburg, Müller of Münster, Heinrich von Hofstätter from Passau, Valentin von Riedel from Regensburg, and Georg Anton von Stahl of Würzburg.

moral character of its students.[51] Möller implied that those two characteristics were reason enough for wanting to establish something similar in Germany.

One of the arguments against establishing a Catholic university in Germany was the claim that the state might use the existence of such a "clerical" institution as a pretense for completely removing all other universities from any influence of the church. Konrad Martin (1812–1879), the bishop of Paderborn, and Pankratius Dinkel (1811–1895), the bishop of Augsburg, were reticent to support the Catholic university project because they feared the de-Christianization of the other universities. Möller, however, anticipated these objections. He pointed out that Louvain had the opposite effect in Belgium. Rather than diminishing the influence of Catholicism in Belgium, the Catholic university of Louvain exerted a beneficial influence on academic developments throughout the country, without the church losing influence at the other institutes of higher learning.

Möller convinced his audience, and they were eager to approve the practical steps he proposed for making the German Catholic university a reality. The first step was to appoint a new University Commission, which would promote and direct the project. Möller's cnadidates were approved, and Heinrich von Andlaw was nominated chair. Andlaw quickly proposed two additional lay members for the commission, including Franz Josef Buss, whom Andlaw praised as the greatest advocate of the Catholic university project.[52] One of the reasons that membership on the Commission was kept lay was that some of the university promoters thought that there would be less opposition to the project if the university did not appear to be a clerical initiative. The project's lukewarm reception or outright rejection among Catholic professors of theology at the state universities was conspicuous. Their reluctance to support the project becomes comprehensible in light of what the university promoters wanted the Catholic university to be.

In the program they formulated in the name of the Commission in 1862 and 1863, Buss and Phillips noted that the freedom and Catholicity of academic disciplines could be vouchsafed only when they were taught in "the most intimate connection with the church," by which the committee members meant the subordination of all

---

[51]Brandt 229.

[52]The Commission included Count Clemens vonn Brandis, Baron Felix von Loe, Baron W. von Ketteler, George Phillips, and Heinrich von Andlaw. The latter proposed August Reichensperger and Franz Josef Buss. Brandt 233.

disciplines to the direction of the pope and the bishops.[53] Johann
Baptist Heinrich, a member of the Mainz Circle, agreed with this
viewpoint, but he hesitated to give his full support for a Catholic
university that was designed and directed by the laity. He claimed
that Louvain was a Catholic university precisely because the Belgian
bishops had planned and established it. The same needed to be
done in Germany. Heinrich said further that a truly Catholic university would take "as its highest principle the divine and infallible
authority of the Catholic Church in its teaching office," and that it
would in principle "subject itself in everything to this highest
authority."[54]

The close supervision of all academic disciplines by the episco-
pate, the requirement that all professors be Catholic, the limitation
of creative theology were the characteristics of the proposed Catholic
university that caused concern among a number of prominent,
progressive Catholic theologians.

Döllinger's Changing Position

In 1848 Ignaz von Döllinger (1799–1890), who attained fame as a
distinguished church historian and as speaker for the Catholic
delegates at the Frankfurt National Convention, became a member of
the University Committee. Throughout the year he regularly proposed the Belgian model as something that would benefit the Catholic Church in Germany. He explained, however, that he did not
envision the total separation of the church from the state, but rather
wanted the church to be independent in certain respects.[55] In the
course of the next few years, Döllinger came to disagree with Buss,
his colleague on the Committee. He felt that not only were the
necessary funds unavailable, but also the requisite teachers and
intellectual resources. For this reason, he suggested that attention
first be turned to improving the secondary schools. Moreover, he
feared that the erection of a Catholic university might mean that the
Catholic Church would lose all influence upon the already existing

---

[53]See the *Sammlung von Aktenstücken bezüglich der Gründung einer freien katholischen Universität in Deutschland* (Mainz: 1865) 12–13.

[54]See the *Verhandlungen der General-Versammlungen des katholischen Vereins
Deutschland: Amtlicher Bericht* (Aachen: 1863) 180–183. Cited in Brandt 231–232.

[55]Brandt points out, 211, note 388, that Döllinger's temporary sympathy for the idea
of a Catholic university coincided with his demotion, in connection with the Lola
Montez affair, from his university post and transfer to Dillingen (1847–1850).

universities by destroying the Catholic departments of theology in them.[56] At the third general convention of the Catholic Association (Katholischer Verein) in Regensburg (1849), Döllinger predicted that a Catholic university, if desirable, still could not be brought into existence within the next fifteen years. Buss interpreted this statement to mean that Döllinger was really opposed to the university plan, even if he only voiced indirect criticism of the project.[57]

By the 1860s there was no doubt about Döllinger's opposition to the plan for a Catholic university. At the Gelehrtenversammlung of 1863, Döllinger argued that relative freedom of research and critical, academic rigor were required if theology were to prosper. And he suggested that, under present circumstances, that was possible only in the state universities. He pointed to the contrast between the quality of theological work at French or Italian seminaries, on the one hand, and that at the German universities, on the other, to underscore his claim.[58] Two years later (1865), during a conflict between the Bavarian government and the bishop of Speyer, he had an opportunity to explain in detail why theology was best left in the state universities.

The conflict had arisen when the bishop of Speyer, Nikolaus von Weis (1796–1869), announced his intention to employ a number of men to teach theology at his seminary and to make their status equal to that of professors at the state universities. According to the Bavarian Concordat of 1817, Seminar referred to the educational institute to which a candidate for the priesthood went after completion of his theological studies at the university; it did not refer to a college for those who study theology. Döllinger not only supported this interpretation of the concordat, but also specified the dangers to the health of the church inherent in the bishop's plan.[59]

Döllinger identified three serious problems in the bishop's plan. First, the bishop's candidates for teaching theology were drawn from the clergy of the immediate area around Speyer, namely, men who were already engaged in other matters and who could therefore "at

---

[56]See Johannes Friedrich, Ignaz von Döllinger. Sein Leben auf Grund Seines Schriftlichen Nachlasses, 3 vols. (Munich: C. H. Beck, 1899–1901) 3: 90–99.

[57]Buss, Reform 500. See Brandt 213.

[58]Ignaz von Döllinger, "Die Vergangenheit und Gegenwart der katholischen Theologie," Kleinere Schriften, gedruckte und ungedruckte, ed. F. H. Reusch (Stuttgart: Cotta, 1890) 180–190.

[59]See his "Die Speyerische Seminarfrage und der Syllabus," in Reusch 197–227; here 198–99.

best" be "theological dilettantes."[60] Second, the bishop would have
the right to install or fire whomever he wished without having to
follow established, formal procedures. To the assurance that the
bishop would exercise this power responsibly, Döllinger replied:

> Every unbounded force for whose use the possessor is not accountable
> to anyone else is misused, often misused in the best intention. Only
> that person is wise who, possessing the correct knowledge of his own
> fallibility and shortsightedness, welcomes the boundary that is set up
> for his discretion.[61]

Third, this measure, if followed by other bishops (as in the case of
Mainz), would make all the bishops more dependent upon Rome. If
Rome wanted a theologian out, he would be out. Such a situation
would make the professor less secure in his position than the pastor
in his. And knowing this, theologians would hesitate to undertake
extensive, critical research or to publich their results. In the end, the
church would suffer. Again, Döllinger pointed to the theological
works produced in France and Italy to substantiate his claims.[62]

Döllinger staunchly opposed stricter episcopal control over the
teaching of theology because he saw that development connected to
the spread and strengthening of ultramontanism. Pius IX's *Syllabus
of Errors*, which had been recently published (December 8, 1864),
was becoming the symbol of the ultramontanists. And its condemnation of error #80 ("The Roman Pontiff can and ought to reconcile
and harmonize himself with progress, with liberalism, and with
modern civilization.") gave clear indication of what to expect from
theologians who shared the papal view. Döllinger rejected ultramontanism not only because it threatened to worsen the political situation of Catholics around the world, but also because it threatened to
undercut the beneficial pluralism that existed in Catholic theology
and church life. He observed that "the ecclesial ideal of the ultramontanists is the Romanization of all individual churches and the
greatest possible suppression of everything distinctive to the life of
national churches." In short, it meant "complete uniformity."[63]

The uniform theology that would result from greater episcopal
and Roman control was the neoscholasticism represented by the

---

[60]Döllinger, "Seminarfrage" 199.
[61]Döllinger, "Seminarfrage" 200.
[62]Döllinger, "Seminarfrage" 201–02.
[63]Döllinger, "Seminarfrage" 215. See also 212.

students of the German College in Rome.[64] This theology was antithetical to the historical research and critical scholarship currently exercised in the German universities; and the use of the Index seemed to be its favorite and most potent weapon against alternative theologies. Döllinger summarized the effect of the spread of this kind of theology: "Where it reigns, there science and literature die off."[65] Therefore, it was not surprising to Döllinger to think that this neoscholastic-ultramontanist party would celebrate the removal of Catholic theologians from state universities as a great victory, especially if in their place "episcopal special schools would then come into operation."[66]

The Position of Johannes Kuhn

Johannes Kuhn (1806–1887), the dogmatic theologian from Tübingen, also came to express his opposition to the idea of establishing a Catholic university in Germany. Shortly after the publication of the Aachen program, Kuhn sketched his "Observations" about the program and sent them to Baron Heinrich von Andlaw (1802–1871), who had become the leading spokesperson for the proposed Catholic university. Although he had not intended his "Observations" for publication, Andlaw sent a copy to the editors of the Historical-political Newspaper for Catholic Germany and to Konstantin Schäzler, both of which parties openly attacked Kuhn.[67]

Kuhn focused his criticism upon two points in the Aachen program. First, he criticized its claim that the task of the university was not only to teach (lehren), but also to rear (erziehen). As Kuhn saw the matter, the university's task was "to mediate insight and cultivation, knowledge and science, and the practical professional abilities that rest upon scientific insights." "Raising" or "rearing" students was something different: "To plant and to make firm in people's souls religious and moral convictions is the task of education at home and in the church."[68] If rearing were anywhere a task

---

[64]Döllinger, "Seminarfrage" 205.

[65]Döllinger, "Seminarfrage" 220. See also 218.

[66]Döllinger, "Seminarfrage" 220.

[67]Johannes Kuhn, "Bemerkungen zu einer Abhandlung des Herrn Freiherrn von Andlaw über die Gründung einer 'freien katholischen' Universität" in: Heinrich von Andlaw, Offenes Sendschreiben an Herrn Dr. Joh. von Kuhn, Professor der Theologie an der Universität Tübingen, über die Frage der "freien katholischen Universität" (Frankfurt, 1863) 15–32. Cf. Brandt 322, 324–27.

[68]Kuhn, "Bemerkungen" 18. Cf. Newman's Introduction to his original sixth discourse, especially the twelfth proposition. See also Ker's Introduction to Idea, lix–lx.

of the schools, then it was at the lower levels, where education took place primarily through the use of authority. At the university level, however, stimulation of the students "to think for themselves and to do research" were the appropriate educational aims. The Catholic university proposed by Buss, Andlaw, and their supporters would *train* students to be Catholic, but it would not educate them.[69]

The second point Kuhn criticized in the Aachen program was its demand for Catholic parity at the existing universities. The Aachen promoters seemed to want the number of Catholic professors in the various academic disciplines to equal the number of Protestants; moreover, they wanted the Catholic professors to let their instruction be guided by the official teaching of the church. Kuhn admitted that Catholics had a right to want competent Catholics to be given consideration in filling university chairs. But he thought it immoral to suggest that there be Catholic law, Catholic medicine, or Catholic philosophy. In Kuhn's mind, all academic disciplines, with the exception of theology, are to be pursued independent of confessional points of view. Kuhn insisted that Catholics respect the academic freedom that already existed in all the various departments of the state universities since that freedom belonged to the essence of "science" and was ultimately in the Catholics' own interest.[70] In addition to these internal arguments against the Aachen program, Kuhn offered an external consideration. He observed that the currently existing theology faculties (in state universities) already provided theology students "both a truly Catholic, ecclesial as well as fundamentally scientific education."[71]

Kuhn's theological opponents used his observations concerning the founding of a Catholic university as an opportunity publicly to portray Kuhn's theology as heterodox. Kuhn's understanding of the relationship between philosophy and theology diverged from the view held by neoscholastics.[72] Although Döllinger and Bishop Lipp of Rottenburg advised him not to respond to the attacks of Andlaw or the *Historical-political Newspaper*, Kuhn felt obligated to respond. In the process, he turned the tables on his critics by suggesting that they were the ones whose position was heterodox.

Kuhn defended his point of view in detail in his lengthy article, "Science and Faith, with Special Reference to the University Ques-

---

[69]Kuhn, "Bemerkungen" 20.
[70]Kuhn, "Bemerkungen" 24–25.
[71]Kuhn, "Bemerkungen" 26.
[72]See Brandt 325–27.

tion" (1864).[73] He began his defense with the observation that the Catholic university project, as described in the *Historical-political Newspaper*, is "nothing else but the eminently practical realization" of the theoretical principle that science ought to be subordinated without restriction to faith.[74] Kuhn's thesis was that such a principle was un-Catholic. As he understood it, Catholic teaching affirmed a double source of truth: the natural and the supernatural revelation of God. These two sources of truth could not lead to any ultimate contradictions, and the fact that supernatural truth transcends reason did not mean for Kuhn that faith stood in no relation whatsoever to reason.[75] He insisted that "just as reason must agree with faith, so too must faith, on the other hand, agree with reason."[76] And he accused the neoscholastics of misinterpreting Albert the Great and Thomas Aquinas when they thought that these medieval theologians could be used to support their construal of the relationship between reason and revelation, philosophy and theology.[77]

With regard to the Catholic university question, Kuhn stated that, in principle, there could be no objection. If, however, a Catholic university denoted an institution in which science was not allowed to operate according to its intrinsic principles, then there was serious reason to object. Kuhn maintained that the sciences possess their own criterion of true and false and that they rightly resist all attempts to let divine revelation determine both their form and content.[78] To hold a contrary view meant that one presupposed that the human mind, outside of supernatural revelation, is completely subject to error and darkness. Such a conclusion, Kuhn argued, is excluded by a proper understanding of Catholic faith; and whatever is built upon such a faulty conclusion (viz., the proposed Catholic university) is a dubious enterprise. Kuhn declared that the one universal bond "that binds all together in unity" is human reason. The proponent of the Catholic university at the *Historical-political Newspaper*, by contrast, implied that there is such a thing as Catholic

---

[73]Kuhn, "Die Wissenschaft und der Glaube mit besonderer Beziehung auf die Universitätsfrage," *Theologische Quartalschrift* 46 (1864): 583–645.

[74]Kuhn, "Wissenschaft" 583–84. The article to which Kuhn was responding is "Die freie katholische Universität," *Historisch-politische Blätter für das katholische Deutschland* 51 (1863): 325–56.

[75]Kuhn, "Wissenschaft" 598.

[76]Kuhn, "Wissenschaft" 593.

[77]Kuhn, "Wissenschaft" 585–87, 630–33, 636–42.

[78]Kuhn, "Wissenschaft" 602–03, 629.

philosophy, Catholic mathematics, and Catholic geology. Kuhn un-equivocally rejected this notion as mistaken and absurd.[79]

Kuhn, however, was not suggesting that faith had nothing to do with science. He granted that "religious education and academic instruction do not exclude each other;" in fact, they get along best together. Kuhn's point, rather, was that religious training and academic instruction were not to be confused. No one—including good Catholics—should "demand such a subordination of instruction to training" such that "the former cannot prevail as scientific instruc-tion." Insofar as the advocates of the Catholic university did exactly that, they were to be opposed.[80] It was ultimately in the best interests of Catholics to be exposed to the insights of science and modern thought. Only in this way could Catholics be equipped to provide creative service to the world and the church.

Conclusion

The Catholic University of Ireland, which began its educational functions in 1854, failed by 1882. The "pure, Catholic university of the German nation" was never established. Yet the discussions that attended the question, whether they should be established, can be a resource in our own reflections on the nature of Catholic universities and on the place of theology within a university curriculum.

John Henry Newman tells us that religious studies and theology should have a place in the university curriculum insofar as univer-sities teach "universal knowledge." Theology not only is a signifi-cant branch of human knowledge, but also has contributed tremen-dously to the present shape of human culture. He cautions, however, that teaching theology does not have as its primary aim the inculca-tion of certain convictions or the evocation of religious feelings. As he put it concisely: theology in the university is not for the purposes of "pulpit or catechism." Its purpose, rather, is to search for and disclose truth about ultimate reality in an intelligible fashion.

Ignaz von Döllinger warns us of the dangers—in the short run, for theology; in the long run, for the entire church—that attend narrow construals of the term "Catholic" and strict episcopal control over

---

[79]Kuhn, "Wissenschaft" 603–06. Cf. Kuhn's "Die historisch-politischen Blätter über 'Eine freie katholische Universität und die Freiheit der Wissenschaft,' " *Theologische Quartalschrift* 45 (1863): 569–667.

[80]Kuhn, "Wissenschaft" 609. See also 635.

theological reflection. He urges the church and its theologians to eschew Romanization and uniformity.

And finally, Johannes Kuhn reminds us ever to distinguish between training our students and educating them. He calls on Catholic universities to be in open and critical dialogue with all that the modern world has to offer, so that they can contribute significantly to the humane formation of our society. "For only when we conduct academic disciplines" according to the principle of academic freedom ". . . will we become effectively involved . . . in the course of social and political movement;" only then will university education "become for us what it can be: power."[81]

---

[81]Kuhn, "Bemerkungen," cited in: Heinrich Fries, ed., *Johannes von Kuhn*, Wegbereiter heutiger Theologie (Graz: Verlag Styria, 1973) 339.

THEOLOGY IN THE POSTMODERN UNIVERSITY: REFLECTIONS FROM POLITICAL PHILOSOPHY AND THEOLOGY

Steven T. Ostovich

"Postmodernism" has become a catchword applied to an unclear but real sense of crisis in modern culture and the consequent desire to move beyond "modernism." As a response to this vague feeling within society, postmodernism is a concept that admits of a variety of contextually-dependent definitions. In philosophy, the aporias in modern (i.e., post-Enlightenment) understandings of human reason have led to several attempts to frame a postmodern model of human understanding. The presupposition of this paper is that such changes in models of understanding entail changes in the definition and organization of colleges and universities, i.e. those institutions that embody understanding.

The connection between modern models of reasoning and the current university system has been described and criticized by Alasdair MacIntyre in his book, *After Virtue: A Study in Moral Theory*. MacIntyre's starting point is a belief that contemporary moral theory has suffered a catastrophe for there seems to be no rational way to settle moral debates: The language of modern morality has ceased to be "rational." This loss of meaning MacIntyre associates with the "*ethos* of the distinctively modern and modernising world," i.e. a post-Enlightenment world.[1] MacIntyre stresses that the problems of post-Enlightenment culture have been built into the curricular divisions of modern universities. Philosophical ethics is divorced from the human or social sciences even though both ostensibly deal with the realm of human action. The division rests upon the distinction between value and fact that is a part of modern

---

[1]Alasdair MacIntyre, *After Virtue: A Study in Moral Theory* (Notre Dame: University of Notre Dame Press, 1981), p. viii.

understanding. The social sciences define human action in mechanistic terms, i.e. terms of objectifiable fact. A philosophical understanding of action in terms of value therefore becomes unintelligible
in social scientific terms. The goal of scientific objectification of
human action is social control stemming from predictive accuracy.
This control is incorporated in public and private bureaucracies
wherein managerial expertise is the hallmark of excellence. For
MacIntyre, this project is doomed to failure because human action
cannot be controlled: There are no rules or law-like generalizations
that govern human conduct. Society (modern) in general and universities in particular may be organized according to the ethos of the
Enlightenment, but "nothing less than a rejection of a large part of
that ethos will provide us with a rationally and morally defensible
standpoint from which to judge and act."[2] Insofar as the ethos of the
Enlightenment has been built into universities, MacIntyre's challenge to modernism is a challenge to the university to change.

The goal of this paper is to offer some suggestions as to the
direction the process of redefining and reorganizing colleges and
universities might follow based on descriptions of postmodern understanding and interdisciplinary dialogue found in the political
philosophy of Juergen Habermas and the political theology of Johann
Baptist Metz and Helmut Peukert. Special attention will be paid to
the role of theology in the postmodern university.

We will begin with a description of Metz's failed attempt to
establish an Institute for Interdisciplinary Research at the State
University of Bielefeld. The thesis here will be that this attempt fails
at an ideological level because it proceeds from a modern conceptualization of "subjectivity" and "objectivity" and therefore accepts
the existing university organizational distinctions between the
"soft" sciences and the "hard" sciences. We will then turn to
Habermas' *Der philosophische Diskurs der Moderne* as providing
both a critique of modernism and a postmodern model of human
understanding based on community discourse. Helmut Peukert's
*Wissenschaftstheorie—Handlungstheorie—Fundamentale Theolo-
gie* will serve to illustrate how the notion of communicative reason
can be used to locate theology in the university. Finally, several
suggestions for opening up the structure and curriculum of the
postmodern college or university will be proferred.

---

[2]Ibid., cf. pp. 8, 76–102, 111.

1. Metz: Theology in Interdisciplinary Dialogue

Beginning twenty years ago, Johann Baptist Metz was involved in an attempt to establish a Center for Interdisciplinary Research at the State University of Bielefeld. The plan was to have more than just a few courses that touched on interdisciplinary dialogue or a mere cross-fertilization of faculty from various departments. The Center was to be fully independent within the university with its own staff. It was to concentrate on interdisciplinary research and have authority to grant doctoral degrees. Further, it was to be biconfessional, i.e. both Roman Catholic and Evangelical theologians were to be represented on the faculty. This last part of the plan has been a problem for both the German Catholic and Evangelical churches, and the Center has not reached its potential level of activity. Nevertheless, some of Metz's clearest statements of his understanding of the relationship between theology and the sciences in the university stem from his involvement in the project.

For Metz, theology must enter into interdisciplinary dialogue given the complexity of contemporary society. There is no longer a single science or philosophy that can provide a unified theory of reality as did natural theology in the past. There is a contemporary pluralism of knowledge that calls for theology to dialogue with technology and politics in the planning of the future. If the church is to remain an effective instrument of social criticism, it cannot isolate itself from the dialogue process by claiming to be the only real avenue to saving truth in the contemporary world.[3] This pluralism of knowledge, however, also means that the exact shape and definition of subject of interdisciplinary research can only be anticipated at present. No a priori concept of "science" or model of knowledge can be the ground for the division of labor in interdisciplinary dialogue or serve as a standard for admission to the community of interdisciplinary discourse. Insofar as Metz is correct here, the entire postmodern university and not just such centers for interdisciplinary research will have to be much less structured than is currently the case.

Participation in interdisciplinary dialogue raises several opportunities for theology. An open-minded vision of interdisciplinary research offers theology the possibility of overcoming its isolation

---

[3]Johann Baptist Metz, "Technik-Politik-Religion in Streit um die Zukunft der Menschen," *Erwartung-Verheissung-Erfuellung*, ed. W. Heinen and J. Schreiner (Wuerzburg: 1969), p. 158f.

in the university by examining its own claim to universality based
on faith and its connection to the church as well as to the university.[4]
This tearing down of walls is not only an external action, however;
internally, there is the opportunity for theology to combat its disin-
tegration into separate disciplines based on various historical sciences and to reintegrate systematic, practical and historical theology.[5] For Metz, the most important opportunity presented by
theological participation in interdisciplinary dialogue, however, is
the chance to define the scientific character of theology. This is
important because, "historically, theology has been thrown into
crisis by its often tragic inability to assimilate critically the import
of modern scientific and scholarly methods."[6]

Curiously, Metz does not follow through by producing an outline
of the scientific character of theology. He is clearer, however, about
what defining theology as a science does not entail: Critical assimi-
lation of scientific and scholarly methods does not mean acquiess-
ence in the face of scientific methodological claims to universality.
This is because the nature of the discourses carried on in the
scientific and theological communities differ. While theology depends primarily on narrative or story-telling, science proceeds by
arguments. For Metz, there can be no abandonment of the narrative
potential of religion in order to take part in scientific or argumentative discourse. Argument does have a role to play in theological
discourse, but theology does not become critical simply by becoming
argumentative and abandoning narrative. A purely argumentative
theology would be a reductionist theology. For example, the transformative power or the biblical story would be lost if that history
were reduced to objectively verifiable "fact."[7] The role of argument
in theology is restricted to the defense of religious narratives in a
scientific world.[8] This restriction of the role of argument in theological discourse does not render theology uncritical or unscientific for

---

[4]Johann Baptist Metz, "Zu einer interdisziplinaer orientierten Theologie auf bikon-
fessioneller Basis: Erster Orientierungen anhand eines konkreten Projekts," *Theologie
in der interdisziplinaeren Forschung*, ed. Johann Baptist Metz and Trutz Rendtorff
(Duesseldorf: Bertelsmann, 1971), pp. 10–25, 51.

[5]Ibid., p. 14f.

[6]Matthew Lamb, "The Exigencies of Meaning and Metascience: A Prolegommenon
to the God-Question," *Trinification of the Word*, ed. Thomas A. Dunne and Jean-Marc
Laporte (Toronto: Regis College Press, 1978), p. 16.

[7]Johann Baptist Metz, *Glaube in Geschichte and Gesellschaft* (Mainz: Matthias
Gruenewald, 1977), p. 197f.

[8]Johann Baptist Metz, "A Short Apology of Narrative," *Concilium* 85 (1973): 93.

Metz because being critical cannot be limited to a matter of using the scientific method of argumentative discourse. Here again, Metz's observations could use development in light of the awareness of the role of narrative even in natural scientific traditions as illustrated in the work of MacIntyre referred to above as well as such philosophers of science as Thomas Kuhn and Paul K. Feyerabend.

A more important problem with what Metz writes about the place of theology in interdisciplinary dialogue (and made especially important in the context of this paper's concern with the place of theology in the postmodern university) is his implicit acceptance of the modern distinction between the Geisteswissenschaften and the Naturwissenschaften. While he is not explicit about this, Metz seems most comfortable locating theology among the "softer" historical sciences. The discourse of natural scientific communities is taken to be characterized by an argumentative concern with the theoretical control of objective reality. Theology is more like the historical sciences that necessarily have recourse to narrative and are more aware of the role of the knowing subject. Despite theological differences between them, Metz here seems to echo the distinction made by Wolfhart Pannenberg between the natural, epistemological sciences and the historical, hermeneutical sciences like theology,[9] a distinction mirrored in the structure of the modern German university.

It is this very distinction that is criticized by many postmodern thinkers. Richard Rorty, for example, explicitly denies that the differences between "hermeneutics" and "epistemology" ground the distinction between the Geisteswissenschaften and the Naturwissenschaften. In the modern world, the natural sciences are perceived to be the realm of "nature," of "hard" facts; these are the (true) sciences that are "objective" because they accurately mirror nature. On the other hand, the human sciences are understood to be the realm of the "spirit," of "soft" knowledge; these are the (pseudo-)sciences wherein knowledge is "made-up" by convention. Essential to Rorty's postmodern and deconstructionist project, however, is the rejection of the model of knowledge as mirroring nature. There is no natural scale to serve as the standard for objective knowledge as opposed to "something squishier and more dubious."[10] Metz's acceptance of

---

[9]Wolfhart Pannenberg, *Theology and the Philosophy of Science*, trans. Francis McDonagh (Philadelphia: Westminster Press, 1976).

[10]Richard Rorty, *Philosophy and the Mirror of Nature* (Princeton: Princeton University Press, 1979), p. 321.

this modern distinction limits the usefulness of what he has to say about the place of theology in interdisciplinary dialogue if such dialogue is to take place in postmodern institutions.

2. Habermas on Postmodernism

A criticism of modernism in philosophy and an attempt to move beyond it is provided by Juergen Habermas, especially in his recent book, *Der philosophische Diskurs der Moderne.* The subtitle of this book, *Zwoelf Vorlesungen,* indicates its format: A collection of twelve lectures (with added excurses), four of them delivered at the College de France in Paris, the fifth actually a previously published article, and the rest delivered or at least worked on at Cornell University and Boston College during 1983–84. The coherence of these assembled lectures is testimony to the coherence of perspective of the author. The audiences, at least for those lectures delivered in Paris, might also explain the selection in several of these lectures of contemporary French philosophers like Derrida, Bataille and Foucault as dialogue partners. Habermas admits being moved to an analysis of postmodernism as a philosophical (rather than artistic) phenomenon by the work of French Neostructuralists like Lyotard who coined the term, "postmodern."[11]

For Habermas, Hegel is the central figure in the process of modern philosophy becoming self-conscious as distinct from ancient philosophy and medievel philosophy (through Kant). Hegel began with the distinction in modern reason between the knowing subject and the known object and recognized as the task of philosophy the overcoming of the division between the two. This was to be accomplished by delineating within the subject the structures of reason productive of knowledge and was made possible by the reflexive quality of subjectivity, i.e., the ability philosophically to turn the subject into an object. Habermas sees here an attempt to assign to philosophy an integrating function formerly fulfilled by religion.[12]

Hegel's own method for integrating subject and object was in terms of a dialectical reconciliation he believed was built into the structure of reason in the individual, but the first generation of Hegel's interpreters already recognized the problems associated with mod-

[11]Juergen Habermas, *Der philosophische Diskurs der Moderne: Zwoelf Vorlesungen* (Frankfurt: Suhrkamp Verlag, 1985), p. 7.
[12]Ibid., p. 105.

ern reason (at least as it played a role in society and politics): In the name of the critical and political freedom of the subject, reason unmasked the hidden forces of oppression and alienation at work in society only to take their place. Marx and the Linkshegelianer responded with a hope in the revolutionary power of practical reason to break through the ideology of rationalism. The Rechtshegelianer looked to overcome tensions between the political subject and society by the rationalization of the latter.

There was a third reaction to Hegel's framing of the modern philosophical and political project that Habermas examines in some detail: Nietzsche's reduction of reason to the will to power.[13] For Nietzsche, no rational integration (not even a dialectical one) of subject and object or subject and society was possible. Nietzsche turned instead to "die rettende Kraft der Kunst"[14] in the form of a new, Dionysian mythology as providing the integrative function mistakenly sought in reason in the modern era and formerly provided by religion. Habermas focuses on Nietzsche because there is a "deconstructionism" at work in Nietzsche regarding subject-centered reason that is carried on by Heidegger, Bataille, Derrida, and Foucault, among others. Each of these critiques of modern philosophy and society suffers, however, from an acceptance of subject-centered reason as the only possible locus for rational activity. The result is to be caught on the horns of a dilemma: The options are either a transcendental objectivism (Heidegger's Seinsgeschichte or Derrida's structuralism) or an empirical relativism (Foucault's theory of power).

Habermas sets as the task of the postmodern philosopher the completion of the deconstructionist critique of modern reason by the reconstruction of reason in terms of community interaction.[15] Modern thinking focuses on the subject and aims to frame a theory of rational consciousness. Postmodern thinking looks for standards of rationality as emerging from the interaction between members of a community of discourse; a theory of consciousness is replaced by a model of understanding arising out of communicative praxis; subject-centered reason is replaced by communicative reason.

While pure theoretical definition of what these standards are or how communicative praxis produces these standards is impossible

---

[13]Ibid., pp. 70f, 110f.
[14]Ibid., p. 122.
[15]Ibid., pp. 279, 344–351.

given the practical character of communicative interaction, Habermas does describe how communicative reason avoids the pitfalls of
subject-centered reason. There is, on the one hand, a tendency in
modern thinking to isolate a privileged position for the subject often
by making the subject the seat of transcendental criteria of knowing
as a means to guaranteeing the objectivity of reason. On the other
hand, there is the modern attempt to be strictly empirical even in
the analysis of subjectivity, thereby reducing the subject to the status
of an object, but also facing the danger of sinking into relativism. By
rejecting subject-centered reason, postmodernism breaks free from
the limits of both transcendental and empirical analyses of subjectivity and escapes the objectivism/relativism dichotomy.[16]

It might be objected that Habermas remains optimistically objec-
tivistic by still believing in the possibility of some form of transcendental standards developing out of community discourse to allow
the commensuration of contributions to that discourse.[17] Perhaps
Habermas is too dependent on a social scientific perspective that
looks at the behavior of groups as statistically relevant in a manner
the behavior of individuals can not be; he has substituted the
rational structure of the community for what is missing at the level
of the individual subject. Nevertheless, Habermas' analysis of the
turn in postmodernism to communicative reason and the interactive
praxis of communities of discourse accurately portrays the direction
followed by other postmodern thinkers (including Rorty and Habermas) and is useful for situating theology in interdisciplinary discourse as the work of Helmut Peukert illustrates.

3. Peukert on Handlungstheorie

Helmut Peukert's dissertation has been published as a book entitled   Wissenschaftstheorie—Handlungstheorie—Fundamentale
Theologie. Directed by Metz, Peukert's approach to interdisciplinary
dialogue in this book is both more thorough and more sophisticated
than that of his director outlined above. Peukert characterizes theology as at a crisis point in modern society caused by the rise of the
sciences (both natural and historical). Scientific language seems to

---

[16]Richard Bernstein, *Beyond Objectivism and Relativism: Science Hermeneutics
and Praxis* (Philadelphia: University of Pennsylvania Press, 1983).

[17]Cf. ibid., pp. 197–207, 223–331 for criticism of Habermas by both Bernstein and
Rorty.

preclude the meaningfulness of theological discourse insofar as experience and subjectivity scientifically conceived do not have transcendental dimensions open to theological elaboration.

For theology to make sense, then, or for dialogue between theology and the sciences to be possible, some common ground must be found where both theological and scientific statements make sense. Peukert follows Habermas' lead in locating this common ground in reason understood in terms of Handlungstheorie, i.e., a theory of communicative interaction.[18] The book, therefore, is divided into three section: Fundamental theology as Handlung; science as Handlung; and the implications of the convergence of theology and science in Handlungstheorie.

Peukert's dialogue partners in tracing the development of fundamental theology are Rudolf Bultmann, Karl Rahner and Metz. Bultmann sets the parameters for the discussion in the demand that talk about transcendence must be existential, i.e. rooted in the structures of historical human subjectivity, but Peukert criticizes Bultmann's existential subject as too privately conceived and limited to the present.[19] Rahner's transcendental anthropology provides a more adequate understanding of subjectivity with its orientation towards transcendence as experienced in interaction with the neighbor. Metz develops this notion of subjectivity by pointing to its necessary social and eschatological aspects. Fundamental theology is grounded in the activity of believing communities aimed at realizing God's promises for the future of history.[20] Expressed in Peukert's terms, fundamental theology is based on a type of communicative interaction and can be described in terms of Handlungstheorie.

Peukert turns to an examination of scientific theory as conceived by logical positivism and critical rationalism. This context is chosen not only for its influence in the philosophy of science but because it represents very often a direct challenge to the meaningfulness of theological statements. The principle figure of this second section is Ludwig Wittgenstein, whose later writings represent for Peukert the abandonment of the more usual quest for a unifying language as the

---

[18]Thomas McCarthy, "Philosophical Foundations of Political Theology: Kant, Peukert and the Frankfurt School," Civil Religion and Political Theology, ed. Leroy S. Rouner (Notre Dame: University of Notre Dame Press, 1986), p. 31ff.

[19]Helmut Peukert, Wissenschaftstheorie-Handlungstheorie-Fundamentale Theologie: Analysen zu Ansatz und Status theologischer Theoriebildung (Duesseldorf: Patmos Verlag, 1976), pp. 21–42, 58.

[20]Ibid., pp. 43–64.

basis of scientific theory in favor of an examination of ordinary language as it is used concretely. It is in this examination of ordinary language that Wittgenstein is led to develop the notion of language "games" or logics of usage that vary by community. Peukert interprets this development in Wittgenstein as a turn to Handlungstheorie. Scientific language, like theological language, is rooted in the activity of a community of investigation and discourse.[21]

The third section of Peukert's book takes as its starting point this convergence of theology and scientific activity in Handlungstheorie. Peukert follows two directions in examining this convergence: A survey of linguistic theories of science open to theological discourse as meaningful (e.g. Ian Ramsey); and an exploration of attempts to describe a metatheory of theology that would be scientific.[22] Guiding this examination is the conviction that the convergence of theology and the sciences in Handlungstheorie entails certain aporias shared by both. Chief among these aporias is the inadequacy of Handlungstheorie as theory for addressing questions of ultimate meaning, the questions that appear in the history of any community and in every individual in the quest for critical appropriation of the self through the other. These questions arise in the limit-experiences of existence, e.g. in the confrontation with death. Meaning arises in such situations not out of theoretical reflection but out of praxis. Peukert describes this praxis as anamnetic solidarity, the preservation of individual and communal meaning through the remembering activity of a living community. Death is overcome not in the individual's ahistorical resolve but in the memory and activity of the community of which the individual is a part. The meaning arising from anamnetic solidarity is made possible only by an appeal to transcendence, i.e., God. In the face of alienation, oppresssion and injustice, only a transcendent reality can render the dead their due and thereby preserve universal meaning.[23]

Peukert concurs with Metz that the only access to transcendentally grounded universal meaning is through the particularity of a community of activity. Meaning is not derived from conceptual truths disclosed by a transcendent reality; meaning arises from the transformative activity of transcendence within an historical tradition.[24] Theology and the sciences share this grounding in the activities of

---

[21]Ibid., pp. 75–86, 146f, 201ff, 244–282.
[22]Ibid., pp. 212–230, 236f, 273–285.
[23]Cf. McCarthy, op. cit., pp. 23–40.
[24]Peukert, op. cit., pp. 317–323.

communities of discourse as well as the methodological explication of this activity in terms of Handlungstheorie. This turn to a theory of communicative activity provides a type of logic for interdisciplinary research for Peukert, i.e. it establishes the common and, in Habermas' terms, postmodern ground for the theological and scientific enterprises.

As a model for establishing a place for theology in interdisciplinary dialogue, Peukert's analysis of theological and scientific activities in terms of Handlungstheorie works admirably. Problems arise when trying to move beyond this apologetic task to a more complete picture of how theologians participate in the discursive interaction of the university community. Peukert turns to the necessity and experience of transcendence as grounding the meaningfulness of theological discourse. This could be interpreted as a call for a return to religion as the integrating medium lacking in modern subject-centered philosophy: Theology addresses religious experience of transcendence to the aporias inherent in every community's theoretical discourse in the face of limit experiences. Such a move would be both retrogressive (an attempt to return to the pre-modern era) and subject to the hermeneutic of suspicion vis-a-vis theology in the academic community. In a less imperious light, Peukert's turn to transcendence might be seen merely as an attempt to identify a subject matter, i.e., limit experiences and transcendence, as the bailiwick of theology. This would leave theology isolated in the university community, however: It is difficult to establish dialogue solely at the level of methodological principles. Fortunately, if the postmodern university is characterized by the open-ended dialogue implied in Habermas' (and Peukert's) model of communicative reason emerging from interactive praxis, neither of the above assignments of theology to a place in the university is necessary.

4. Theology in the Postmodern University

Habermas describes the move to postmodernism as beginning in the deconstruction of modern philosophy. The same approach might be followed in analyzing the impact of postmodern thought on the university and theology's place in the academic community: If postmodernism entails a radically new understanding of rationality it must entail also radical changes in the structure of the community that embodies and fosters (communicative) reason. The assumption in what follows, therefore, is that university structure must be opened-up to explore new avenues for communicative interaction. Further, what are offered here are a few directions or pathways that might be followed to good result in pursuing Habermas' program for the reconstruction of rationality, here as embodied in the university.

At a fundamental level, postmodernism in the university calls for a new delineation of what constitutes the communities or divisions and departments within the larger academic community. Reliance upon actual patterns of communicative praxis precludes defining communities of discourse simply on the basis of subject matter.

Thomas Kuhn provides both reasons why this is so and a picture of how communities of discourse should be identified with specific reference to scientific communities. Modern science typically is pictured as the production of knowledge primarily by the individual scientist rigorously following rules of abstract method, a type of great-person view of discovery and the history of science. Kuhn proposes instead viewing scientific knowledge as produced by scientific communities. Such communities are not to be defined, however, by subject matter. This mode of definition runs afoul of the actual history or science. One subject matter, e.g. heat, may be divided and shared among several different scientific communities over the course of time. Other communities have come into existence as the result of mergers between formerly separate communities so that, e.g. what currently is the subject matter of physics previously was divided between mathematics and natural philosophy. And, within a single scientific community there may be competing schools that define their subject matter differently. There is no simple one-to-one correspondence between "scientific community" and "subject matter."

Kuhn's own definition of community might be termed practical: "A scientific community consists, on this view, of the practitioners of a scientific specialty."[25] Identifying scientific communities is not a matter of isolating subject matters but a process that focuses on science as an activity and what scientists do. Kuhn suggests paying attention to "patterns of education and communication," the former involving not just the "similar educations and professional initiations" of the members of a community but their concern for "training of their successors," and the latter involving looking at "subject of highest degree, membership in professional societies, and jour-

---

[25]Thomas Kuhn, *The Structure of Scientific Revolutions*, 2nd edition (Chicago/London: University of Chicago Press, 1970), p. 180.

nals read" and, where the community is small, paying attention to "attendance at special conferences, to the distribution or draft manuscripts of galley proofs prior to publication, and above all to formal and informal communication networks including those discovered in correspondence and in the linkages among citations."[26]

This understanding of what constitutes a community is applicable beyond the realm of science. As applied to theology it offers both the external possibility of abandoning a defensive posture regarding the place of theology in the scientific university and the internal possibility of overcoming the fractionalization of the theological project into isolated areas based on methodologies adopted from other disciplines. Kuhn's understanding of community also catches the spirit of the postmodern desire to let standards of rationality emerge from interactive praxis even to the point of recognizing the configuration of communities will be changing constantly as patterns of communicative activity change. The structure of the postmodern university will have to remain fluid.

Steps that could be taken to foster the development of this type of postmodern university culture include encouraging interdisciplinary dialogue by such means as faculty offering seminars for each other that cut across denominational lines, offering (team-taught) interdisciplinary courses, and special faculty development funds for (team) projects that in their actualization offer new visions of which groups might find interaction productive. Cross-appointments also should be used even where this might involve the deemphasizing of traditional credentials for participating in a community's dialogue with the consequent danger of academic anarchy. Theology offers a model of how this type of grass-roots interactive praxis might issue in new understandings of what it means to be rational as well as human in the activity of basic communities described by Metz and liberation theologians.

At another level, postmodernism affects the nature of educational activity, i.e. the university curriculum. First, more time must be spent examining the histories of communities of investigation rather than merely teaching their respective methodologies. Communicative reason can only be seen to emerge from interactive praxis if that community praxis is viewed historically. Communicative reason is

---

[26]Thomas Kuhn, *The Essential Tension: Selected Studies in Scientific Tradition and Change* (Chicago/London: University of Chicago Press, 1977), p. xvi; cf. Kuhn, *The Structure of Scientific Revolutions*, pp. 176–181.

in this sense historical reason. This is part of the reason why narrative has become a central category for theological understanding. The emphasis on history also can be seen in the philosophy of science where thinkers like Kuhn, Imre Lakatos and Paul Feyerabend, among others, all make the history of science foundational for doing philosophy of science and deny that science can be understood as an activity apart from its history. These three historical philosophers of science have in turn influenced self-consciously postmodernist philosophers like MacIntyre, Rorty and Bernstein.

Second, emphasis must be placed in at least the latter stages of a course of study on the integration of knowledge within a community and between the communities in whose activity a student has participated. Much has been written criticizing the modern cult of the expert.[27] Postmodern education should neither foster the creation of nor rely upon experts insofar as expertise is an individual concept inimical to communicative reason. At the same time, the postmodern university cannot simply be content with a return to the "basics." Basic skills are necessary for but insufficient to elicit integrative ability. As a final caveat, it should be mentioned that talk of integration here is not a call for a return to natural theology as *the* integrative discipline in the postmodern university; theology provides *a* perspective for integration but others are possible and in the course of discussion it may become increasingly difficult to talk about what is meant today by a theological perspective.

---

[27]MacIntyre, op. cit., p. 101.

THE PLACE OF THEOLOGY IN THE LIBERAL ARTS CURRICULUM OF THE CATHOLIC COLLEGE AND UNIVERSITY

Alice Gallin, O.S.U.

The other morning I boarded my usual Metrobus en route to work and was confronted by a new coin box. For the previous ten years I had to fold up my dollar bill into a narrow piece so as to insert it, along with forty cents in change, into the coin box. But now, we had been computerized. The coin box had two separate gadgets to receive our money: one for bills, the other for coins. "String out your dollar . . ." the driver said. Bewildered as to what that might mean, I struggled to figure out what to do. How does one "string out" a dollar?

I mention this only because I was struck once again by the fact that language is both a means of communication and a barrier to it. Language uncovers meaning but also buries it. Language evolves through usage, through creativity, and through history. The title for my paper today contains at least four problematic linguistic expressions in terms of definition and meaning: theology; college/university; liberal arts; Catholic. I think it important that I share with you my understanding of the way I am going to use these terms before we begin.

1. Theology. I am using the term inclusively, as I believe you do in your membership of CTS. I intend it to cover the various ways in which we communicate about questions of religious significance, whether it be Scripture studies, moral and ethical problems, or peace and justice issues. The recent issue of our journal, done jointly with CTS, presented many different ways of "doing" theology. Although conscious of the many distinctions made by those within the profession, I entitled this issue "Perspectives on Teaching Theology."[1] It is in the same sense that I use the term in this paper.

---

[1] ACCU, *Current Issues in Catholic Higher Education*, Volume 7, Number 2, Winter, 1987.

2. College and/or University. Again, I take my lead from CTS usage. Our program is called: "Theology and the University." I take it that university here stands for both colleges and universities. We have this language problem because of the way that higher education developed in the United States. I shall have some reflections on that piece of history later on, but want to declare at this point that I am going to confine most of my remarks to four-year undergraduate programs whether in four year colleges or within universities. The role of theologians on a faculty of a graduate school or of a research university will be covered by others on the program. I will be happy to extend my remarks in that direction in the discussion if you so choose.

3. Liberal Arts. I use the dictionary definition which states that they are the "arts becoming a freeman." The term has come to mean those subjects which are specific to an academic college, as distinguished from professional or technical subjects. In current literature they are often designated as "general education" and ordinarily include literature, languages, history, philosophy, mathematics, natural and social sciences. As human knowledge has expanded, so also has the notion of the liberal arts. They are considered to be the major way in which a cultural tradition is handed on to a new generation. Interestingly, we have not included religion or theology in our formal definition of the liberal arts and that may reflect the way in which theology had related to other faculties in the traditional European model of universities.

4. And, finally, the term "Catholic." This is, perhaps, the most ambiguous of all the terms. I use it when speaking of the 215 colleges and universities that choose to belong to the Association of Catholic Colleges and Universities and of all the other twenty or so that are not members but clearly identify themselves as Catholic. So, basically, it is a matter of self-identification, but there is also the built-in notion that such institutions have been identified as Catholic by both civic and church communities over a fairly long period of time.

Now that you know the meaning of the language I shall be using, let's begin.

The choice of my topic today stems from a conviction that our Catholic colleges and universities in the United States have tried to do a unique thing—to integrate the study of theological disciplines with the liberal arts. In this effort, we were aided by the experience of American higher education itself, for, in the early days most colleges here were church related and therefore had a large component of religion and moral discipline. Unlike our colleagues in Catholic universities the world over, we evolved from Catholic private academies or else from secondary schools sponsored by dioceses, and for a long period of time in the late 19th century it was hard to determine where the high school ended and the college began. With very few exceptions, our universities began with general education for undergraduates, while in Europe universities were comprised by specialized faculties—law, medicine, philosophy, and theology—which presumed that the general or liberal education had been done in the secondary school. While it is true that many of our American Catholic high schools developed strong classical programs they were seen by the colleges as "preparatory" to the liberal arts program for the undergraduate student, leading to the B.A. degree.

This distinctive heritage that we have in the United States is shown in the oft-repeated definition of our mission as "educating the whole person." Mindful of affective and spiritual development as well as intellectual growth, Catholic colleges have spent time, money, and creativity on the "environment" of the campus. By this, they some-times mean residence halls, campus ministry, chapels, health facili-ties, football teams, movies, tennis courts etc. Such things would be of no concern to most universities in Europe and elsewhere. But because of this concern for educating the whole person, we have perhaps thought more than our European colleagues about the im-portance of religion as a factor in higher education. If we look back about fifty years we find that courses in religion were generally required, and the concern about the student's faith was reflected in compulsory chapel attendance and a host of other symbols and regulations. We had "religious" reasons for almost every student activity! The religion courses were designed to continue the knowl-edge and formation begun in the preparatory school—apologetics, sacraments, the life of Christ, moral principles, and sometimes the social teaching of the church. I have not done much research on this topic of curricula, but I think there was little or no conscious effort to relate the courses in religion to the rest of the curriculum—the liberal arts. The type of religion course was more directly related to the desired outcome in terms of faith and Christian practice, and I have not discovered any real effort to promote interaction between religion and the liberal arts.

In 1953, however, a program was introduced at the Catholic University of America entitled "Theology, Philosophy, and History as integrating disciplines in the Catholic College of Liberal Arts." A

workshop held that summer and in several succeeding years promoted this curriculum, and many Catholic colleges—especially
smaller ones—adopted it. The papers given at the workshop in the
summer of 1952 are extremely important for the consideration of
our topic.[2] "The more things change, the more they remain the
same." The foreword to the workshop's publication was written by
Archbishop Richard Cushing, and you will smile at the title "The
Necessity for Theology at the College Level." It was his conviction
that our colleges must become places where lay people could study
theology; at that time only seminaries taught theology and only
clerics could study there. Cushing wrote, "Why should a Catholic
layman or indeed any layman study theology? I answer: Why should
a Catholic or any American study biology, American history, government, literature?" He explained this further in words which may
amuse us by their simplicity but may be key to our understanding
the initial impulse to make theology (rather than religion) a part of
the Catholic college curriculum. Said Cushing:

> We study biology because it is the science of natural life. It is not the
> exclusive domain of medicine. We study theology because it is the
> science of supernatural life. This is not the exclusive domain of the
> seminary. We study American history because we are children of
> America. We study theology because we are the children of God. We
> study American government to learn the laws of our native land. We
> study theology to learn the laws of our eternal home. We study litera-
> ture to know the most important reflections of human life in language.
> We study sacred scripture to share God's words to us, His children.[3]

Cushing went on to denounce, in the spirit of the early 50's, the
secularism of the public schools and colleges—their Godlessness—
and the importance of our Catholic schools and colleges if we were
to produce the intelligent, mature Catholic with "adult dynamic
knowledge and love of his Creator."

What I find significant in this introduction to the new program is
the use of the term "theology" instead of "religion" and the way in
which Archbishop Cushing saw the study of theology as analogous
to the other courses in the curriculum. The authors of the report, of

---

[2]Roy J. Deferrari (ed.), *Theology, Philosophy, and History as Integrating Disciplines
in the Catholic College of Liberal Arts,* The Catholic University of America Press,
Washington, D.C., 1953.
    [3]*Ibid.,* pp. 3–4.

whom the major one was Professor Roy J. Deferrari, evidently thought that Cushing's reflections were appropriate for what they were trying to do with their "Integration" of the liberal arts curriculum by philosophy, history, and theology. To play that role, theology taught to undergraduates had to have academic strength; from the 1950s on, that seems to have been the goal.

In the colleges where the Catholic University program took root, the integration of the course of liberal arts studies was achieved in a very structured way. The first two years were given to survey courses in all the various fields: English literature, a foreign language, history, classics, mathematics, sciences, philosophy. By the end of the sophomore year, the student had to choose a "field of concentration"—the use of the word major was avoided because it smacked of specialization. She then moved on to a selection of courses within that field. Requirements in philosophy and theology were heavy— 15 or 18 credits in each. Junior year had a Reading Seminar so that the student might become thoroughly acquainted with the classics in her field. The capstone experience came in Senior year with the Coordinating Seminar: readings and discussion which mandated a cross fertilization of ideas from philosophy, history, and theology with the special field. A comprehensive examination prior to graduation determined whether or not the mature intelligent Catholic had been formed! On one campus a favorite student song was "The Integrated Catholic Woman"—whatever that was. Seriously, this may well have been the best intellectual experience we ever offered our students in Catholic colleges.

But I do not merely wish to take a trip down memory lane. I am not suggesting a return to a golden age. I have unearthed some of the elements of the curriculum of the 1950's only to suggest that: 1) the reason why theology began to be taken seriously in our colleges was to assist a genuine integrated learning experience; and 2) because of this function of theology, the faculty in all disciplines had to regard it with respect.

It seems to me that even though this particular curriculum device may have only been adopted in total by a very few colleges, the spirit of it was fairly widely accepted. Catalogues of individual colleges as well as programs of national meetings suggest a common vocabulary about theology and its integrating function in the liberal arts curriculum. I think this new role for theology may well have inspired those teachers of Sacred Doctrine in Catholic colleges to form their new organization—now called CTS.[4] If theology were to play this new and important role in the Catholic college, then there was need to get state accreditation for it and to improve the professional standards for those who taught in the colleges. I would say that they achieved their purposes very well. It looked as if theology and the liberal arts could make a good marriage and secure the existence of the distinctive purpose of the Catholic college, for surely nowhere else—not Wellesley, Yale, or Princeton—could do exactly the same thing. The Catholic identity now was secure; all we had to do was improve the level of theological teaching and run workshops which explained the integration process. The Catholic identity was in the curriculum itself!

What happened to all that? In a word, the 1960's. We might attribute some of the collapse of our neat system to forces within theology and the Church itself and some to forces in the wider society. Tremendous scholarly work in the 50's brought us a new vision of the Church—Congar, de Lubac, Murray and Weigel—the precursors of Vatican II. The Council itself stressed freedom, cultural pluralism, liturgical reforms, intellectual exploration. By the late sixties, the meaning of "Catholic" in reference to a college campus was already greatly changed. The Civil Rights Movement, the Vietnam war protests, and the war on poverty brought our students and faculties into far greater collaboration with those on secular campuses. Interaction on that level did much to show us the complexity of some of the assumptions we had long made and to challenge their validity. Administrators on our campuses surrendered to pressure, as did those on secular campuses, and curricula became loose and unrestrictive. Required courses were dropped in many of the liberal arts and credits were reduced in philosophy and theology. The clarity and strength of integration-concentration programs became murky at best.

As the 70's and 80's have come and gone, other factors have affected our Catholic colleges. Increasing numbers of older students, of part-time students, of those with very special career goals have changed the disposition of the receivers of our educational package. New sensitivity to other cultures and religions have made us question whether only the Roman Catholic tradition should be taught in our theology programs. The lack of structure in curriculum has led

---

[4]Rose Mary Rodgers, OP, *A History of the College Theology Society,* St. Joseph's University Press, distributed by CTS c/o Horizons, Villanova University, PA, 1983.

to a certain competitiveness among faculty. Increasing pressures on faculty for publication have reduced interest in developing cross-disciplinary courses. Can we see on our campuses today any evidence that the theology faculty play a significant role in the decisions made about curriculum? Is there an attempt to think through the specific contribution of theology as a discipline to the total education?

Sometimes it takes an attack on our assumptions to rouse us from the comfortable acceptance of the status quo. When the draft Schema on Catholic universities reached our shores in the summer of 1985 for consultation with our college presidents, we were shocked, then angry, that the "Catholicity" of our institutions was being questioned.[5] In reviewing the responses and preparing the synthesis of them for the congregation of Catholic Education, I was impressed by the determination of the presidents to assert the Catholic identity of their colleges. It was clear that in their view the "Catholic" character did not arise from some juridical tie to the local Bishop (as suggested by the Schema) but from the way in which the fundamental educational task of the college was carried out. While referring to the services rendered by campus ministry, by counselling staff, by chaplains, and residence hall personnel, they clearly saw the basic Catholic character in the very fabric of the curriculum. They spoke of their strong and vibrant theology departments. They recognized that the key to a Catholic college is a faculty committed to its mission. I think that some of the presidents had an underlying confidence that what had gone on in their own education—strong liberal arts as pre-professional training and Roman Catholic theology courses—was still the mark of their institutions. Others are committed to strengthen and revitalize these indicators of Catholic identity. But as you and I know, presidents (like everyone else) labor under pressures and restraints. Are there ways that we can help our presidents achieve their goal?

If you agree with me that the theological education we give in our Catholic colleges and universities should have a fundamental relationship with the arts and sciences, and that this relationship is an

---

[5]Congregation for Catholic Education, Proposed Schema (Draft) for a Pontifical Document on Catholic Universities, 15th April 1985; ACCU, Synthesis of Responses Received from U.S. Catholic College & University Presidents to the Pontifical Document on Catholic Universities, February 11, 1986; ACCU Board of Directors, Response of ACCU Board of Directors on "Proposed Schema for a Pontifical Document on Catholic Universities," approved by the Board February 4, 1986.

important characteristic of a Catholic institution, let me suggest a few reflections on the present state of the art.

1. I wonder about the continued significance of the theological enterprise in our colleges when colleagues in other disciplines seem so unconcerned about the question of academic freedom for our theologians. I am not at all sure that they understand the full range of your discipline and that they appreciate the impact of serious theological reflection on their own disciplines of anthropology, political science or literature. If you were no longer on the campus, would they miss you? Not just personally, but as essential contributors to the educational process? How important is the on-going dialogue that you and your colleagues engage in? Do they understand why freedom is necessary for theologians if you are to assist all of us in understanding our tradition and in reflecting on our own experience? Is there some way that such relationships can be developed and strengthened?

2. Obviously, the rationale for the old integration-concentration program will not suffice today to undergird the linkage between theology and the liberal arts curriculum. Is there some new way we can get a handle on it? If I were a theologian and had the time to do some research, I would explore the work of Bernard Lonergan in this regard. Is there some understanding of "method" which could furnish the bridge between theology and the other disciplines? Such a project might be a good way to bring faculties together to talk about the curriculum. But someone in theology needs to do the spade work. Are the same basic skills involved in doing theology as in the arts and sciences? What are the significant differences? The exploration of the kinds of evidence used and the ways in which people go about their research in their specialties might give us some new and important insights as to the value of our unique opportunity for integrating religious experience with aesthetic, economic, and pastoral experience.

One area in which several Catholic colleges have begun to do something like this is that of peace and justice issues. Members of theology departments have joined with colleagues in political science and economics to design courses which will address some of the issues which have implicit ethical and religious dimensions. Teacher education, the arts, and many others have done the same. A book published last year, edited by David Johnson of ACCU[6] gives

---

[6]David M. Johnson, *Justice and Peace Education: Models for College and University Faculty*, Orbis Books, Maryknoll, New York, 1986.

many examples of faculty involvement in such curriculum changes. Using the bishops' pastorals on peace and the United States economy, teachers can find topics that are multi-disciplinary and that ought to be explored in a particular way on the Catholic campus.

Are there not also health issues, human development questions, aesthetic values which could be approached in this way? In our day and age, in other words, how do we link "The Love of Learning and the Desire for God?" That's a question that can't be asked formally on too many other campuses. Is it addressed on yours?

3. I said that presidents are aware that if the mission of their Catholic college or university is to be achieved it will require the presence of appropriate faculty. It is true that mission statements are articulated by Boards of Trustees (hopefully only after long consultation with faculty, students, alumnae/i, etc.), but it is also true that the day to day carrying out of the mission statement rests mainly with faculty. Is your college still committed to "educating the whole person"—or some similar phrase? Does your college still speak of its heritage as that of the Roman Catholic tradition? What do these phrases mean? And who decides what they mean? When curriculum committees meet, are these the guiding principles? When new faculty are hired and others are promoted and tenured, are these items significant? If we do not have faculties interested in mediating our specific cultural values, then they will not be mediated. I think we have reached a point in our Catholic colleges where criteria for hiring, promoting, and tenuring need to be carefully rethought. In some instances, I think, we have adopted AAUP guidelines as if they were written on tablets of stone. It may be that they should be regarded as minimum rather than maximum criteria and that we ought to make some additional judgments. The same is true of other elements in our reward system; it may be that we are extolling the virtues of faculty participation in "the education of the whole person" but rewarding the narrow specialist with more frequent sabbaticals.

Finally, the real freedom we need at Catholic colleges and universities is the freedom to accomplish our mission. Franklin Roosevelt inspired our country to fight for four freedoms—two were *from* something (fear and want) and two were *of* something (speech and press). Given those, the question remains: freedom *for* what? In our colleges and universities, the trustees and administrators must be vigilant in defending institutional autonomy. Whether the attack comes from the State, the Church, or corporate donors and alumni/

ae, the trustees must guard your freedom. But you must be clear about the purpose for which you demand freedom. I hope that you want to defend your right to be intrinsic to our liberal arts colleges— not just an add-on-frill—because such a role is necessary if the education we give to our students is to be a Christian education in the Roman Catholic tradition. Obviously, we cannot do that in the mode of the 1950's, nor do we want to, but I hope we can creatively work to develop a new model of theology's relationship to the liberal arts so that we may continue to be Catholic colleges with a distinct mission. That is why our presidents are resisting strongly the proposal by some to set our theologians off in separate "institutes." That would simplify administrative links to Church authorities but would destroy the integration we have sought.

Let me close with a reflection that stems from my work as an historian. My doctoral dissertation, as some of you know, was on the topic of German Resistance to Hitler.[7] I discovered in my research that although there were cells of resistance to the Third Reich in labor unions, churches, the foreign office and the army, there were none in universities. It puzzled me that in the halls of academia no models were offered of the need to resist intrusions on individual freedoms. My further work confirmed the fact that the professors in the period before Hitler actually prepared the way for his take-over by their refusal to deal with violations of individual rights, realities, political *realists* and the need for reform of the universities themselves.[8] Each cadre of professors was a world unto itself; each researcher worked in splendid isolation. Students crowded into classrooms but never exchanged ideas with professors. There was no university forum for debate on significant issues.

If Father William Cenkner is correct in his understanding of theology when he says "Two constants exist at the very center of theological work: the interpretation of tradition, and the interpretation of contemporary experience"[9] then how can those engaged in theological education fulfill their function unless they are in close relationship with those who carry out the same kind of exploration

---

[7]Mary Alice Gallen, *German Resistance to Hitler: Ethical and Religious Factors*, Catholic University of America Press, Washington, D.C., 1955 and 1961.

[8]Alice Gallin, *Midwives to Nazism*, Mercer University Press, Macon, Georgia, 1986.

[9]William Cenkner, "Theology and the Magisterium: What does Athens Have to Say to Jerusalem?" ACCU *Current Issues in Catholic Higher Education*, Volume 7, Number 2, Winter, 1987.

in other fields? Let their analyses of both tradition and contemporary experience be shared and debated. They will thus provide a real Catholic education for our students, an education which will enable them to build a better human community for the 21st century.

Part Four
THE CHARACTER OF CATHOLIC HIGHER EDUCATION

ACADEMIC FREEDOM AND THE CATHOLIC UNIVERSITY

James Heft, S.M.

In recent years controversies among Catholics have been widely aired in the media. Several of these controversies focused directly upon the Catholic university. Controversy erupted over the New Code of Canon Law, especially Canons 807-14 which deal with colleges and universities, and over the proposed Vatican *schema* on Catholic colleges and universities. National media attention was fixed on the case of Fr. Charles Curran at the pontifically chartered Catholic University of America, and to a lesser extent on that of Professor Daniel Maguire at Marquette University. One way of approaching the cluster of complex questions raised by these events is to look carefully at the meaning of academic freedom and the nature of a Catholic university. I intend to do this in three steps: first, a brief review of the history of the development of the idea of academic freedom; second, a description of the growth of Catholic colleges and universities in this country; and third, some suggestions to clarify the purpose of the Catholic university and academic freedom.

I. The Development of the Idea of Academic Freedom

Historians[1] of the idea of academic freedom typically trace its origins all the way back to the Greeks who sought to understand reality apart from the religious beliefs of their society. The example of Socrates, who though charged with corrupting the youth of

---

[1]Valuable studies include Richard Hofstadter and Walter Metzher's *The Development of Academic Freedom in the United States* (Columbia University Press, 1955), Robert MacIver, *Academic Freedom in Our Time* (Columbia University Press, 1955), Louis Loughlin, ed., *Academic Freedom and Tenure* (University of Wisconsin Press, 1967), and George Shuster, "Academic Freedom," in the *New Catholic Encyclopedia: Supplement,* Vol. 1, pp. 65–68.

Athens defended his calling as a teacher, has emboldened scholars throughout the centuries to remain true to their calling in the most adverse of circumstances. The rise of the great medieval universities in the 12th and 13th centuries provided an institutional context for teachers and students that often required protection from princes, prelates, and the local population. In fact, in 1215 and then again in 1231, popes intervened at the University of Paris precisely to prevent the local bishop from meddling in the affairs of the students and the faculty.[2] Medieval theological faculties exercised considerable influence and were called upon regularly by the hierarchy to help in the resolution of theological disputes.[3] More often than not however, the hierarchy intervened in the affairs of the university. That intervention, on the whole, was accepted more readily by the academy than would be the case today:

> The modern academic community in a democratic state, although often unable fully to realize it, assumes the right of free inquiry. The medieval academic community, although frequently and intentionally breaching it, assumed the right of some authority to exercise censorship and proscription in theology and on such conclusions of philosophy as were deemed to encroach upon theology.[4]

Even if the medieval university community acknowledged the right of episcopal authority in matters of theology, it did not readily welcome every exercise of that authority. In 1277, for example, Godfrey of Fontaines, secular master of theology at Paris and later elected in 1300 to the bishopric of Tournai, refused to acknowledge the validity of Tempier's condemnations of 100 propositions, some of which were defended by Thomas Aquinas. Since the matter, explained Godfrey, concerned the whole community of faith, a council or the pope, and not the local bishop, should condemn a doctrine as heretical. Moreover, people should not be bound to one

---

[2]John T. Ellis, "A Tradition of Autonomy?" in *The Catholic University: A Modern Appraisal*, ed. by N. G. McCluskey, (University of Notre Dame Press, 1970), pp. 266–267.

[3]Avery Dulles, *The Survival of Dogma* (Doubleday, 1971), p. 104. Dulles explains further that "the decrees of the Council of Vienne (1311–1312), by order of Clement V, were not made official until they had been submitted to the universities." In 1332, Pope John XXII pleaded with the theologians at the University of Paris not to close off the discussion on the Beatific Vision which he himself had opened for reasons of debate and clarification. See my *John XXII and Papal Teaching Authority* (Edwin Mellen Press, 1986), p. 98.

[4]Hofstadter, *The Development of Academic Freedom*, pp. 16–17.

opinion on which a legitimate diversity of opinions may be had. Finally, not only would a conflict among the learned stimulate discussion, said Godfrey, but it would be more likely that through such discussion the truth would be discovered.[5]

After the Reformation, when individual nations had been formed in Europe, much of the corporate autonomy enjoyed by the medieval universities disappeared. The confessional state brought some peace to the confessionally divided Europe. The same arrangement was used to govern the intellectual life: *cujus regio, ejus universitas*. The faith to be taught in the university was determined by the king or the prince, and whatever freedom was to be had was obtained by choosing the location for teaching and studying. The universities had become confessional institutions.[6]

A confessional character also marked all of the earliest educational foundations in America. Harvard, founded in 1636 by the Puritans, took the mottoes *Christo et Ecclesiae* and *In Christi Gloriam*. William and Mary was founded by the Anglicans in 1693. In the next ninety years, Yale, Princeton, Washington and Lee, Columbia, Brown, Rutgers, and Dartmouth were all organized under religious auspices. The primary purpose of these colleges was to train clergy. All of these educational institutions were Protestant. The medieval universities had been governed internally by guild systems of self-government and were protected externally by the church from the harassment and interventions of kings, princes, and local populations. In the New World, the colleges were governed neither internally by the faculty, nor were they externally protected by the church. Rather, lay boards governed the colleges and held the power to hire, fire, and set policy.

Already in the 18th century, less theology and more science was taught to the students; the curricula gradually became more secularized. "By opening up new fields of college study, both scientific and practical, by rarefying the devotional atmosphere of the colleges, and by introducing a note of skepticism and inquiry, the trend toward secular learning inevitably did much to liberate college

---

[5]*Op. cit.*, pp. 31–32. Godfrey told Tempier's successor, Simon de Bucy, that though he knew canon and civil law, he did not know enough theology to make those condemnations, and therefore should consult those competent in the subject. Godfrey warned about the scandal caused by ignorant prelates: "What a scandal in the eyes of both many believers and unbelievers that prelates should be so ignorant and naive as to hold as erroneous and contrary to faith that which is irreconcilable neither with faith nor with good morals."

[6]*Op. cit.*, p. 71.

work."[7] Despite the gradual "secularization" of the colleges, there was still little of what today we would call academic freedom—at least not until the middle of the 19th century.

One of the main reasons for the late development of the idea of academic freedom was the absence of any professionally developed professorate. As Hofstadter explains, "so long as the bulk of college teaching was only a by-path to more desired careers, faculty self-government was bound to seem less acceptable, indeed less meaningful, than it did in European universities numbering among their masters great and influential men of learning."[8] The modern idea of academic freedom was developed by individuals who drew freely upon several ideas that were influential in the 19th century:

> From modern science they have taken the notion of a continuing search for new truths, fostered by freedom of inquiry, verified by objective processes, and judged by those who are competent. From commerce they have taken the concept of a free competition among ideas—hence the suggestive metaphor of a free market in thought. From the politics of the liberal state they have taken the ideas of free speech and a free press and an appreciation of the multitude of perspectives in a pluralistic society. From religious liberalism and from the long historical development which led to the taming of sectarian animus have come the ideas of toleration and religious liberty by which they have benefited.[9]

To bring this brief history of the development of the idea of academic freedom to a close, I shall consider only three more factors: the German influence, the impact of Darwinism and the foundation of the American Association of University Professors (AAUP). Walter Metzger, who wrote the second half of *The Development of the Idea of Academic Freedom*, places strong emphasis on the impact that science in general and Darwinism in particular had on the idea of academic freedom.[10] Metzger holds that Darwinism provided a "new rationale" for academic freedom by fostering a new idea of truth:

---

[7]*Ibid.*, pp. 185–86.

[8]*Ibid.*, p. 124.

[9]Hofstadter, *Ibid.*, p. 61. Robert MacIver describes the origin of the modern idea of academic freedom as part of a movement that included "the ending of theocratic overlordship, the establishment of the territorial state . . . the crumbling of the oligarchical class system, the growth of the consciousness of nationality, the accelerating advancement of science . . . and the whole proces of socioeconomic change that is summed up in the expression 'Industrial Revolution.' "

[10]Metzger, *Ibid.*, pp. 320–66.

namely, nothing is to be thought true or false until verified through a continual process of inquiry.[11] That process of inquiry had to be disciplined, and therefore had to be performed by "experts," a process which supported the idea that the professional standing or competence of a professor could best be judged only by other experts or professional peers. The emphasis on scientific competence was used to thwart "clerical presumptuousness" and contain "trustee presumption."[12]

Finally, Darwinism and the rise of science gave support to certain values such as tolerance, verification, and cooperation. In particular, it was assumed that real scientists could transcend dogmatism and ideology, and in their disinterestedness in everything but verifiable truth, embody the neutrality which ultimately could "signify the brotherhood of man in science that is akin in inspiration to the brotherhood of man in God."[13]

Another reality that has had an impact on the idea of academic freedom was the influence exerted in the mid-19th century by the German universities. Before 1850 only about 200 Americans had gone to Germany for their doctoral studies; during the 1880s, however, nearly 2,000 Americans were studying in Germany. There, the universities had freed themselves from confessional restrictions.[14] The Americans were impressed with two things—the German idea of *Wissenschaft*, or "knowledge," and the two related ideas of *Lernfreiheit* and *Lehrfreiheit*. *Wissenschaft* assumed that the role of professors was not to pass on truths from the past, but to search scientifically after new verifiable truths. Their only professional

---

[11]*Ibid.*, p. 364.

[12]*Ibid.*, p. 365. "In the attack upon clerical control, no argument figured more prominently than the contention that the clergy were incompetent in science" (p. 351).

[13]*Ibid.*, p. 366. Of course, one of the consequences of this way of thinking was to relegate those disciplines which deal with subject matter not empirically verifiable, such as theology and philosophy, to the realm of mere opinion. James T. Burtchaell sees this attitude as the "single most powerful bias against religious studies in all colleges: state, private, and Church-affiliated." "Hot Gospel in a Cool College? The Questions of Advocacy," in *Religion in the Undergraduate Curriculum*, ed. Claude Welch (Washington, D.C.: Association of American Colleges, 1972), p. 23.

[14]Germany and several other European countries did, however, maintain theological faculties along confessional boundaries. These faculties were separated from the rest of the state-owned university and, for the most part, played no role in the education of anyone but graduate students of theology. Since such faculties represent specific confessions, the respective Churches (Lutheran and Roman Catholic in Germany) usually play a direct role in the selection and dismissal of faculty, even though the state frequently pays the salaries of the professors.

obligation to their students was to train them to enable them to engage in the same sort of research.[15] Unfettered scientific research, for the Germans, constituted Lehrfreiheit, and in effect, for them, "defined the true university."[16] This highly vaunted freedom, however, was enjoyed only within the German university; outside of it, German professors were to remain politically non-partisan or lose their academic positions. Finally, unlike the German professors of philosophy who tried to win over their students to their own personal philosophical views, Americans professors tried in the classroom to maintain a stance of neutrality on controversial issues, and remained silent on issues not in their area of competence. Lernfreiheit, or freedom to learn, meant that

> German students were free to roam from place to place, sampling academic wares; that wherever they lighted, they were free to determine the choice and sequence of courses, and were responsible to no one for regular attendance; that they were exempted from all tests save the final examination, that they lived in private quarters and controlled their private lives.[17]

Given the fact that in the latter part of the 19th century almost all colleges and universities in the United States, with the notable exception of Johns Hopkins University, were centers for undergraduate education, the idea of Lernfreiheit was never adopted. Moreover, the constitutional provision for free speech permitted Americans professors to express publicly, not however without some conflicts, their political views.

Between 1890 and 1914 there were in the United States a number of well-publicized cases in which professors, a good portion of whom had studied in Germany, were dismissed or resigned from universities on account of their views on evolution, pacifism, and economics. All of this led eventually to the formation in 1915 of the AAUP. Their first declaration was entitled "Report on Academic

---

[15]Philip Gleason quotes G. Stanley Hall, an American psychologist trained in Germany, as saying that "research is nothing less than a religion," and that the researcher is "the knight of the Holy Spirit of truth", and compared the "great corporate body of science" to a "church militant yet indivisible." Gleason points out how Wissenschaft, as it was developed in Germany, was hostile to traditional religious institutions. "Academic Freedom and the Crises in Catholic Universities," in Academic Freedom and the Catholic University, ed. by Edward Manier and John Houck (Notre Dame: Fides Publishers, 1967), pp. 48–49.

[16]Metzher, op. cit., p. 393.

[17]Ibid., p. 386.

Freedom." Eight of the original 13 signers had studied in Germany, and seven were social scientists.[18] Their report defined academic freedom so that it included three ideas:

> The term "academic freedom" has traditionally had two applications— to the freedom of the teacher and to that of the student, *Lehrfreiheit* and *Lernfreiheit*. It need scarcely be pointed out that the freedom which is the subject of this report is that of the teacher. Academic freedom in this sense comprises three elements: freedom of inquiry and research; freedom of teaching within the university or college; and freedom of extra-mural utterance and action.[19]

It should be remembered that this statement follows strictly the thinking of the professorate only. In its early years, college presidents and deans were denied membership in the AAUP. Moreover, the statement did not deal at all with the rights of students. The founders' understanding of freedom for research and for teaching was heavily influenced by the German university model. Freedom for extra-mural utterance and action reflects more a unique American perspective, grounded in a spirit of progressivism that wanted the university to develop experts to work at complex problems in modern society.

Concerning the denominational college, the 1915 report acknowledges the right of the board of such an institution to govern according to its religious purpose. It explains that such institutions

> do not, at least as regards one particular subject, accept the principles of freedom of inquiry, of opinion, and of teaching; and their purpose is not to advance knowledge by the unrestricted research and unfettered discussion of impartial investigations, but rather to subsidize the promotion of the opinions held by persons usually not of a scholar's calling, who provide the funds for their maintenance. Concerning the desirability of the existence of such institutions, the committee does not desire to express any opinion. But it is manifestly important that they should not be permitted to sail under false colors. Genuine boldness and thoroughness of inquiry, and freedom of speech, are scarcely reconcilable with the prescribed inculcating of a particular opinion upon a controverted question.[20]

---

[18]*Ibid.*, p. 396, 407.

[19]Cited by James John Annarelli, *Academic Freedom and the American Roman Catholic University* (Unpublished Ph.D. dissertation submitted to Drew University, 1984), p. 174.

[20]*Op. cit.*, p. 183.

Therefore, while recognizing the right of boards of directors to run such institutions, the AAUP did not recognize such institutions as true colleges and universities in the American sense of the term since true academic freedom was judged to be not possible in them. A similar statement about denominational colleges and universities was made by the AAUP in their "1940 Statement on Principles of Academic Freedom and Tenure": "Limitations of academic freedom because of religious or other aims of the institution should be clearly stated in writing at the time of the appointment."[21] Just how to interpret this clause has presented continual difficulties.[22] But in 1970 the AAUP endorsed the following comment on their 1940 Statement: "Most Church-related institutions no longer need or desire the departure from the principle of academic freedom implied in the 1940 Statement, and we do not now endorse such a departure."[23] In 1982, however, the AAUP stated in its *Recommended Institutional Regulations on Academic Freedom and Tenure* that a "college or university is a marketplace of ideas, and it cannot fulfill its purpose of transmitting, evaluating, and extending knowledge if it requires conformity with any orthodoxy of content and method."[24]

To understand part of the reason why, in 1970, the AAUP seems to admit church-related institutions of learning into the ranks of true universities, that is, institutions which support "true" academic freedom, we turn now to a consideration of the recent developments in Catholic higher education and academic freedom.

---

[21] *AAUP Policy Documents and Reports* (1984 Edition), p. 3.

[22] One way of interpreting it is according to the confessional commitment of the particular institution. Thus, while generally affirming the principles of academic freedom as proposed by the AAUP, the American Association of Theological Schools explained in 1960 that "so long as the teacher remains within the accepted constitutional and confessional basis of his school he should be free to teach, carry on research and to publish. . . ." It is further stated that "A concept of freedom appropriate to the theological schools will respect this confessional loyalty, both in institutions and their individual members." See "Academic Freedom and Tenure in the Theological School," in *A.A.T.S. Bulletin* 24 (1960), p. 35, cited by James John Annarelli, *Academic Freedom and the American Roman Catholic University*, p. 186, n. 43.

[23] *AAUP Policy Documents and Reports* (1984 Edition), p. 5.

[24] *AAUP Policy Documents and Reports* (1984 Edition), p. 21. It may be asked whether the image, "marketplace of ideas," given its economic coloring, serves well when what is really being attempted is not the bartering of goods, but the development of traditions. These and similar statements of the AAUP need a more careful analysis and interpretation than can be given them here.

II. Catholic Higher Education and Academic Freedom

In the late 1960s two major changes took place in Catholic higher education in the United States: first, several major Catholic universities endorsed the concept of academic freedom as developed by the AAUP; and second, several of the same institutions owned and run by religious orders turned over their ownership and control to lay-dominated boards. Both of these changes were rapid in coming and, in the judgment of Philip Gleason, were made when Catholic higher education was "entering its identity crisis in a state of virtual amnesia, with no meaningful grip on the history that has played so crucial a role in forging its present identity."[25] Having surveyed the history of the development of Catholic higher education, Gleason concludes his essay with the disturbing question: "In what sense is a university Catholic if it is composed predominantly of lay professionals who employ, in their teaching and research, the same methods and norms as their counterparts in secular universities, and who are engaged in the pursuit of knowledge in autonomous spheres that are in no way dependent upon any over-all 'Catholic position'? What, in short, is the reason for being of the *Catholic* college or university."[26]

Besides these two easily identifiable changes, there were also the pervasive cultural shifts, perhaps even "revolutions," that expressed themselves through the civil rights movement, opposition to the Vietnam War, a heightened emphasis on individual freedom, the use of drugs, and the huge gatherings at rock concerts such as Woodstock in New York in 1970. The polarization on the campuses was often not between the faculty and the students, but between the board of trustees and the administration on the one hand, and many of the faculty religious and students on the other. These indeed were difficult and turbulent years when fixed academic requirements in place for decades collapsed along with the uniform offerings in Catholic universities of Thomism in philosophy departments and Thomistically-inspired systematic theology in theology departments.

Before delineating the main lines of the intense and well-publi-

---

[25]Philip Gleason, "American Catholic Higher Education: A Historical Perspective," in *The Shape of Catholic Higher Education* (University of Chicago Press, 1967), ed. Robert Hassenger, p. 53.
[26]*Ibid.*, p. 52.

cized debate in circles of Catholic higher education from 1967 to the present, it is important first to understand the history of the rise of Catholic colleges and universities in the United States. If the history of the idea of academic freedom, as we have already seen, can be extended back to the times of the Greeks, the history of Catholic higher education, at least as we understand colleges and universities today, is less than 100 years old.

First of all, consider the very rapid growth of Catholic colleges in the 20th century. In 1916, for example, there were 32,000 students enrolled in 84 colleges for men (and more than half of these men were high school students). By 1940, 160,000 men and women were enrolled, a fivefold increase in 25 years. By 1966, the number had increased to about 400,000 students.[27] It was not until 1920 that all prep departments were clearly separated from the colleges, which enabled the colleges, for the first time, to concentrate on a four year program that would correspond to the American pattern.

Another indicator of the rapid maturation only in this century of Catholic colleges and universities is the number of Ph.D. degrees that they have awarded. Writing in 1967, Gleason states that:

> Graduate education—and true graduate education is measured by the production of Ph.D.'s—is a relatively new phenomenon in American higher education; it dates back only to the closing decades of the 19th century. But in Catholic schools, regardless of whether they called themselves universities or not, it is hardly older than yesterday.[28]

With a few notable exceptions, an emphasis on graduate education and the development of Ph.D. programs is mainly a post-World War II phenomenon. Until the 1940s and 1950s, most Catholic colleges and universities emphasized the formation of character as much as, and in some cases more than, intellectual excellence. At Notre Dame, in 1928, the religious emphasis was strongly expressed in their *Religious Bulletin*: "It is the hope of this school that if it can cloister a boy for four years from the ways of the world and can give him a demonstration of the workability of its principles, it can send him out ready to pay tribute to Caesar without losing his soul."[29]

---

[27]Gleason, "Academic Freedom and the Crisis in Catholic Universities," pp. 39–40, and in "American Catholic Higher Education," pp. 18–19.

[28]Gleason, "Academic Freedom and the Crisis in Catholic Universities," p. 41.

[29]J. T. Ellis, "A Tradition of Autonomy?" in *The Catholic University: A Modern Appraisal* ed. Neil G. McCluskey, S.J. (University of Notre Dame Press, 1970), p. 217.

Many institutions stressed both moral and intellectual development. Even though the 1917 Georgetown University catalogue stated that religious instruction was considered "of the first importance in education," and that "the discipline in force at Georgetown is paternal,"[30] many Catholic colleges and universities strove to provide excellence in undergraduate education, especially the sciences or some of the humanities, such as English and languages.

Until around 1940, however, only philosophy was taught for credit on the undergraduate level. Theology was taught mainly in seminaries to men who had gotten their B.A.'s in philosophy. Religion departments on the college level existed mainly for purposes of catechesis and apologetics, and religion began to be taught for credit on the undergraduate level only in the 1940s.[31] In the 1950s and 1960s many religion departments changed their names to "Department of Theology," only to change them once again in the 1970s to "Department of Religious Studies," ostensibly in an effort to emphasize their non-sectarian character and academic rigor.

Almost all Catholic colleges and universities were founded and run by religious orders.[32] These self-perpetuating bodies seemed to be the most capable groups in maintaining and developing educational institutions. Sometimes this resulted in a lack of cooperation between colleges and a needless duplication of efforts. Given the fact that throughout Christian history the precise relationship between religious orders and the hierarchy has been unclear, the relationship between the colleges run by orders and the hierarchy in the United States has been, in the words of David O'Brien, intimate but undefined: "Juridically, some colleges, sponsored by dioceses or religious congregations established under diocesan auspices, resembled parochial and diocesan elementary and secondary schools, but those under the control of religious orders enjoyed a certain autonomy."[33]

---

[30]*Ibid.*, p. 217.

[31]See David O'Brien, "The Church and Catholic Higher Education," unpublished paper read at the DePaul University Conference on "American Catholic Higher Education and Academic Freedom" held April 30–May 1, 1987.

[32]Gleason, "American Catholic Higher Education," pp. 31–32. He explains further: "By 1866 . . . there were 60 Catholic colleges, all men's schools; three were operated by laymen, ten by diocesan priests, and 47 by religious communities. Fifty years later there were no lay-operated men's colleges among the 84 surveyed by the Catholic Educational Association, only six were in the hands of diocesan priests, and all the rest—roughly 93% of the total—were run by religious orders."

[33]O'Brien, *Art. cit.*, p. 15.

There seemed, however, to be few conflicts between the religious orders and the hierarchy and those few were usually resolved through the vow of obedience. A survey done in 1942 indicated that in 65% of all Catholic colleges and universities there were no provisions for tenure; religious could be transferred at a moment's notice or could be ordered to stay at the college for life. The vow of obedience made a system of tenure unnecessary and potentially troublesome. Given, however, the rapid growth in enrollment after World War II, the number of lay faculty increased dramatically. Once several religious orders transferred ownership and control of their colleges and universities to lay-dominated boards, the precise relationship of those institutions to the Church became even more complicated and a point of controversy.

In July of 1967, 26 college presidents, teachers, and bishops gathered at Land O'Lakes, Wisconsin to prepare a statement on the nature and role of a Catholic university as a preparation for the meeting of the International Federation of Catholic Universities (IFCU) scheduled for 1968. Their statement emphasized in terms stronger than any made before the necessity of institutional autonomy and academic freedom for the Catholic university.

> The Catholic university today must be a university in the full modern sense of the word, with a strong commitment to and concern for academic excellence. To perform its teaching and research functions effectively the Catholic university must have a true autonomy and academic freedom in the face of authority of whatever kind, lay or clerical, external to the academic community itself.[34]

The best-known champion of this conception of a Catholic university is Fr. Theodore Hesburgh, who for the last twenty years has stressed the importance of academic excellence in Catholic higher education. Since 1967, however, a number of conferences and symposia have been convened by the International Federation of Catholic Universities and by the Vatican Congregation for Catholic Education.[35] More recently, in 1979, the Vatican Congregation for Catholic

---

[34]In The Catholic University: A Modern Appraisal, p. 336. For a lengthier treatment of the history of the development in Catholic higher education in the U.S. to the present, see Ann Ida Gannon, B.V.M., "Some Aspects of Catholic Higher Education Since Vatican II," in Current Issues in Catholic Higher Education, vol. 8 (Summer 1987), pp. 10–24.

[35]For example, in 1968, the IFCU met at the Catholic University of Kinshasa (since taken over by the government) in the Congo; a special symposium convened by Cardinal Garrone that met in Rome in 1969; and another that met in Rome in 1972 to produce a document entitled "The Catholic University in the Modern World."

Education (formerly, until 1968, the Sacred Congregation for Seminaries and Universities) released the Apostolic Constitution *Sapien-
tia Christiana*, which addressed directly the meaning of academic
freedom in universities and faculties that are canonically erected,
and required that in them all "who teach disciplines concerning
faith and morals must receive . . . a canonical mission from the
chancellor or his delegate." Moreover, faculty, whose competency is
not to be judged only by peers, are to be marked by an uprightness
of life. The revised *Code of Canon Law*, published in 1983, no longer
spoke of a "canonical mission," but spoke more broadly of a "mandate" (Canon 812) to teach in the name of the church. This mandate
represents an official commission to teach granted by the competent
ecclesiastical authority, who could be the conference of bishops, the
local bishop, or his delegate. It should be obvious that the spirit and
content of the 1967 Land O'Lakes statement, which stressed academic freedom and juridical autonomy, is apparently at odds with
several recent Vatican statements and the new *Code of Canon Law*.

In the United States, the debate may be described, in admittedly
somewhat simplified but not completely inaccurate terms, as one
that, unfortunately and artificially, pits those who want academi-
cally first-rate institutions over against those who want educational
institutions faithful to the church. For example, in 1973, St. John's
University in New York organized a symposium to discuss the 1972
IFCU document and to make clear their fidelity to Rome. The goals
of secular higher education are consistently depicted by the speakers
as hostile to Catholic universities. For example, Jeremiah Newman,
the rector of St. Patrick's College in Maynouth, Ireland, identifies the
description of a Catholic university contained in the Land O'Lakes
statement with that of the "American liberal universities" that seek
to remain value neutral and, in the process, are rendered incapable
of standing for any values. George A. Kelly, the editor of the volume
that contains the proceedings of the symposium, criticizes what he
exaggeratedly describes as the "absolutely unrestricted conditions"
of existence claimed for the Catholic university by the Land O'Lakes
statement, and counters it with a statement drawn from the 1972
IFCU document "The Catholic University in the Modern World":
"When we affirm the autonomy of the university we do not mean
that it stands outside the law."[36] Thomas Greenburg criticizes the

---

[36]George A. Kelly, ed., *Why Should a Catholic University Survive?* (St. John's
University Press, 1973), pp. xiv–xv. In the end, the 1972 IFCU document "recognized

Land O'Lakes ideal for uncritically appropriating the model of the
19th century German graduate school,[37] which Germain Grisez,
another participant in the symposium, describes as the product of
the German Enlightenment, which in effect banished faith from the
/ intellectual life.[38]

   A division of opinion is also to be found in the interpretations of
the 1972 IFCU document. In January of 1973, Fr. Robert Henle, the
president of Georgetown University, described the 1972 document
as one "that endorses the principles of academic freedom and
autonomy for Catholic colleges and universities," while Fr. Joseph
Cahill, the president of St. John's University, described it as a
reaffirmation of the "necessity of a Catholic university's fidelity to
the Christian message as it comes to us through the Church."[39]

   In 1985, the Congregation for Catholic Education drew up a
Schema on the nature and purpose of the Catholic university and
sent it out to all Catholic college and university presidents for
comment.[40] Most of the presidents who are members of the Association of Catholic Colleges and Universities (ACCU) sent their responses to the national office in Washington where they were synthesized
and forwarded to Rome.[41] The response of the majority of the college
presidents was negative, especially when it came to the Schema's
desire for juridical links between the university and the church that
would permit the local bishop, if he judged it to be necessary, to
intervene in the life of the university or college directly, to ensure
that orthodoxy is maintained. The exasperation of these college
presidents is well stated by Theodore Hesburgh:

---

that some universities, while not under canonical jurisdiction, were nonetheless
authentic or 'real' Catholic institutions." See Joseph A. O'Hare, S.J., "The American
Catholic University: Pluralism and Identity," in Current Issues in Catholic Higher
Education, Vol. 8 (Winter 1988), p. 32. O'Hare adds: "This notion is missing from the
present working document (the 1985 vatican Schema), and this represents not an
advance but a retreat."

   [37]Thomas Greenburg, "The Problem of Identity in Catholic Higher Education: The
Statement of the Question," op. cit., p. 21.

   [38]Germain Grisez, "American Catholic Higher Education: The Experience Evaluated," ibid., p. 49. This same line of argument has been picked up by the Fellowship
of Catholic Scholars who stated in 1980 that "it is an undeniable fact, however, that
Catholic universities recently have understressed the importance of witnessing the
Catholic faith, choosing instead to adopt a university model designed mostly by
unbelievers" (The Priest, October, 1980, p. 13).

   [39]Quoted by J. Newman in Why Should A Catholic University Survive? p. 63.

   [40]"Proposed Schema for a Pontifical Document on Catholic Universities," Origins
15 (1986), pp. 706–711.

   [41]"Catholic College and University Presidents Respond to Proposed Vatican
Schema," Origins 15 (1986), pp. 697–704.

What Europeans find hard to believe, because it is contrary to all their experience, is that most of our Catholic colleges were not founded by the hierarchy, but by religious orders of men and women; that we are not funded by the church or state, but privately by tuition, gifts and grants; that religious and bishops do not govern most of our Catholic colleges and universities, but lay boards do, and that these lay boards will observe the university requirements whatever is said by others. The terrible basic dilemma is that the best Catholic universities are being asked to choose between being real universities and being really Catholic when, in fact, they are already both.[42]

The compiled response of the ACCU has been criticized by some who again see in it a refusal to be truly Catholic. Leonard A. Kelly, the Dean of Philosophy at the University of St. Thomas in Houston, Texas wrote: "To put the matter mildly, the Association is not pleased with the proposed *Schema*. To put it more strongly (but not unfairly), its response is a clear 'I will not serve.' The Association wants no episcopal authority over its institutions."[43] Also unfair and sweeping is the comment of William Ball, a lawyer who had argued First Amendment cases before the Supreme Court: "It is bootless to say that without government aid many such colleges would have gone under; *with* government aid they *did* go under as to the only thing that justified their special existence: the informing of minds and lives with the riches of the ancient faith."[44] In a more nuanced

---

[42]Theodore Hesburgh, "The Vatican and American Catholic Higher Education," *America*, November 1, 1986, pp. 250 and 263. In an unpublished paper, Alice Gallin, O.S.U., the executive director of the ACCU who prepared the response to the *Schema*, explains the intent of the Vatican in this way: "In this *Schema*, another freedom is being asserted: the freedom of the Church to have universities, and to have Catholic theologians teaching in them who teach in the name of the Church. In the light of the nationalization of Catholic universities in Africa and the continued harassment of Catholic universities in many countries around the world, such a defensive posture is understandable. But, in the United States, our situation is quite different." "Academic Freedom and the Catholic College/University," in *Current Issues in Catholic Higher Education* (published by the Association of Catholic Colleges and Universities), Vol. 8 (Summer 1987), pp. 32–33.

[43]Leonard A. Kennedy, "Academic Freedom and the Vatican," in *Catholicism in Crisis*, November, 1986, p. 23.

[44]William Ball, "A Symposium: Curran, Dissent and Rome," in *Catholicism in Crisis*, May 1986, p. 8. In the Summer 1986 issue of the *Educational Record*, Alice Gallin is quoted as saying that "if Rome takes away our academic independence, and insists that bishops determine who can teach theology, then our right to federal funds (500 million in state and federal money each year, including tuition aid for approximately 60% of the students in Catholic schools) might soon be challenged in the courts. Without this aid, most Catholic institutions simply would be forced out of business," in Jerome Cramer's "Academic Freedom and the Catholic Church" (p. 37).

and penetrating criticism, Mark Jordan, of the Program of Liberal Studies at Notre Dame, wrote that "the ACCU might well have been more candid about the many good reasons for worry on Rome's part."[45]

In early March of 1988, the Vatican Congregation for Catholic Education released a summary of the responses it received to its *Schema*. The introduction states that both the "depth and quality" of the responses exceeded expectations. The combined evaluation of the ACCU was fairly summarized. A unique characteristic of the U.S. episcopal response emerged: in contrast to the single response of the episcopal conference, which for the most part supported the response of the ACCU, seven individual bishops wrote "in strong support of the proposed norms." The lay people consulted believed the institutions to be "excellent as universities" and "truly Catholic," offering to the students both an intellectual foundation and a pastoral formation.

Concerning academic freedom, most U.S. responses stressed, according to the Vatican summary, that the 1985 *Schema* was too one-sided and stressed "authority and fidelity at the expense of legitimate freedom." Concerning theologians, the summary indicates that "while they must respect the prerogatives of the hierarchy, theologians in a university setting require trust and support from the broader church if their efforts are to bear fruit." A few Catholic institutions, however, took exception to this stress on institutional autonomy and academic freedom, fearing more the loss of the Catholic identity of the institution and the endangering of ortho-

---

For a different opinion of the impact that sacrificing institutional autonomy would have on government aid, see Kenneth Whitehead, the Deputy Assistant Secretary for Higher Education Programs at the U.S. Department of Education, "Religiously Affiliated Colleges and American Freedom," *America,* February 7, 1987.

[45]Mark Jordan, "On Defending Catholic Higher Education in America," *Communio* 13 (1986), p. 259. The joint response to the Vatican *Schema* drawn up by the Fellowship of Catholic Scholars states that "dissenting scholars insist on freedom of research, but the issue really is the indoctrination of undergraduate students against received Catholic positions without the Church's position ever being presented in its integrity. Required courses, required first so that Catholic students would come to know and be convinced of their faith, are often taught by professors who no longer believe the Catholic faith as the Church receives and teaches it" (*Fellowship of Catholic Scholars Newsletter* Vol. 9, #1, December 1985, p. 7). When this occurs, there is indeed a serious problem. See my article, "The Response Catholics Owe to Non-Infallible Teachings," in *Current Issues in Catholic Higher Education,* Vol. 8, #1 (Summer 1987) pp. 54–62, soon to appear in *Raising the Torch of Good News: Catholic Authority and Dialogue With the World,* Bernard Prusack, ed. (University Press of America, 1987).

doxy: "These institutions, along with two of the professional associations and some of the U.S. bishops, approve the substance of the
Schema in its present form and insist that it is needed in order to
preserve Catholic values and teach Catholic doctrine in the Catholic
university." In a final section entitled "Questions Arising from the
Responses," it is asked: "In theological teaching and research by a
member of the Catholic faith . . . how is academic freedom to be
reconciled with fidelity to the magisterium?"[46]

This summary was produced by the Vatican to prepare the way for
the next step in the process: an international meeting of representatives of Catholic universities and other institutions of higher education scheduled for April of 1989 in Rome. The summary makes quite
clear the enormous complexity of the question of the nature of a
Catholic university and the meaning of academic freedom. A certain
polarization continues to exist to the point where, at least for some,
it would appear that there is some truth to the famous dictum of
George Bernard Shaw: a "Catholic university" is a contradiction in
terms.[47] Must Catholic educational leaders in the United States
choose between running real universities or faithful ones?

III. Toward a Catholic University: Some Suggestions

I chose to describe my comments as suggestions and not as
solutions. It should be evident from what I have already written that
the question of academic freedom and the Catholic university is not
only complex, but unfortunately is also today a point of deep
division. Moreover, concern over the nature and limits of academic
freedom has arisen only recently, especially in American Catholic
higher education. To complicate matters further, those who in the
past century consciously attempted to define academic freedom
were, for the most part, hostile to traditional religion. This means
that Catholic educators now must come to grips with an idea which

---

[46]"Summary of Responses to Draft Schema on Catholic Universities," in Origins
17:41 (March 24, 1988), pp. 694–705.

[47]In 1967 John Cogley wrote that in the United States, Catholic universities, for
which he could see no future, "will one day seem as anachronistic as the papal states,
the error-has-no rights 'Catholic State,' or the Catholic penitentiary." Moreover, he
asserted that "Today, Notre Dame is the best Catholic university in the nation. But
this is precisely because, in a certain sense, Notre Dame is the least 'Catholic'
university." Cogley was a member of the group that wrote the Land O'Lakes Statement. See The Catholic University: A Modern Appraisal, pp. 291–306, originally
published as "The Future of An Illusion," Commonweal, June 2, 1967.

"has been evolving not only apart from the influence of traditional religious institutions, but in active hostility to them."[48] It would be, therefore, naive and premature to presume to offer *solutions* to such a complex problem. Nevertheless, it does seem possible, at least to me, to offer several *suggestions* which I hope will contribute to an eventual solution.

Influence Rather than Control

It seems to me that given the unique structure of Catholic higher education in the United States, the Vatican would be unwise to seek juridical control over Catholic colleges and universities. I say this not to avoid losing financial aid from the government, or to keep the Church hierarchy at arm's length, fearing as John Leary, S.J., president of Gonzaga University put it in 1968, that even an embrace might become a bear hug. I say it because self-governance can be the most effective way to bring Catholic educational institutions to realize their special mission.

Obviously, there is a risk inherent in such a suggestion. It cannot be denied that some individual colleges and universities have either been unable or have chosen not to maintain their own internal procedures which would make it more likely that their Catholic identity would remain visible and strong. Colleges and universities need, in my judgment, to make it clear that they recognize, respect, and welcome the role of the bishops as official definers of what constitutes true Catholic teaching. Such recognition, however, does not require juridical control of universities by bishops. The 1972 IFCU document offers some helpful clarifications that respect the great diversity in juridical structures of Catholic educational institutions: "some have been directly established or approved by ecclesiastical authority, while others have not; some have a statutory relationship with this authority, while others do not." It continues to explain that "the latter, provided that they maintain the essential characteristics of every Catholic university . . . are no less Catholic, whether by a formal, explicit commitment on part of their founders, trustees or faculty, or by their implicit tradition of fidelity to Catholicism and the corresponding social and cultural influence."[49]

---

[48]Gleason, "Academic Freedom and the Crisis in Catholic Universities," p. 48.

[49]Paragraph 15 of "The Catholic University in the Modern World." The essential characteristics of any Catholic university are set forth in the first paragraph as numbering four: "(1) a Christian inspiration not only of individuals but of the

Careful Hiring of Faculty

One of the most important and effective ways to set the tone for any educational institution is to hire as faculty people who accept the purposes of the institution. As Raymond Schroth recently put it, "hiring is the first step in a million-dollar relationship more permanent than most marriages, a forty-year opportunity to affect the beliefs of young people and the character of the institutions." Even though a college should hire faculty that support its values, "not all faculty need share all the values; indeed, for the free exchange of ideas to flourish, the university needs thinkers who contradict established wisdom."[50]

Several critics of the 1985 Vatican *Schema* have singled out for negative comment the rule that requires that professors of theology be distinguished, as the *Schema* put it, "by integrity and uprightness of life." Rev. William C. McInnes, S.J., president of the Association of Jesuit Colleges and Universities, was quoted as saying that "this means that a local bishop might have the power to fire a professor of theology for being divorced, for being homosexual, or for being anything they [sic] determine does not demonstrate uprightness of life.[51] I too believe that it is important to oppose any unjust applications of such a rule. On the other hand, I believe that it is just as important to admit that the character of faculty members, as difficult as it would be to evaluate in an objective and precise way, is of great importance. As Schroth states: "A teacher is a role model, not an impersonal conveyer of academic stuff. To separate the teacher from what is taught denies human experience. The interaction of students and teachers involves emotions as basic as greed, ambition and

---

university community as such; (2) a continuing reflection in the light of the Catholic faith upon the growing treasury of human knowledge, to which it seeks to contribute by its own research; (3) fidelity to the Christian message as it comes to us through the Church; and (4) an institutional commitment to the service of the people of God and of the human family in their pilgrimage to the transcendent goals which give meaning to life. All universities that realize these fundamental conditions are Catholic universities, whether canonically erected or not." The text of the Document may be found in *Why Should The Catholic University Survive?*, pp. 110–29.

[50]Unpublished paper on "Academic freedom and Catholic Identity," presented at Depaul University, April 30–May 1, 1987, p. 12.

[51]Jerome Cramer, "Academic Freedom and the Catholic Church," p. 36. If, however, for example, a homosexual were sexually active and were promoting his or her lifestyle in the classroom, even the AAUP might find grounds on the basis of incompetence or moral turpitude to dismiss the person.

possessiveness, and as deep as love, sexual attraction or Christian sacrifice."[52]

Few professionals exercise as much autonomy as do faculty in the typical American university. They play key roles in the selection of its members, as well as in their promotion. They exercise direct influence on the students and certify the extent of their knowledge and professional competence. As J. Patout Burns recently put it, "The entire success of the college or university depends upon its faculty's commitment to the institution's ideals and creativity in pursuing them. The true challenge facing the Catholic institutions is of corporate leadership within the faculty."[53]

An Operational Academic Freedom

Philip Gleason distinguishes three meanings of academic freedom: operational precision, vague abstraction, and ideology.[54] He suggests that on the first level it should be possible to combine academic freedom and Catholicism as an institutional commitment. By the operational level Gleason is referring to "specific requirements and prescriptions designed to shield professors from arbitrary action on the part of administrators," and to "tenure" and "academic due process (written charges, hearing, appeals, etc.). . . ." Much of what the AAUP stated in 1915 concerning academic competence is valuable and should be adopted: for example, that in dealing with controversial matters the professors should set forth divergent opinions without suppression or innuendo and remember that their business is not to provide the students with ready-made conclusions, but to train them to think for themselves; professors should aim at education and not indoctrination.

---

[52]Schroth, art. cit., p. 15. Fr. John L. McKenzie, commenting in his usual forthright style on the credibility of bishops as official teachers, writes: "I know that it is 'authentic' doctrine that the charisma of authentic teaching is separable from the charisma of Christian life. From this authentic teaching I dissent. I find no support in the New Testament for the belief that one can teach authentic Christianity with no efforts to live authentic Christianity. Christian doctrine is taught with more persuasion when it is taught by teachers whose conviction of the truth of what they are teaching is transparent" ("The Vatican: The Palace vs. The Council," in *Woodstock Report*, February 1987, p. 4). It may be asked if what McKenzie says about the value of the "charisma of Christian life" for bishops would apply *mutatis mutandis* to faculty who teach theology.

[53]"How Is the University Catholic?" in *Current Issues in Catholic Higher Education*, vol. 8 (Winter 1988), p. 13.

[54]Gleason, "Academic Freedom," *America*, July 19, 1966, p. 61.

On the operational level, academic freedom should be able to function within a Catholic university without difficulty. Where the problems enter, according to Gleason, is on the ideological level. To the extent that academic freedom is taken to mean that the commitment of faith, which most theologians accept as an integral part of the process of theologizing, compromises the status of theology as a true academic discipline, or that academic freedom requires one to believe that the only tenable truth is one which is empirically verified, or that adherence by a professor to a religious tradition inevitably leads to indoctrination of students—to the extent that such ideology clothes the concept of academic freedom, one meets profound problems in trying to incorporate it into a Catholic college or university.

In the area of theology, where conflicts are most likely to become apparent, potential problems are not resolved by stating that faith is not required for doing theology, or that theology should give way to religious studies. This is quite a complex matter that I cannot deal with here. Suffice it to say that even though the discipline of religious studies has enriched theology in many ways, theology, understood as the Catholic tradition has understood it, differs in some ways from other disciplines. As Richard McCormick writes: "The facts (truths) that found and energize the believing community and influence its moral behavior are not like data from other disciplines. They concern God's nature, intentions and actions as experienced and interpreted by a historical religious community. To reject such a context (Catholic) is to misunderstand either theology and/or its Catholic specification."[55]

In an article published in 1982, Charles Curran explained that the academic freedom that a Catholic theologian enjoys brings with it duties of responsibility and competency:

Competency requires that one be true to the presuppositions, sources and methods of the discipline. Specifically, the theologian should

---

[55]Richard McCormick, S.J., "The Search for Truth in the Catholic Context," *America*, Nov. 8, 1986. Charles Curran also accepts this understanding of the nature and sources of theology; that is why he explains in his defense against Rome's charges that he has never dissented from any infallible teaching—which, if he were to do so, would remove him from the "Catholic context." John J. Annarelli argues that to require a professor to have a personal faith commitment to the dogmas of the Catholic Church reduces the theologian to a spokesperson for the magisterium and turns the Catholic campus into a vehicle for "higher catechesis" (see his *Academic Freedom and the American Roman Catholic University*, p. 275ff.).

distinguish between the data of revelation and theories or hypotheses
that have been proposed. The official teaching of the Church should be
carefully spelled out and interpreted in accord with accepted hermeneutic principles. Personal hypotheses and opinions should be labeled
as such. The personal responsibility of the competent theologian forms
the best safeguard for protecting the rights of all concerned.[56]

In a lecture on "Academic Freedom" given at the University of
Dayton in January 1988, Curran expanded the list of safeguards to
three: (1) discussion and mutual criticism by peers (something, I
might add, which is hardly done often enough today, and when it is
done, too frequently is mean-spirited and divisive); (2) the right of
bishops to point out errors and ambiguities of a theology of particular theologians; and (3) competency, which for the Catholic theologian requires that he or she theologize within and not against
dogma.[57] It should be noted, however, that the second and third
safeguards are not formulated by theologians alone, but ultimately
by the Church as a whole. Many bishops are not professional
theologians, yet they play a key role in judging what constitutes
dogma. These last two safeguards would likely appear to the secular
academy as mechanisms that include more than merely peer review,
even though bishops should not be permitted, in my view, juridical
control of theology faculties at non-pontifical colleges and universities. What all this means is that academic freedom for theologians in
particular, will operate in a Catholic university in ways that can
only appear to be different, if not perhaps alien, from the way it is
understood by the secular academy.
    One of the risks that all theologians take, especially if they attempt
to work at the edges of their disciplines, finding new ways to
articulate the tradition and rethinking that tradition in the face of
current questions, is that of being misunderstood and accused of
departing from sound teaching. Theologians encountered difficult
times during the Modernist crisis at the turn of this century, and the
examples of Baron von Hügel's commitment both to scholarship and
the church is worth recalling. Two years before he died he wrote:

I saw that during the past fifty years it has been my life's purpose to
conduct myself scrupulously as a critical historian and uncompromis-

[56]Charles Curran, "Catholic Theology and Academe," in *Moral Theology: A Continuing Journey* (University of Notre Dame Press, 1982), p. 25.
    [57]Charles E. Curran, "Academic Freedom and Catholic Institutions of Higher Learn-
ing," given at the University of Dayton, January 21, 1988.

ing philosopher of religion; that my allegiance to the Roman Catholic Church cost me more than ten years of intense struggle and wrestling, precisely because, though I needed a large measure of freedom to carry out the task I had proposed to myself, I was beset by temptations to discard all the obligations of authority and seek complete freedom in individual effort; but that, finally, my fidelity to the Church saved me from skepticism and spiritual arrogance, being, when rightly understood and practiced, completely reconcilable with the healthy freedom necessary to my studies. I am not, therefore, recommending something the price of which I do not know. This price is really so great that only a strong faith can pay it. But the reward is great—the greatest a soul can receive, or God by his grace can offer.[58]

Finally, what should be done about a professor of theology who no longer accepts what McCormick describes as the "Catholic context"? First of all, he should realize that it is not for him to define officially whether he is a Catholic. Secondly, as long as such a professor follows the rules of competency described above, continues to respect the mission of the university, it would be possible to retain him as a member of the faculty as someone who would contribute to a dialogue with Roman Catholicism. As Raymond Schroth puts it:

In general practice it [academic freedom] means that no professor who, in the judgment of the scholarly community, otherwise meets the criteria for academic excellence—in scholarship, teaching, and academic citizenship—should lose his job because of his ideas. Period. If his ideas disturb the peace of the community and threaten to destroy its public image, the university will have to protect its image in other ways. It can insist that a professor distinguish his position from Church teaching, choose which courses he teaches, meet his arguments with better ones; but it shouldn't fire him.[59]

---

[58]Friedrich von Hügel, "Der Mystiker und die Kirche/aus Anlass des Sadhu", *Das Hochland* XXII (December, 1924), p. 330, the English translation printed in *The Month* (June, 1927), p. 560, cited by John A. McGrath, *Historical Christianity: The Contribution of Baron Friedrich von Hügel to the Controversy over History and Dogma (1902–1905)*, an unpublished Ph.D. dissertation submitted to the University of St. Michael's College, Toronto, p. 314–15. Von Hügel explained his commitment to an intellectual appropriation of his faith to his niece as follows: "I am determined to do all I can to make the old Church inhabitable *intellectually* as ever I can—not because the intellect is the most important thing in religion—it is not; but because the old Church already possesses in full the knowledge and the aids to *spirituality*, whilst, for various reasons which would fill a volume, it is much less strong as regards to needs, rights, and duties of the mental life" (also cited by McGrath, p. 16).
[59]Schroth, *art. cit.*, p. 10.

What is really unfortunate, however, is when such a professor or any professor for that matter, acts in a way that indicates that he no longer respects the mission of the university, does not contribute positively to the department and does only a mediocre job teaching, but stays on for reasons of security protected by tenure. It is also unlikely, as experience teaches, that other institutions would want to hire such a person. And, unfortunately, incompetency is notoriously hard to prove. As I have already pointed out, hiring is a critical part of building a fine university. Yet, no one can or should try to coerce through administrative pressures the direction of a person's thought over the years. It is one of the risks that a university takes in being a university that respects tenure.

Finding Ways to Stress the Rights of Institutions, Parents, and Students

If there is one idea that comes through clearly in the deservedly widely read book *Habits of the Heart* by Robert Bellah and his associates, it is that in the United States there is firmly in place a deeply ingrained individualism that makes the formation of communities extremely difficult. I have already pointed out how the founders of the AAUP set out to protect the rights of individual professors, as well as improve the profession. Deans and presidents, persons who represented larger areas of concern in the university, were not at first permitted membership. The American Civil Liberties Union also represents a focus on individual rights. What is needed is a complementary emphasis on institutional rights.

Catholic universities, for example, need to take seriously the expectation of many parents that their sons and daughters will be exposed to theology courses that will present an accurate and persuasive account of the Catholic faith. Catholic parents regularly express concern for both the academic and the pastoral. Some parents, however, have a narrow idea of how theology should be taught at a university level. They believe that only Catholic content should be presented, that other points of view from other denominations and religions should not be introduced, and that there should never be any critical evaluation of the Catholic faith. Theology at the university level, even though some students (despite 12 years in Catholic grade schools and high schools) arrive on campus practically religiously illiterate, needs to challenge the students to think both accurately and critically about religion.[60] Competence on the part of the professor requires, of course, that the content of courses on Catholic theology, or on any theology or religion for that matter, be complete and accurate. It would be helpful if courses that specialize in Catholic content be designated clearly in catalogues and registration guides so that students could choose them knowing precisely what to expect.

Some theologians think of their role in the classroom as having nothing to do with the development of the faith of the students. I believe that this way of thinking is narrow and naive. There is, of course, a distinction to be made between teaching theology and catechizing. To catechize is to teach a believer the truths of the faith; it is not to explore the meaning of the Christian faith intellectually and critically. Catechesis is done typically in parish settings and through religious education in grade school and high school. In most university classrooms, there are students who are not Catholic and sometimes not Christian. In such a setting, it would be inappropriate for a theology professor to assume that every student is there to deepen his or her Catholic faith. And even if all the students in the classroom were Catholic, it would still be inappropriate to expect that in a university there would not be an intellectually rigorous and critical investigation of the Catholic tradition. Yet, if research is understood as faith seeking understanding, the theologian will and should be perceived by the students as a believer. In such a course, the Catholic students at least should find their faith strengthened, sometimes by being challenged, sometimes by critical analysis, and regularly by clear, coherent, and complete exposition. If students who are not Catholic feel uncomfortable in the classroom, it may be because the professor is proselytizing, does not welcome criticisms and challenges from the students, or has a narrow view of what it means to teach theology at the university level.

All of this remains complex and admits of no easy formulation. If before 1950 almost all theology courses in Catholic universities and

---

[60]Paul J. Reiss, president of Saint Michael's College in Winooski, Vermont writes: "We must also take recognition of the fact that many students advanced in other areas of knowledge come to the College with a very meager understanding of their Christian faith which may then be subjected to critical evaluation and analysis. We should not, for example, emphasize issues in dispute among leading theologians before the student has had an opportunity to grasp at least a rudimentary understanding of the principles of the faith that are at issue. It is simply poor pedagogy." "St. Michael's College: Its Catholic Character and Academic Freedom," in *Current Issues in Catholic Higher Education*, Vol. 8, (Summer, 1987), p. 44.

colleges were aimed mainly at catechesis, we need to understand that in the 1980s university theology courses do not need to reject all catechetical purposes. While maintaining a high level of intellectual rigor and critical examination, the Catholic theology courses should have as one of their principal purposes the effective handing on of the Catholic tradition to the students who wish not only to learn more of it but also to live it more deeply. I believe that this is a legitimate expectation of students and parents and should therefore be met by the Catholic university.

More Than Theology and Campus Ministry

Many attempts to bring into sharper focus the identity of Catholic higher educational institutions make the mistake of limiting their efforts to strengthening the theology department and campus ministry. John Paul II has spoken frequently about the importance of Catholic universities as centers where men and women learn to make a personal synthesis of faith and culture. He has also described the Catholic university as a place where partial visions of the human reality are rejected and where human problems are studied on the deepest level.

It should be obvious that the faculty of theology and campus ministry play key roles in the pursuit of such goals. What is not so obvious is how important it is that faculty members from the arts, the social sciences and natural sciences, for example, and from the professional schools be willing to explore together some of the ethical dimensions of their disciplines, and the issues that fall in between their disciplines. I am not suggesting that there is such a thing as Catholic mathematics or physics, but I am suggesting that the ubiquity of the computer and the sub-atomic structure of reality do have profound implications for how we think about ourselves and our planet. Surely the social teachings of the church, and particularly the most recent letters of the bishops on peace and the economy, should generate spirited discussion across disciplines. It is even more important that such concerns be integrated into the curriculum, despite typically narrowly defined disciplines and the tyranny of accrediting agencies.[61]

---

[61]As Alice Gallin recently put it, "In all academic areas there must be a willingness to surface questions that deal with fundamental human experience. A course in economics cannot ignore the ethical problems that occur to the student when he or she learns about international trade or multi-national corporations. A course in

None of these remarks is intended to minimize the value of theology. It is impossible in my opinion to have an excellent Catholic university without an excellent department of theology. It is sad when the faculty of that department is not respected by faculty in other departments for its scholarship, teaching and willingness to dialogue. For the first time in our nation's history, our colleges and universities can provide a forum for theological exploration. It is unlikely to happen at state universities. William Shea, who taught theology for 11 years at a Catholic university and then 7 years at a state university recently wrote that "the most immediately noticeable difference to my mind . . . is the fact that the denominational university has a powerful assumption that religion is important and in some sense true as a form of life, while the state university and its faculty can only agree that religion is or at least might be worthwhile as a field of study. . . ."[62]

From the Ghetto to the Open Circle

There is something valid, I believe, in the criticism of those who warn against the Catholic college becoming a ghetto. While it is much less likely today that students on Catholic campuses will be sealed off from the distractions of the invasive and pervasive media and from the destructiveness of drugs and drinking and "safe sex," it still might well be far from being a vital part of a community of learning who with their teachers seek the truth through dialectic and dialogue. I turn again to William Shea who links the existence of a ghetto to diminished intellectual challenges and opportunities:

We must consider whether Catholic academics, theologians in particular, and administrators are to some extent obscurantists, protectionists,

---

European history cannot ignore the Judaeo-Christian faith that underlay many of the decisions made at particular moments of that history. A pre-med or nursing student cannot be taught about genetic engineering without being encouraged to think about the questions of life and death that are implicit." And further she explains that what she is calling for is an "open treatment of human history and development in all its richness, including its religious dimension. This is something that students cannot expect in other institutions; they surely have a right to expect it from us." "Academic Pluralism and Catholic Identity in Higher Education," in *Current Issues in Catholic Higher Education*, vol. 8 (Winter,, 1988), p. 27.

[62]William M. Shea, "Religious Pluralism in the State University: Lessons for a Theologian," in *Current Issues in Catholic Higher Education*, Vol. 7, (Winter, 1987), p. 13. He adds, "the state university is far more readily regarded by some of its faculty members solely as a place to work, while the Catholic university with its religious mission makes it difficult for faculty members to regard it so."

and cultural introverts, and to what extent Catholic higher education does not live up to the simple but rigorous ideal of contemporary scholarship. Perhaps, after all, Catholic institutions are separatist and particularist, parochial in their concerns, operating on the assumption that a Catholic public ought to be carved out of the general American public for educational purposes.[63]

If a Catholic university is not well served by turning itself into a "ghetto," it also ought to avoid becoming merely a "marketplace of ideas." We should be prepared to challenge the liberal assumption that truth is best found and differences most effectively overcome through the free exchange of ideas, for "whoever knew Truth put to the worse in a free and open encounter."[64] The purpose of a Catholic university is not to become a "marketplace of ideas," but a place where all ideas can be encountered and thought through, but from a certain perspective that might be called "the Catholic intellectual tradition." At a Catholic university I would expect to find a certain concentration upon "Catholic issues" researched and taught by a highly influential part of the faculty in a way that welcomes dialogue across disciplines. I propose the image of an "open circle," suffi- ciently circumscribed to constitute a community of discourse, but open enough to welcome others with different perspectives. There is therefore a need on a Catholic campus for students and faculty from other religious traditions, precisely to keep the dialogue more honest and open. Rather than carry on in a manner that would confirm the suspicions of those who think that adherence to reli- gious truths atrophies the intellect, academics at Catholic universi- ties should engage the ethical and religious dimensions of all issues, no matter how secular or even anti-religious they may appear to be.

There are individuals, of course, parents, wealthy benefactors, administrators and even some students, who think that the only points of view permissible on a Catholic campus should be those consistent with Catholicism. Such people do not understand the nature of a university. They need to be reminded that the Latin word *campus*

means field. It designates the arena where armies settled disputes with lance and sword. College campuses exist in part to render such incivil-

---

[63]*Ibid.*, p. 16.
[64]John Milton, *Aeropagitica*, cited by Metzher in *The Development of Academic Freedom*, p. 405, n. 124.

ity obsolete. The vigorous exchange of ideas by the open minded in the university setting is the way to reconcile our differences. That is why colleges have campuses, open forums for discussion and clash of ideas.[65]

In some way, however, the discussions and clash of ideas should be aimed at contributing to, among other things, the development of the Catholic intellectual tradition. There may be a need on a number of Catholic campuses for a certain "affirmative action" to populate and strengthen the "open circle." For the vigorous exchange of ideas to bear fruit I am presupposing that Catholic campuses maintain on their faculties individuals of sufficient academic merit and familiarity with the Catholic tradition to ensure that at the heart of the campus there stands an "open circle," that is, a community of scholars who are committed to the Catholic tradition, and others who are committed to engaging it and the religious and moral issues raised by it and by modern society.

Many Risks and No Assurances

We have already noted how most of the great Ivy League universities were founded by denominations precisely to train clergy, and how they gradually became non-sectarian simply because that is the way things evolved. All of these colleges were originally Protestant establishments. History shows how vulnerable that tradition was to fragmentation. Catholicism has a strong emphasis on community and a body of normative doctrine authoritatively determined. While individuals are always free to leave the Catholic tradition, they are not free to dissolve it.

The Catholic tradition exists in identifiable forms which shape beliefs, doctrines, ethical teachings and liturgical practices. Some of these forms embody the very core of the Catholic faith. Catholic scholars accept that core as a "given," or, even more accurately put, as a "gift," and understand their vocation as the careful handing on of that gift to others, contributing what they can to understanding the gift and articulating in fresh but faithful ways its value for the age. The Catholic tradition is, as it can be put in German, both a

---

[65]Richard McCormick, *art. cit.*, p. 281. The image of the open circle, incidentally, has been borrowed from the English title of Cardinal Ratzinger's book, *The Open Circle: The Meaning of Christian Brotherhood* (Sheed and Ward, 1966), originally published as *Die christliche Brüderlichkeit* (Kösel-Verlag KG; Munich, 1960).

Gabe and an *Aufgabe,* a gift and a task, a revelation and a responsibility. But for a culture such as our own that views the past as an
empty and uninteresting museum and sees tradition as rigidity and
mere repetition and describes the acceptance of a revelation as
intellectual suicide, Catholic scholars in a Catholic university dedicated to the intellectual exploration of that revelation must surely
appear as sincere but misguided individuals committed to the impossible: the deepening of faith through the cultivating of the intellect.[66]

But for those who have discovered through faith a deepening of
the range of intellect, there is good reason to see in a "Catholic
university" not an oxymoron, but an exciting blend of faith and
reason. To the extent that faculty and administration so committed
in Catholic universities and colleges welcome the influence of the
church, hire faculty carefully, accept an operational definition of
academic freedom, balance individual rights with institutional
rights, and involve the entire campus in a dialogue on ethical and
religious issues, there is, I believe, reason to be confident about the
future.

---

[66]James Monroe Cameron describes the current situation and opportunity of the
Catholic university in the West as follows: "There is a serious threat to the freedom
of the Catholic university. It comes, not from Rome, from the Curia, from bishops, but
from the dominant culture of western society, filled with the hatred of life and of
human virtue, lost in a maze of ephemeral intellectual fashions. (This is not the
whole truth about western society, but it is the aspect of it we are tempted to forget.)
I think we—Catholics engaged in higher education—owe it to our society to challenge
it in the sharpest possible way, to draw from the rich resources open to us—the
prophetic tradition, the theological tradition, the words of the Gospel—words of
warning and consolation. But mostly we have simply to go on doing our own work in
the traditional academic disciplines, to cultivate skepticism in the face of the claims
made by the pundits of the day, and not, emphatically not, to try to emulate them in
their own style. I think these are general duties binding on *all* universities. But
Catholic universities have available to them, if they seek it, something that goes
beyond the highest accomplishments of intellect relying upon its own resources. If
God had not already shown himself in Jesus Christ we could still have done theology;
but what a pitiful affair it would have been. Think of how poor, at the level of
theology, a Plato or an Aristotle is as compared with an Athansius, an Augustine, an
Aquinas. . . . We find the treasure of revelation in earthen vessels (these vessels are
ourselves), but what a treasure it is, one so great that we ought to sacrifice every
worldly advantage in order to preserve it." (Unpublished address, "Academic Freedom in the Catholic University," given at the University of Dayton, September 14,
1978, p. 11).

THE MISSION OF A CATHOLIC COLLEGE

William L. Portier

During the 1980's, education in the United States has been the subject of much academic soul-searching. The danger of cultural illiteracy for entire generations, we are told, places our very future as a nation in jeopardy. This agonizing reappraisal of education, especially higher education, comes as part of a wider body of commentary on the state of American culture as fragmented and lacking any shared vision of life. Voices which span the range of our political spectrum call for more attention to values in the educational process. Ernest Boyer's Carnegie Foundation report, *College, The Undergraduate Experience in America* recognizes that, if colleges are to be real "learning communities," they need some "sense of common purpose."[1] The advantage of a shared experience of learning is often used to justify limiting student choice in the curriculum. "You have to guide kids toward the real stuff," as Education Secretary William Bennett has put it with reference to his model high school curriculum.[2]

The provocative subtitle of Allan Bloom's bestseller, *The Closing of the American Mind,* charges American higher education with having failed to provide this guidance: "How Higher Education Has Failed Democracy and Impoverished the Souls of Today's Students." The "absolute certitude" with which Bloom begins his book is this: "almost every student entering the university believes, or says he [sic] believes that truth is relative."[3] Bloom, correctly in my view, identifies this belief as a "moral postulate" rather than a theoretical insight. Perhaps this is why he never feels the need to define

---

[1] Ernest L. Boyer, *College, The Undergraduate Experience in America,* The Carnegie Foundation for the Advancement of Teaching (New York: Harper & Row, 1987), p. 250.

[2] *Washington Post*, December 30, 1987, p. A5.

[3] Allan Bloom, *The Closing of the American Mind* (New York: Simon and Schuster, 1987), p. 25.

relativism except in the vaguest terms or to offer theoretical arguments against it. Neither Bloom nor Bennett address the situation so
insightfully described by the authors of *Habits of the Heart* (University of California Press, 1985), namely the lack in the United States
of an accepted public language for talking about the meaning of
human life and the value of the shared experience we do have. In
the absence of serious arguments directed against relativism as a
diverse set of possible philosophical positions and toward Bennett's
"real stuff," the denunciation of some ill-defined relativism is no
more than an exercise in elitist lamentation for the passing of a time
that never was.

One might think that the unique experience of Catholic higher
education in the United States, and specifically that of the undergraduate colleges, would have something to contribute to a wider
discussion which seems at last to have become dimly aware of the
limitations of a value-free posture in education. But one searches
the current literature on higher education in vain for any substantive
reference to the existence and mission of the nation's more than 200
Catholic colleges and universities.[4] Perhaps this is due to the fact
that many of them appear indistinguishable from their secular counterparts.

In the context of the present discussion on values and vision in
higher education, the time is ripe for those involved in undergraduate education at Catholic colleges to reflect on what their mission in
the contemporary United States ought to be. What can the experience of trying to fulfill this mission contribute to the broader discussion of such issues as the role of shared values in creating a learning
community and the question, ever present in a pluralist environment, of the relativity of truth? Can we explain to ourselves and to
the wider academy why there are Catholic colleges and how they
can provide a limited but real example of true humanistic education
in an environment of shared basic values and vision? These questions will be treated in this essay under the following headings: I. A
Preliminary Philosophical Case for Education With a Point of View,
II. The Vision of Christian Humanism as the Foundation for Catholic
Liberal Arts Education, III. How A Catholic College Works, IV.
Academic Integrity in a Catholic College.

---

[4]Bloom notes in passing that "scholasticism, the use of Aristotle by the Roman
Catholic Church," has helped to exacerbate the schism between ancients and moderns
he so decries. *Ibid.*, p. 264.

I. A Preliminary Philosophical Case for Education With a
Point of View

There is a belief abroad in the American academy that education, in order to protect students from brainwashing and indoctrination, must be done from a "value-free," "neutral" and virtually "objective" Archimedean point of view. Archimedes, the reader may recall, was that buoyant Greek who promised to move the world, if only he could have a fulcrum. If one supposes the necessity of value-free education, there follows the rather widespread belief that the last place one would want to go for an education is a "sectarian" college. The very word *sectarian* sets visions of witch-burnings and heresy-hunts to dancing, like the flames that lick the heretics, in the heads of the enlightened. It follows that the absolutely last place one would want to go for an education is a "sectarian" college that is "Catholic." That very word, nearly synonomous with *dogmatism* and *intolerance*, conjures images of rapacious crusaders, corrupt renaissance popes and unscrupulous inquisitors. These latter are often vivid preoccupations of value-free surveyors of western history. *Catholic* and *university* are, as George Bernard Shaw is said to have put it, "a contradiction in terms."[5] Bound to the pre-determined conclusions of the tradition, Catholics, therefore, are not free to follow the often heroic path which leads out of the ignorance and superstition of the murky past and into the light of objective truth.

Although I have overstated this view of Catholic education, it is not in my experience an uncommon one. To verify this observation, the reader need only disguise him or herself as a Catholic and wander the groves and cattle markets of academe for a while. In the present essay, I would like to submit that this view of Catholic education, as somehow a privation of the objectivity required for academic integrity, is, on its own terms—i.e., those of Western enlightened thought—outdated and prejudiced, not to mention philosophically and historically untenable. The first step in developing such an argument is to rescue the notion of tradition from its modern detractors. This requires something like a "post-Enlightenment," or rather "late-Enlightenment," notion of tradition as the *de facto*

---

[5]Cited in John Tracy Ellis, "A Tradition of Autonomy?," in Neil G. McCluskey, ed., *The Catholic University, A Modern Appraisal* (Notre Dame: University of Notre Dame Press, 1970), pp. 206–270, 262. Although this dictum of Shaw's is often cited in discussions of Catholic higher education, I have been unable to find its original source in his works.

condition of the possibility of Western thought and education. Objectivity in such a view would consist in the capacity for self-criticism.

Developments in late-Enlightenment Western thought, e.g., the culture critiques of Nietzsche, Marx and Freud, as well as the rise of the social sciences, have tended to mitigate the Age of Reason's emphasis on the autonomy of the free inquiring subject. Marx, for example, has taught us to be very suspicious of members of professional elites who claim value neutrality in their descriptions of human behavior. Such descriptions often reflect their interests as usually white, usually male professionals. But Marx too believed that "science" would free us from the illusions of our forebears. He too in spite of himself stood in the Enlightenment tradition, carrying on the scientific spirit of Archimedes and the Greeks, often quite innocent of his naive faith in scientific reason, and uncritical of what the philosopher Hans-Georg Gadamer has called the Enlightenment's "prejudice against prejudice."[6]

But the point of view of early Enlightenment, in its delusion that it had no point of view, has been unmasked. As the Enlightenment heritage, even as the Church it loves to hate, gives rise to the various movements of self-criticism mentioned above, the role of tradition, e.g., language, society, culture, in the very constitution of the free inquiring subject's selfhood has become more and more difficult to leave out of account. In such an approach to human consciousness as historical, the word *tradition* need not retain the pejorative connotations it tended to acquire during the early Enlightenment. The word *tradition* can be legitimately used to refer to the matrix of linguistic, social and cultural influences within which an historical self or human subject is constituted as such.

Given such a notion of tradition, critical thinking need not imply an iconoclastic process of storming some imagined Archimedean bastion above and outside of tradition. This would be more like naive self-delusion than scholarly objectivity. Academic integrity might be seen to consist rather in the scholarly reflection on our inevitable presuppositions as Westerners, Americans, Catholics, pro-

---

[6]"And there is one prejudice of the enlightenment that is essential to it: the fundamental prejudice of the enlightenment is the prejudice against prejudice itself, which deprives tradition of its power." Gadamer goes on to give an account of how the term *prejudice* acquired its present pejorative sense. Hans-Georg Gadamer, *Truth and Method* [1960], no translator given (New York: The Seabury Press, 1975), pp. 238–39.

fessional academics or whatever. Such reflection can lead to the critical appropriation and creative reshaping of tradition in terms of the very symbols which the tradition has handed on. Western academics, for example, tend to be especially sensitive to their tradition's tendencies toward economic and political imperialism, racism, etc. But that sensitivity itself is testimony to the fact that Western tradition is resilient enought to be self-critical. Western tradition retains the capacity to provide those who are educated in it with the resources to recognize such tendencies, judge them as perversions in terms of the West's own inclusive symbols and resist them.

People who think out of a tradition, therefore, are not necessarily lacking in objectivity, although they may be. They are simply thinking in what, to present appearances at least, is the only way that humans can think. The methodological integrity or objectivity of scholarly inquiry and teaching, therefore, depends on the scholar's or teacher's ability to be self-critical and reflective in the appropriation of the data of his or her discipline.

The historicity of human consciousness which I have been trying to describe means that we are born into a conversation which has been going on for centuries. If we are to think at all, it will be as active participants in that conversation. To think critically is to become systematically aware of that fact. However unfair it may seem, this is an inevitable consequence of human finitude. We do not think from a divine or Archimedean standpoint. This can be regarded as a privation of objectivity only if, on the basis of some prior assumption, we believe that we ought to have such a point of view.

If tradition and the process of critical thinking can legitimately be understood as I have described them, certain consequences follow for the way liberal arts education is to be understood. Its purpose is to help students develop the wherewithal to take part in the conversation which is our tradition in the West and to make critical contributions to it. If the notion of tradition sketched above is at all proportionate to experience, then the process of liberal education implies built-in value judgements about the worthiness of carrying on the conversation which is Western culture. These judgments will find expression in the organization of curriculum and in the process of designating some subjects as part of a liberal arts "core."

In my own experience, the most effective teachers have been those who visibly embodied their conviction that the part of Western tradition with which they were concerned, science, literature, philosophy, was worthy of being brought to the attention of those who came after them. Within the assumptions of Western culture, time spent with Plato or Shakespeare is time well spent. Finally the notion of tradition at work here implies that liberal arts education is not concerned merely with imparting a form of thinking, i.e. critical. It extends inevitably to the content of thinking in terms of which the form itself can be judged as valuable and worthy of being passed on.

I have argued that those who think from a point of view need not be damned since that is the only way we can think. This line of argument raises two difficulties. First, is the tradition or point of view in education which I wish to defend, namely that of Roman Catholicism, compatible with the ideals of the Western tradition which I have sketched? To put it in another way, am I equivocating in my use of the word *tradition,* so that the defense of tradition in general which I have offered does not apply to the specific tradition in question? Second, does the notion of tradition I have sketched condemn me unawares to an historical relativism which lacks a position from which to carry out the self-criticism which I have claimed scholarly objectivity requires?

I would like to address both concerns briefly by way of commenting on Max Weber's 1918 essay on "Science As a Vocation."[7] In this essay, Weber makes a chastened but eloquent profession of the Enlightenment's faith in science. He carefully circumscribes the sense in which scientific activity can be free of presuppositions and glories teutonically in its methodological integrity. He separates the person with his or her beliefs or presuppositions from the scientist who must, as far as he or she is able, let the data speak for themselves. Weber admits that in order to do this, he must be critically aware of his own presuppositions. The contemporary reader would profit from critically attending to the nuanced self-reflection of Weber's description of the relationship between scientific work and its presuppositions. About the ultimate meaning, if any, of what it studies, and about the worthiness of that endeavor, science cannot, according to Weber, speak scientifically. Since the German *Wissenschaft* has a much broader extension than our word *science,* Weber's reflections refer not only to the physical scientist

---

[7]The essay is found in *From Max Weber: Essays in Sociology,* translated, edited and with an introduction by H. H. Gerth and C. Wright Mills (New York: Oxford University Press, 1946), pp. 129–56.

but to scholarly activity in general. He begins the discussion of the relationship between scientific activity and what it must presuppose with this quotation from Russian novelist and Christian pacifist, Leo Tolstoy: "Science is meaningless because it gives no answer to our question, the only question important for us: 'What shall we do and how shall we live?' "[8]

If scholars in the American academy would admit with Weber the import of this statement and accept the modest yet significant task which he bequeaths them as a vocation, the first difficulty would be mitigated considerably, though not entirely. Scientists would then refrain from putting forth as science their beliefs about the meaning of human life and the nature of the human person. This would go a long way toward alleviating the so-called conflict between science and religion, between the critical spirit and religious faith.

But this would still leave us with the second question, that of the historicism into which the stream of thought for which Weber spoke, the *Geisteswissenschaften*, tended to flow. The notion of any meaningful sense of a Western tradition would then fracture on the pluralism of positions about how we are to live, all of which are historically, linguistically and culturally conditioned or relative. Weber refused to plead scientifically his own practical and political stands in the classroom because he found such pleading "meaningless in principle because the various value spheres of the world stand in irreconcilable conflict with each other."[9] Bloom's chapter on the "German Connection" indicates that it is this "value relativism" of Weber's that he thinks has become "the everyday language of the United States" and of his students.[10] This question of the historical relativity of the true and the good is one of the major preoccupations of modern Western thought. I cannot provide a complete account of it here.

Whether from what the scientists, in Weber's broad understanding of the term, must presuppose in order to do their work, the metaphysicians left among us can construe an answer to Tolstoy's question, however minimal and negative, I leave to my colleagues in philosophy.[11] I must note in doing so, however, that the Roman Catholic

---

[8]*Ibid.*, p. 143.

[9]*Ibid.*, p. 147.

[10]Bloom, *Closing of the American Mind*, p. 147.

[11]The most disappointing aspect of Bloom's provocative book is his failure to argue substantively for why his students should choose the faith in reason perspective he sees represented by Socrates and Locke rather than the perspective he attributes to

tradition is committed, on theological grounds, to the proposition that they can, as philosophers, come up with a minimal answer to Tolstoy's question.

The precondition to such an answer is the rather simple demonstration that the position of historical relativism is in the end logically incoherent and hence intellectually untenable. The statement that all beliefs about the ultimate meaning of life and human nature are historically conditioned self destructs as soon as the speaker realizes that the statement which claims universal validity, is itself historically conditioned. There is an informal contradiction here between the universal validity intended by the statement and its historically conditioned form.[12] It is this very transcendence of history at which the historical relativist incoherently aims that the metaphysician traditionally seeks.

Thus the Socratic challenge to the internal coherence of an absolutely relativist perspective opens up a radical choice between two possible directions for further movement. The first, let us call it Alternative A, would lead to a limited or contextual relativism in which truths relative to a time and place could in principle be related, sometimes with great difficulty, to truths relative to other times and places. The ultimate meaning of all of this limited meaning could be meaningfully questioned. The notion of tradition for which I am trying to argue rests in the end on the possibility of some such philosophical account of the more than meaninglessness of human life.

The second direction, let us call if Alternative B, would reject the Socratic challenge as inadequate to the radical ambivalence of experience and embrace an absolute relativism in which the various finite contexts would remain ever closed to one another. At this point, the value of further public conversation would come into radical question. The notion of Catholic tradition which I will describe below would be set off from the various humanisms and

---

Nietzsche and Weber. His impassioned argument that value relativism cannot ground American democracy lacks any corresponding argument in favor of some form of natural rights theory. His modest conclusion is that the university ought not be a place where Weberian "value relativism" is simply taken for granted. Rather it should be challenged in dialogue with the perspective of Nietzsche's mortal enemy, Socrates. With this I heartily agree.

[12]While Gadamer doesn't accept the logical argument presented here, his comments on it and on the use made of it by Leo Strauss (Bloom's mentor) are instructive for anyone engaged in the present discussion of "relativism" in American higher education. Gadamer, *Truth and Method*, pp. 406–407; 482–91.

materialisms of modern secular thought in a chaos of pluralism. The Catholic tradition would be one among the many voices competing in the cacaphony of the absolutely relative.

From the perspective of Alternative B, the very project of liberal arts education would appear as a quaint relic of a previous historical period, to be propagated according to the self interest of a diminishing number of eccentric initiates, until their general uselessness should become more universally apparent. Both liberal arts education in general and its Catholic variant in particular would have to be defended with the kind of resentful ideology of decline we find in *The Closing of the American Mind*.

According to Alternative A, on the other hand, liberal arts education and its Catholic variant represent an enduring and inclusive vision, variously expressed in literature, etc., of the meaning of human life. Western tradition from the Greeks through the Enlightenment even to the recent past is based on the conviction that there is an abiding *humanum* which it is the purpose of society and education to preserve and enhance. We recognize this *humanum* most readily in our common abhorrence at its violations in various forms of inhumanity. The ethical consequences of absolute relativism, therefore, provide the basis for one of the more persuasive arguments in favor of Alterntive A. The Western tradition is committed to the proposition that we can express the *humanum* positively as well. One such attempt is the vision of Christian humanism as mediated through the Catholic tradition.

II. The Catholic Vision of Christian Humanism as the Foundation For Catholic Liberal Arts Education

Liberal arts education in a Catholic college takes place within the three concentric spheres of basic Western humanism, Christian humanism as an animating religious vision, and Catholicism as mediating Christian humanism through its beliefs, worship and church structure. In the medium most proper to the academic setting of a college, Catholics carry on the mediation of Christian faith by means of what can justly be called the longest lived intellectual tradition in the West.

Western humanism is recognizable as a tradition by its characteristic concern for the dignity and worth of individual human persons. Pointing out that this concern has not always been inclusive is a form of internal criticism. This specifying concern finds expression

in the literary and legal classics of the West and in the very form of
scholarship itself as an instance of free inquiry. Depending on the
foundation that is proposed for this broad and vague consensus on
individual worth, the relationships among individuals and between
individuals and society are variously conceived.

That strain of Western humanism which sees the Enlightenment
as a radical break with the past, rather than as a development of it,
is, for all practical purposes, in control of the academy. From this
perspective, Christianity, especially in its Catholic form, often appears as inherently hostile to humanism. Indeed, it cannot be denied
that in the Christian vision of things, individual sovereignty cannot
be absolute. It must be subordinated to what both Ignatius Loyola
and John Calvin liked to call the "glory of God." Individual worth
must be understood in accordance with what Aquinas might have
called the "last end" of human beings and the inner purposes of
God's creation.

One of the greatest challenges to Christian thought in the twentieth
century has been to respond to the Enlightenment's charge that
Christianity, and particularly Catholicism, is an anti-worldly ideology which places no inherent value on individuals and their lives in
the world. The second Vatican Council addressed this concern at
length in its "Pastoral Constitution on the Church in the Modern
World" (Gaudium et Spes). Scholars from Edward Gibbon to Fran-
çois Guizot and Max Weber have tried to assess the impact of
Christianity on Western civilization. Catholic writers from Jaime
Balmes and Charles de Montalembert to J.-B. Metz have sought the
very ideals of Enlightenment in the influence of Catholicism on
European civilization.

What specifies Christian humanism, regardless of how we answer
the historical questions above, is the foundation it proposes for its
commitment to human dignity. This foundation is ultimately a
theological one grounded in Christian revelation. To the questions
which human beings ask about the meaning of their lives, with their
concomitant sorrows and exhilarations, Christianity proposes the
figure of Jesus Christ, crucified and risen, the fulfillment of God's
promises and Israel's hopes as we find them in the Hebrew scrip-
tures. This revelation provides a fourfold vision of what it means to
be a human being. This vision is based on the biblical doctrines of
creation, fall, incarnation and redemption.

Human beings are in the first place creatures who stand in relationship to a creator. This places them in a cosmos, good as it comes

from the hand of God, and ordered both physically and morally according to God's purposes. But we do not find these blessed creatures apart from the simultaneous curse of sorrow and death, the threat of meaninglessness and the extinguishing of order. Scripture, in what to the enlightened spirit is one of its hardest sayings, attributes this condition to the abuse of human freedom, i.e., to sin. Human beings find themselves and their world scarred to their very cores by the accumulated effects of centuries of deviation from God's order. This order finds its most concise expression in the first commandment's claim that only God should be treated as God. Scripture teaches that the condition in which we find ourselves makes it difficult to perceive the order by which God is God and creatures are creatures, and still more difficult to live by it. According to the biblical vision, any attempt to absolutize human freedom and to regard it as ultimate must stand convicted of the sin of idolatry. For a humanist of the Sartrian stripe, this means that humans are not really free to be human until they have disposed of God.

According to the Christian doctrine of the incarnation, as expressed, for example, in Jn 1, God entered human history in the human nature of the first-century Palestinian Jew, Jesus of Nazareth. This means, among other things, that a human being is not so low a creature that God could not become one. By his cross and resurrection, Christ redeemed creation from the power of sin, and offers to us, not only as God's creatures but as his adopted children, the wherewithal to live in a new way, according to the order in which only God is God. Thus the *imitatio Christi* provides Christians with the embodiment of the *humanum* which philosophers can perceive only dimly.

This is the biblical vision of a human being. I have tried to state it in such a way that it could be received by other Christians, and, in part, by faithful Jews as well. This vision of human beings as created, fallen and redeemed in Christ as God incarnate, must animate all Christian life in the power of the Holy Spirit, and hence the lives of those Christians who would undertake Christian education.

But what specifies the Catholic mediation of this Christian vision of the *humanum* as it might appear in a Catholic college? Other Christian bodies sponsor schools which identify themselves as affiliates of a particular Christian church. I do not know how much of their own self-understandings other Christians will recognize in my description, but I will try to emphasize what in my experience marks the distinctively Catholic mediation of the Christian vision as embodied in education.

Taking for granted that all Christian schools should be concerned with addressing the basic questions of human life from a Christian perspective, what is specific to the way Catholics have done this? My own view, and perhaps it is colored to some degree by the fact that I am a theologian, is that the doctrines of creation and incarnation, as they were received by those who began the great medieval universities at Paris, Bologna, Oxford, etc., have had a tremendous impact on the way Catholics think they should organize colleges and universities. Specifically, these doctrines affect the conception of what philosophy and theology are and the integrating role that is ascribed to them in any conversation among Catholics about what humans can know and how they should act. Space does not permit a discussion of the Jesuit *ratio studiorum* and its possible historical relationship with Calvin's ideas on Christian education. I must assume that the remote origins of both are located in the medieval universities.

The goal of medieval education as articulated by Albert the Great and carried out by Thomas Aquinas in his teaching and writing was a synthesis of faith and reason, an integration of what we can know of ourselves and our world as relatively autonomous, with what God has revealed. This involves casting "faith seeking understanding" (theology) into the mold of Aristotelian science, which for our purposes has the occupational hazard of emphasizing the cognitive dimension of revelation in methodological abstraction from its personal dimension. Philosophy, autonomous in its own right in abstraction from revelation, becomes the organon of theology when the two are joined.

Aquinas at his best affirms the created world with vigor and uses the doctrine of creation as a bridge to join Christian revelation and Aristotelian science. Thus Aquinas was able to answer the challenge to Christian thought posed by Aristotle's self-sufficient explanation of reality apart from any reference to Christ or biblical revelation. The truth of one could not therefore contradict the truth of the other. Conflicts between science and faith could, in the medieval view, only be apparent. Thus Aquinas emphasized a certain continuity between the orders of creation and redemption, between reason and faith, between nature and grace. This continuity is expressed in his oft-repeated dictum "grace presupposes nature."[13]

---

[13]St. Thomas Aquinas, *Summa Theologica*, 3 vols., translated by the English

By the sixteenth century, however, this medieval synthesis had deteriorated to such an extent that the reformers could accuse Aquinas and the scholastics in general of neglecting the doctrines of the fall and redemption, of suggesting that nature is self-sufficient and salvation in Christ superfluous. A certain hostility toward philosophy as a purely human endeavor apart from grace, as well as a certain disdain for theology as "science" ensued.

In spite of the fact that many of the reformers' criticisms are well taken, Catholic education is to this day premised on the belief that something like the medieval synthesis is still possible. There need not be a conflict between science and faith. According to this time-honored ideal, then, the goal of education in the Catholic tradition is to facilitate in the hearts and minds of those being educated this integration, first between the various branches of human knowledge as in Aristotle, and then between what they know and what they believe as in Aquinas. Faith that such synthesis is possible and desirable rests on the doctrine of creation. Remembering the doctrine of the fall, however, reminds us that this integrative ideal is difficult to achieve. The doctrines of creation and incarnation provide the theological basis for affirming and studying our culture as worthy. The doctrines of fall and redemption caution Christians as Christians to be inherently suspicious of the cultures in which they live, and remind them of the need to criticize those cultures in the light of the gospel of salvation in Jesus Christ and no other.

Because most students in Catholic colleges were lay people who would be immersed in largely secular tasks after graduation, the methodology or form of public discourse used to talk about the integrative ideal was what Etienne Gilson and Jacques Maritain called "Christian philosophy." This is a theologically sensitive form of realist philosophy which gives Catholics a theoretical way of affirming simultaneously both the relative autonomy and the physical and moral order of God's creation. The emphasis of this tradition on "natural law" made it potentially well-suited, in the American context especially, for political discussion in the public forum. As more lay people began to study theology after the second Vatican Council, that discipline began to assume a share of the integrative task. Although the methodological distinction between philosophy and theology remains clear, their relative roles in working out the synthesis are no longer so.

Dominicans (New York: Benziger Brothers, 1947), Vol. 1, p. 12; Part I, Question 2, Art. 2, reply obj. 1.

As a community of scholar/believers, a Catholic college at its best should bring to life an ongoing conversation between students and professors and professors among themselves. This is a conversation about the integration between disciplines and ultimately the integration between faith and reason. It will not always be a calm conversation. Such a goal is relatively foreign to the secular university where "specialization" reigns. In the context of Christian humanism, "specialization" must ultimately be unsatisfactory.[14] The Christian humanist vision strives for a comprehensive view of reality. Philosophers and theologians play a key role by acting as catalysts who continually raise value questions and who consult and challenge colleagues in their respective areas of expertise.

III. How a Catholic College Works

The vision of a Catholic college as a community of scholar/believers who are concerned to situate their respective areas of specialization with respect to a comprehensive view of reality is like Plato's republic only an ideal. It presupposes that the people who make up the community of discourse which is the college have a genuine concern for the integrative task and the Christian vision which inspires it. It further presupposes that basic competence in various areas of specialization can be achieved and that these areas are methodologically autonomous from philosophy and theology.

It is difficult to imagine how a Catholic college could long retain its identity as such unless its across the board hiring policies actively sought out and gave reference to, all other professional considerations being equal, people who, on the basis of sharing the vision of Christian humanism, were committed explicitly to the goal of integration and synthesis. Although it is possible and even likely that others, especially other Christians, would share this vision to greater or lesser degrees, and thus contribute significantly to the community of scholar/believers, it seems equally obvious to me that the ideal requires at the very minimum a "critical mass" of committed Catholics. Hiring practices must either take cognizance of this situation or place the Catholic identity of the college in jeopardy.

If the goal of Catholic education is anything like what I described,

---

[14]"Pastoral Constitution on the Church in the Modern World," Para. 8 in Walter M. Abbott and Joseph Gallagher, eds., *The Documents of Vatican II* (Piscataway, N.J.: New Century Publishers, 1966), p. 206.

then the ideal of synthesis and bridge-building between faith and culture would be a subsidiary interest and an elementary component of every discipline in the college. This need not impair the methodological autonomy of any discipline, whether its research is directed primarily toward the analysis of texts or in a more empirical direction. The vision of Christian humanism must come into play, however, in what might be called "extra-methodological" situations, Weber's value questions. Value postures are engaged, for example, in any considerations about what to investigate, what to use as an example of the method under study, or in the questions which arise whenever people think about what to do with this or that methodology or scientific construct.

Can professors of literature, for example, really presume that there is some Archimedean body of classic texts apart from their provenance in either the Western tradition in general, Christian humanism or its specifically Catholic mediations? How, for example, could they justify excluding from the college's curriculum the very body of works which literarily render and reflect upon the experience of trying to live the Christian vision of human life in the form mediated by Catholicism. I am thinking of authors such as Dante, George Bernanos, Sigrid Undset, Graham Greene, Flannery O'Connor, etc.

Can empirical and social scientists really pretend that the methods they teach ever exist apart from a value-committed person faced with ethical decisions about how to use them? Over the course of the present century, the popes and bishops have brought the traditional wisdom of the Church to bear on various questions of personal and social morality. These attempts to apply traditional moral principles to contemporary situations range from economics and war related issues to questions of sexual morality and reproductive technology. In the first instance, the Church's positions are usually to the left of the general population's. In the second, the Church's positions are clearly "counter-cultural." Regardless of how these teachings stand up against the scales of public opinion, are professors who deal with these issues in extra-methodological class discussion really free to ignore or make light of these positions? How can an economist or a sociologist at a Catholic college be ignorant of the Church's social teachings? Shouldn't we expect students who graduate from Catholic colleges to understand the differences between statistical descriptions of what most people happen to do or think and ethical reflection about what human beings ought to do? These are two very disparate senses of the term *human behavior*.

How can students be expected to understand the difference between these two levels of discourse if their professors never address it in forms of interdisciplinary conversation?

Although the problem applies primarily to research-oriented universities, colleges cannot ignore the reality that research topics have value dimensions. If scholars as people are living out the vision of the human person offered by Christian humanism, it should not come as a surprise if these concerns surface in connection with the research topics they choose as scholars. Consider the timely example of the economics of the arms race. In the recent past Church leaders have consistently spoken out in authoritative form against the arms race. *Gaudium et Spes* calls it "an utterly treacherous trap for humanity, and one which injures the poor to an intolerable degree."[15] This is a statement about a matter of economic fact. No intelligent person could believe that an authoritative statement of the Church could make a matter of fact other than it is. The critical inquirer, therefore, might wonder if there really is an empirically demonstrable correlation between spending on behalf of the arms race and injury to the poor. Further, if such an analyst were to conclude that there is indeed such a correlation, he or she might become interested in developing economic and political strategies for diverting resources to less harmful uses. Research is inevitably political. Allegedly "neutral" and "purely descriptive" researchers simply affirm as "objective" whatever happens to be the case. In so doing, they unwittingly, or perhaps all too purposefully, lend the deservedly honored mantle of science to the *status quo*.

IV. Academic Integrity and Catholic Education

I have proposed an ideal of a Catholic college as a community of scholar/believers who are in conversation about the value questions which impinge upon the society as a whole and upon their scholarly endeavors as well. The controlling perspective of this conversation is the Christian vision of humanism as mediated through Catholicism. Practically speaking, this means that philosophy and theology should both try to push the conversation toward the integration which it seeks and try to provide the public vocabulary or form of discourse in which the conversation about values can take place. The ultimate goal of this process is to prepare students to live their

---

[15]*Ibid.*, Para. 81, p. 295.

worldly vocations as embodiments of Christian humanism. This means that they must not only have achieved methodological competence in their respective disciplines, but also that they have learned to raise and answer the inevitable value questions of their disciplines from within the perspective of Christian humanism.

Such a conversation usually includes dissenting voices. If the ideal sketched above is to be credible, the integrity of the academic process at the Catholic college must be guaranteed. This raises the issue of academic freedom. Any educational institution which officially espouses a point of view, a mission, is incompatible with academic freedom abstractly and absolutely conceived. But it need not be so conceived. A Catholic college is committed to a vision which has brought it into existence in the first place and upon which its espousal of freedom of inquiry is based. Such a commitment implies that academic freedom is a relative rather than an absolute good. Nevertheless, scholars and teachers generally function with relative autonomy within the freely accepted and pluralist vision of Christian humanism. Under ordinary conditions, the conversation of the college community regulates itself.

I do not see this as differing dramatically in practice from the way in which academic freedom might function in a state university. It too presupposes a vision of a democratic society in which freedom of inquiry is an important value. This is why Bloom can meaningfully charge higher education with failing in its mission to educate people for democracy. But even Bloom does not pose legal solutions to the problems he sees. It is interesting to speculate on what the trustees and administrators of an hypothetical state university ought to do if they awoke one morning to find that a tenured geneticist had become a militant neo-Nazi or a political philosopher an ardent Leninist. But our understanding of academic freedom ought not be guided by nightmares of such limit cases.

Experience shows that the professionalism of the scholars and professors involved can usually be relied upon. As Rev. Theodore Hesburgh has put it, "The university is not the kind of place that one can or should try to rule by authority external to the university."[16] It is difficult to imagine how, given the religious and political traditions of the United States, recourse to legal sanctions to turn responsible scholarly discussion in a particular direction could ever work to the long range good of either church or academy. Recent

---

[16]Cited in Ellis, "A Tradition of Autonomy?," p. 262.

discussions of the Vatican's 1985 draft of proposed norms for Catholic higher educational institutions tends to support such a conclusion. If theology ever came to be seen as a conspicuous exception to this ordinary way of dealing with academic freedom at Catholic colleges, then we would have to admit that it had ceased to be an academic discipline in any meaningful sense.

In defending academic freedom at the Catholic college, or at the state university for that matter, one must carefully note the radical disparity between academic freedom as it is conceived by those who tend to see the Enlightenment as a radical break with the past, and academic freedom as it is conceived by those who interpret the Enlightenment as one self-critical moment in the wider Western tradition. In the first case, academic freedom comes perilously close to functioning as an empty absolute, apart from the content required to ground its desirability in the first place. Critical thinking comes to be valued as an end in itself. The critical foundations for such an evaluation rarely come to light. Freedom of inquiry so conceived is deeply ambivalent. Because of its unexamined foundations, it can, once established, function just as effectively to suppress dissent as its dogmatic counterpart.

Freedom of inquiry in the Catholic college, by contrast, ought to have its foundation in the Christian vision of the human person. Academic freedom in this context is based on the same trust in the continuity between faith and reason that inspired the medieval scholastics. It should never be forgotten that one of their primary teaching devices was the *disputatio*. Such a faith assumes that truth is solid enough to withstand critical scrutiny. Indeed, if believers are to appropriate critically and internalize it, the truth of faith needs to be challenged by the best arguments its secular detractors have to offer. Such *disputationes* should take place in the class room and in the faculty lounge. On such a view of academic freedom, church officials and college administrators who are too quick to repress dissent will appear to have lost faith in the truth of the vision for which they claim to speak.

BEYOND TOLERANCE: PLURALISM AND CATHOLIC HIGHER EDUCATION

William M. Shea

Catholicism and Pluralism

The demands of American cultural pluralism and the choices of Catholic educators have, over the past two decades, heightened the public character of Catholic higher education.[1] Catholic higher education may be legally private, but it is morally public. This fact presents both educators and the church with new problems. I wish here to discuss the dilemma of Catholic higher education when, in pursuit of its publicness, it confronts pluralism within and without its walls. I will rely heavily on the educational philosophies of John Dewey and Bernard Lonergan in doing so,[2] but before I do, I need to state briefly my belief on three matters relevant to a consideration of the task of higher education.

First, Lonergan writes that the task of education is "constructing a world of meaning and value," and discovering a "vocation" in that world (finding "something to do in the world" is another way he puts the latter).[3] Are these legitimate goals of higher education? The

[1] This piece was written during a fellowship at the Woodrow Wilson Center in the Smithsonian Institution, 1986–1987. I am grateful to the Center for its hospitality and to Michael J. Lacey, Program Secretary on American Society and Politics, for his criticism and encouragement.
[2] Dewey's fullest text in philosophy of education is *Democracy and Education: An Introduction to the Philosophy of Education* (New York: The Free Press, 1944.1916). Bernard Lonergan's work on the philosophy of education is unpublished. His "The Philosophy of Education: Lectures by Bernard Lonergan," delivered at Xavier University in 1959, was transcribed and edited by James and John Quinn in 1979 and is available at the Lonergan Research Institute at Regis College of the University of Toronto. It will appear in critical edition in the complete works of Father Lonergan to be published by the University of Toronto Press. For a commentary and extension of Lonergan's work on education, see Frederick J. Crowe, SJ, *Old Things and New: A Strategy for Education* (Atlanta: Scholars Press, 1985).
[3] Lonergan, "Philosophy of Education," pp. 133–135.

phrases sound suspiciously religious, do they not? I would say yes;
they are not only legitimate goals of students but also legitimate
hopes and intentions of universities for their students, and not only
for private but also for state educational institutions. Interestingly
enough, I would get little argument from the recent investigators and
critics of higher education. Both Derek Bok and Ernest Boyer, for
example, are clear that the college experience is a time for grappling
with the questions of values and vocation.[4] Bok especially seems
nervous about indoctrinating students into a predigested set of
values, but nonetheless has praise for those educators who help
students clarify what their lives are for and what they are worth.
And so, aside from those who think that values and commitments
are matters of feeling and essentially private, we can take it as a
matter of not uncommon opinion that terms such as "commitment,"
"values," and "vocation" name important human realities which
are personal rather than private, and which can and ought to be
dealt with in the educational system. I do not think that even John
Dewey would disagree, except insofar as the language might suggest
a return to what he thinks of as supernaturalism.[5]

A second question is this one drawn from a reading of Dewey: Is
there a special character to education in a democratic society?
Dewey's position here is that every society shapes its education
according to its political and social structure and ideals, and that
democratic society is not different in this respect.[6] The ideal, at
least, of a professedly democratic society is anti-elitist and anti-
classist. The ideal includes free and open communication among
essentially equal citizens and among the various social groups included. Education, of course, is torn between the actual elitism and
classism of American life and its egalitarian and communitarian
ideal. But education must foster the ideal and attempt to incarnate it
in its own communal life if, as Dewey claims, education is not an
antechamber to social and political life but is that life being lived in
continuity with the larger society around it.[7]

---

[4]On values and vocation, see Derek Bok, *Higher Learning* (Cambridge: Harvard
University Press, 1986), pp. 35–72, and Ernest L. Boyer, *College: The Undergraduate
Experience in America* (New York: Harper and Row, 1987), especially chapters 13 and
18.

[5]Dewey, *A Common Faith* (New Haven: Yale University Press, 1934), *passim*, and
"Anti-naturalism in Extremis," in Yervant Krikorian, ed., *Naturalism and the Human
Spirit* (New York: Columbia University Press, 1944), pp. 1–16.

[6]*Democracy and Education*, pp. 81ff.

[7]*Ibid.*, pp. 55ff; and *The School and Society* (Chicago: University of Chicago Press,

Dewey was not wrong to point to the special tension that exists between a society dedicated to an egalitarian ideal, to freedom of communication and to a common approach to common problems on one side, and on the other side religious communities and institutions whose internal life is authoritarian and hierarchic, and who are inclined to put their own interests before those of the civic community.[8] But this is simply another example of the strain between a culture and its subcultures which the Catholic church, among others, has shown can be mediated in various constructive and even prophetic ways. The Catholic church's educational institutions have been among the most ardent supporters of American democratic ideals and procedures, and so have displayed the fact that tension between political democracy and hierarchic religion is not unmediable. So clear is the success of American Catholic education in this regard that the American church has often felt the breath of Rome upon its more egalitarian and democratic neck.

A third belief, this one relying on both Lonergan and Dewey, is that community is established upon common meanings, values, decisions, action, and communication.[9] While the Roman Catholic church is unquestionably a community with its own meanings and values, constituted as a community by common decisions of faith, the church understands itself as included in the civil community and not separate from it. The Catholic church is, then, not a sect. But doesn't pluralism combined with "free and open communication of meaning" imply the dissolution of the differences among the many worlds of meaning?

The effect of the presence of other worlds and communities on one's own unquestionably makes a difference to one's perception of one's own world and community, but the precise effect depends on how one constitutes that presence.[10] My own view is that if the

---

1899). While the schools have not fulfilled Dewey's hope that they would carry through a democratic reform of American society, they have had sufficient reformist impact to provoke cries of protest from the more conservative leaders of both church and state. See note 25 below.

[8]The anti-democratic and anti-scientific cast of traditional religions are major themes in Dewey's rejection of them. See note 5, above.

[9]On meaning, value, community, and communication see Dewey, *Democracy and Education*, pp. 4–6; and Lonergan, *Method in Theology* (London: Darton, Longman, and Todd, 1972), pp. 79ff, and on communications as a functional specialty in theology, see pp. 355ff.

[10]The other can be present as an oppressor, as was Antiochus IV Epiphanes to Israel in the second century BC; and the British to the Irish for a good part of the last millenium. Or one can be present to another as a sect fending off communication as

presence is freely chosen and on equal terms, then the presence should modify one's own world as well as that of the other, and that one's world will be stronger and healthier for it if one's world includes an affirmation of the values of intelligence and freedom. This is a typical liberal assumption, I grant. But I have seen innumerable times in my devilishly pluralistic classes in religious studies at the University of South Florida that dialogue need not, indeed most often does not, mean the dissolution but rather the reappropriation and transformation of a heritage.

And now to the dilemma, of which there are two forms, one confronting state education and another denominational education:[11]

1. Since our society is culturally plural, how can its state education present a norm of any sort that goes beyond what all can agree to (and that, in our society, seems precious little)? In the worst case, aren't public education and educators condemned by the logic of pluralism to a value-free professional training in which all meanings are left to a private sphere, or, where meanings and values appear, to a strict neutrality in their regard?

2. If denominational education has an evangelical or religious norm, how can it serve any but its own communicants and prospective converts? Isn't denominational education in the worst case sectarian, conversionist, anti-public, and anti-democratic?

The glory of state higher education in my experience of it is its ability to reproduce the national environment on the classroom scale. It brings the range of worlds of learning and value into contact with one another and permits and, at its best, encourages a look beyond the limits of one's own community and into the mind and life of other communities. We may have in the classroom of the state university the closest thing to a non-classist situation one can find in American life.

The liability of state higher education is its tendency to soft-pedal differences, to ignore the processes by which students integrate their beliefs and values with their educational experience, to avoid the

---

many American fundamentalists tend to behave in the American university where they habitually avoid taking courses which will involve them in discussion of religious beliefs. Or the presence can be dialogical, as it has been in the case of the Roman Church's attempt after the Second Vatican Council to engage other communities of religious meaning in conversation.

[11]I mention state education here only to highlight the problem that pluralism presents to Catholic higher education. The state college and university's problem with pluralism deserves discussion on its own.

problems of clarifying and defending values, to balk at the question of the truth of the many meanings presented in the culture and studied in the humanities, to talk tolerance and yet work with positivist assumptions in determining what questions and subject-matter are relevant to the actual working of the educational system, and to be unable to say anything serious from a moral perspective. The reasons for this are many, and they include both constitutional law and the conviction of the American liberal democratic tradition that tolerance allows America to work as a political and social system.

In spite of its liabilities, public higher education is crowded with faculty and administrators who resist these tendencies and habitually act against them. Whereas in the denominational institution the context supports affirmations of meaning and value and the practice associated with them, in the state institution the people who give their lives to education must provide moral and intellectual fiber to a context which can demand very little of either from its constituencies, aside, that is, from the standards developed by the professions and specializations themselves. Like the nation, American public higher education is a set of operations, abilities, and interests in search of a community, a many which needs to be welded into one.

The glory of denominational education is that it presents to society what public education thinks it cannot, a perspective from which one can sort out what rings true to human experience and what does not, and what is right from what is wrong. Denominational education has displayed to the American public two things: that one can believe and yet think, and that one can serve the common good while deeply involved in the life of a particular community of meaning and value. Throughout its history denominational education, even when it has played to its own special public, has been deeply concerned with the American public and has not conceived itself as unattached to the republic. Catholic higher education in particular has been clear on this, that in addition to preserving its religious tradition, it meant its students to serve the republic. In other terms, the vocations in this world which Catholic educators have sought to encourage in their students have never been restricted to the "religious life," but to the service of the republic and humankind in "secular" life.

On the other hand, denominational education is caught between its loyalty to its own religious community and its service to the

260

public. Is the denominational college dedicated to augmenting a democratic and pluralist vision of our common life, or is it a sectarian institution dedicated to preserving and furthering the special truth discovered by its founding religious community? The earliest evangelical colleges included among their statutes a statement that no one would be excluded because of denominational affiliation and that all denominations would be treated with respect.[12] Philip Gleason, in a recent lecture at Holy Trinity Parish in the District of Columbia, remarked that the founders of the early Catholic colleges, including Bishop Carroll, viewed Catholic colleges as a service to the nation and not only to the church, and included a similar statement in their statutes.[13] Cynics will point out that all these institutions needed every student fee they could scrape up and so were not in a position to exclude students of any sort; and they will wonder as well just what sorts of pressures students were under to convert to the denomination that ran the college. But cynicism aside for the moment, it is just possible that at the outset of denominational education there was the notion that the college was meant to serve the nation as well as the church, and that in this sense it was conceived to be a public institution.

Tension exists for our institutions of higher learning. Dewey wondered whether there was a contradiction between truly democratic education and the interests of a nation that was deeply flawed by elitist and classist interests.[14] Contrary to popular notions of his views, Dewey was highly critical of the practice of democracy in America, and thought that if, as he hoped, education would be the instrument by which America might be truly democratized, the educational institutions must rise above capitalist and individual self-interest and educate the students to the same.[15]

---

[12]The statutes of the College of Rhode Island (1764) read: ". . . it is hereby enacted and declared that into this liberal and catholic institution shall never be admitted any religious test; but on the contrary, all members hereof shall forever enjoy full, free, absolute, and uninterrupted liberty of conscience . . ." This, of course, does not include Catholics, Jews, or atheists. The limits become clear when in the next sentence the founders tell us that the body is open to all denominations of Protestants. See Richard Hofstadter, *American Higher Education: A Documentary History* (Chicago: University of Chicago Press, 1961) I, 134–136.

[13]Gleason lectured on "Two Hundred Years of Catholic Higher Education" on 12/3/86. He pointed out that in the early nineteenth century the Catholic schools included up to one-third non-Catholic students; only later in the century, under the pressure of nativist bigotry, did we have the exclusion of non-Catholics. On the same subject, see Edward J. Power, *A History of Catholic Higher Education in the United States* (Milwaukee: Bruce Publishing Co., 1958), pp. 55, 114.

[14]*Democracy and Education,* pp. 97–98.

[15]Dewey's Marxist critics, for example, took him to be an ideologist of bourgeois

There is bound to be a parallel tension felt in the higher education caught between the church and culture, for some church leaders may not consider the church itself in any sense a public institution and may find it suspicious that educators have two publics and two tasks in mind. The tension will be especially acute when the academic specialists begin to turn their academic-critical apparatus on the church as they are used to doing on society and begin to raise questions about the interests of the church.

As there are questions raised for the church by the college's attachment to the larger culture, there are problems—deeply felt— in the college itself. What justification is there for a Catholic college 80% of whose student body is non-Catholic? For Catholic colleges which take in students without inquiring into their religious status? Who keep no record of the percentage of non-Catholics in the student body? Who admit that there is no religious test for admission and no quota? Or a Catholic college which claims that religious belief and practice is irrelevant to hiring and tenuring? Or how do we explain a college which insists that its president be a member of a religious congregation and at the same time has no obligatory religious services and reduces its theology requirement to six credits or fewer which can be fulfilled by taking courses in those religions which only three decades ago we still termed false and even demonic?

However we may justify all this, and I am interested in justifying some of it, it does present one with a problem. Something serious has happened to Catholic education. The Roman Catholic Church in the United States chose long ago not to recommend the public educational system to its young. It chose, rather, to construct its own system, to confirm students in its own constructed world of meaning. It still supports a vast educational establishment and, if Andrew Greeley's figures can be trusted, the Catholic population is prepared to go on doing so.[16]

Roman Catholic education, and especially higher education, has

---

democracy. That he philosophically defended the democratic ideal is unquestionably true, and on the basis of that ideal he became a severe critic of Marxism in its Soviet form. That he identified the ideal with American practice and defended middle class interests is another matter and highly debatable in my opinion. For Marxist criticisms of Dewey and pragmatism see Harvey K. Wells, *Pragmatism: Philosophy of Imperialism* (Freeport, New York: Books for Libraries Press, 1971.1954) and George Novack, *Pragmatism vs. Marxism* (New York: Pathfinder Press, 1975).

[16]Andrew M. Greeley, *American Catholics: A Social Portrait* (New York: Basic Books, 1977), chapter 9.

fled neither its own religious vision nor its public function. It has
expanded its attention to its neighbors' visions and realities. And
over the past quarter of a century, in a particularly vigorous way, it
has reaffirmed its embrace of American pluralism and, for all its
powerful ecclesial sentiments and convictions, it has refused to
become sectarian. In fact, American Catholic higher education is
already public. It is chartered by the state; its existence is entrusted
to boards which are not ecclesiastical in makeup; for most of this
century it has sought and found accreditation from public bodies; it
uses no religious test for admission and, in many cases, for hiring; it
is recipient of large amounts of public money; its course requirements in theology are taught according to American academic criteria and not under ecclesiastical supervision; its campus ministers
are ministers and not proselytizers; and even when it clearly affirms
its Catholic heritage, it does not impose it even upon its Catholic
students. The problem of Catholic higher education is no longer
with its public commitment; it is now with its ecclesial definition,
and with those Catholics and their ecclesiastical leaders who do not
understand and thus reject what the leaders of the educational
institutions have been up to for the past quarter of a century. The
colleges have been redefining their Catholicism.[17]

Let us recall the range of response to the American ethos of
colleges of other American religious bodies. I will name only a few:
Dartmouth, Yale, Oberlin, St. Olaf, Mercer, Baylor, Liberty, Bob
Jones, Wheaton. A recent case is the severing of its relationship with
the North Carolina Southern Baptist Convention by Wake Forest
University, which, according to its president, does not in any way
presage a surrender of its dedication to the Southern Baptist heritage.[18] Catholic colleges are passing through the same process of
assessment and realignment as did their evangelical cousins and
will in all likelihood find similar modes of response to the challenge—although one would hope that very few will go the way of
either Dartmouth or Bob Jones University.

Moreover, there is an interesting point of comparison between the
evangelical polity and the Catholic colleges. The Catholic colleges
are, by and large, free of hierarchic control. They are the most

---

[17]The change in Catholic educational institutions is merely one facet of a pervasive
change in the contemporary church as a whole. Educational institutions, however,
have experienced peculiar economic, social, and political pressures in American
society.
[18]The Chronicles of Higher Education, v. 33, #17 (January 7, 1987), p. 3.

congregational of all Catholic institutions from the point of view of their organization. They are quite often, to my experience, jealous of their ecclesiastical independence. They are far more dependent on their boards and presidents and faculties for their Catholic identity than they are on local bishops and religious congregations. This proves a danger, from the point of view of those who would wish a single solution to the problem to hold the field; but from another point of view, the flexibility which this arrangement affords makes it possible for Catholic colleges to be on the front line of the relationship between the church and the culture, to be exploring new ways of being Catholic which are hard to come by for other Catholic institutions. This possibility is important for the Catholic church in the United States and perhaps in the world. It may be as important to the church's future as the Polish Catholic experiment in working out a constructive relationship with a Marxist state or the experiments of people's Catholicism in central and south America.

Of overwhelming importance from my point of view in trying to understand the relationship between higher education and a culture full of options in meaning and value is this: Catholic higher education is dealing with American culture as it in fact is in all its plurality, and it has chosen to take that plurality into itself in terms of students and faculty. Although that poses a difficulty to the definition of its Catholic nature, it also affords us a unique experiment in understanding the public responsibilities of academic institutions and the flexibility of Catholic identity.

Is Catholic higher education for the church or for the culture? Is it denominational, or is it public? Is its ideal the Kingdom of God, or is it the Great Community? The dichotomies are simplistic, for both sets are true of Catholic higher education. Catholics must converse (intellectually and spiritually) with the many other communities of meaning in our culture. We need dialogue as individual persons and as a religious community, and nowhere more intensely than in our educational institutions. We are in need of others if we are to clarify ourselves. Dictation and repetition are the worst of methods for achieving self-understanding. We will not solve our problems, except nominally, by turning to ecclesiastical authority for definitions.[19]

---

[19]I am not denying to authorities a decisive role in the community's definition of its meaning. For the conditions under which authority is authentically exercised, see Lonergan, "The Dialectic of Authority" in A Third Collection (New Jersey: Paulist Press, 1985), pp. 5–34.

The rest of the church and its leadership obviously has a legitimate concern in all this, and part of the difficulty for educational
leaders is negotiating that concern so that it contributes construc-
tively to solutions. The leadership of the church has shown itself
highly ambiguous on this question of inculturation and pluralism.
Vatican II was a turning point of monumental significance, but the
results of it remain at least mixed, indicating a conflicted judgment
and a divided heart. The church has to some degree shucked classical consciousness and taken on historical consciousness. It has
dropped the notion of a single cultural norm and accepted the
empirical notion of culture. It has redefined its relation to other
religions and even to negators of religion, and taken them as dialogue
partners, seeking common ideals wherever they may be found.

Yet, as classicism identifies common understanding with identity
of word or concept, language and behavior, so Rome continues its
drive for tight universal legislation for higher education and shows
itself unhappy with theological pluralism within the church. We
educators have shown ourselves hesitant as well. For example, in
spite of the genuinely ecumenical bent of Catholic theologians and
religionists, we have yet to see a genuinely ecumenical major faculty
of theology under Catholic auspices. It would seem that many
Catholic institutions of higher learning have accepted responsibility
for the public nature of higher education, but there remain problems
of ecclesiastical reaction and of a coherent theological defense of a
new relationship between Catholicism and its cultures. Nor is it a
question whether Roman Catholics can live in a pluralist culture, for
the church is thoroughly engaged in it. The final question which the
church must answer is how far it will tolerate pluralism within its
walls. To that question the experiment of Catholic educational institutions may provide a great deal of the answer. But how shall a
pluralist culture be met?

Beyond Tolerance

Tolerance is a central virtue in the American civic tradition. God
knows we have had a massive amount of intolerance in fact—and we
Catholics know that as well as any religious group—but we have had
the rhetoric of tolerance to appeal to in breaking down the cultural
and political hegemony of White Anglo-Saxon Protestantism, for

example. We American Catholics believed in tolerance before we were the recipients of its practice.[20]

To tolerate means, according to Webster, to endure or resist action without grave or lasting injury; to suffer to be or to be done without prohibition, hindrance, or contradiction. One can see the political usefulness of a virtue of this sort, even if it is immediately clear that the virtue is essentially negative. It means the willingness and the ability to put up with something the elimination of which might be more difficult or dangerous. So far as it goes, tolerance has stood the citizens of our land in good civic stead. But it carries some connotations and associated meanings with which one might quarrel. There are three possible meanings of the term that I want to mention.[21]

There is the tolerance of the Enlightenment, at least as it has reached us in our academic and civic traditions. It serves as no answer to the questions surrounding pluralism, except in the minimal sense that it at least occasionally has restrained its possessors from acting against those whose cultures differ from its own. It has two huge flaws. One is its arrogance and concealed classicism; it takes its own truth for granted, along with the falsity or inauthenticity of the tolerated. Although it is willing to allow the other opinion or way of life to exist, it merely watches from a distance, certain of its own truth. Its second flaw is that it leads nowhere, and most especially it does not lead to understanding, either of the other or of oneself. At its worst it is the tolerance of the bigot.

There is as well the tolerance of that chastened child of the Enlightenment, the American liberal for whom all beliefs and values are relative and ungrounded and who, although he or she espouses values and has beliefs aplenty, is so struck by their limitations that he or she cannot imagine that there may be very good reasons for holding them. This is the tolerance of the muddle headed liberal who is so often the subject of mockery by conservatives and neo-liberals, the relativist tolerance that will not engage in serious

---

[20]Though Catholicism has been far from a tolerant religion historically, we are fortunate that through our ecclesial tradition we have inherited a strong sense of community and of doctrine which has enabled us to curb some of the not so attractive aspects of the Enlightenment, namely individualism and the inability to believe.

[21]See G. Dalcourt, "Tolerance," in *The New Catholic Encyclopedia* (New York: McGraw-Hill, 1967), 14: 192–193. There is an interesting development of the author's view in the supplementary volume of a decade later, apparently as a result of the Vatican II Council's teaching on religious liberty: see 17: 666. See also Maurice Cranston, "Toleration," *The Encyclopedia of Philosophy* (New York: Macmillan Co., 1967), 8: 143–146.

critical conversation about beliefs and values because, in the final analysis, no belief or value is incorrect or wrong.

The tolerance of the Enlightenment and the tolerance of liberalism are no longer adequate for dealing with the realities of American political, academic, and ecclesial life. They either permit us to avoid and ignore the other or they permit us to talk with the other without taking the conversation seriously. They militate against the very task of education: they may allow the other, whether student or faculty member, to "construct their world of meaning" but they do not aid in it or lead to it. Neither of these versions of tolerance befits the teacher or the administrator who cares about the integrity of education and of religious belief and practice.

The third type of tolerance recognizes the limits of historical consciousness and the need for concrete communities of symbol and understanding and custom and finds other views, perspectives, and values a challenge and a possible source of blessing. This tolerance is based on humility and on respect for the minds and hearts and history of others. It is active tolerance, not arrogant or condescending. It is the Protestant tolerance practiced so movingly by Martin Luther King who could learn from Augustine, Tillich, and Gandhi, and the Catholic tolerance of Pope John XXIII. When it is practiced with full heart, it is the sort of tolerance that seeks the truth in the life and words of another and assumes that there is a truth there to be found. This tolerance is extremely difficult for orthodox Christians to practice since it may do funny things to one's sense of doctrines, but it is the sort of virtue that is crucial to both the interreligious and the academic situation. Perhaps this virtue, at its best, ought to be called something other than tolerance, for it seems to take us beyond tolerance.

Derek Bok in his recent book *Higher Learning* makes some helpful comments on tolerance:

> The questioning of values and the emergence of many contrasting beliefs and lifestyles present an entirely different set of challenges for the university. On the one hand, if we are to remain true to our pluralistic traditions, it is crucial to encourage undergraduates to respect contrasting attitudes and conflicting points of view. Fortunately, the American college does well in this endeavor . . .
>
> On the other hand, if the universities do nothing but emphasize tolerance, they may simply succeed in fostering a kind of moral relativism that looks upon ethical questions as matters of individual

preference immune from rational argument or intellectual scrutiny. Such attitudes will further weaken the ethical restraints essential to society and further loosen the bonds that join human beings together.

Bok understands the problem. Now listen to his solution:

> Such prospects call for greater efforts to search for common values and explore their contemporary meaning. This has long been the province of the humanities. The challenge now is to renew this effort and to seek fresh syntheses that reconcile new insights and needs with more enduring human values in order to bring coherence and diversity into a healthier balance one again. . . . Whether the humanities can possibly live up to their traditional aspirations at a time when the surrounding culture offers so little encouragement is itself an open question. It would surely be mischievous to berate humanists for failing to succeed in an enterprise that may be beyond anyone's capacity.[22]

If I am not mistaken, Mr. Bok has just finessed the solution to the question on pluralism and ethics. Bok states the problem, tells us its alternate dangers, indicates in whose province the solution lies, suggests that the poor humanists may not be able to measure up to the burden, which failure would be the fault of the surrounding culture that has the problem to begin with, and concludes with the admission that the problem may be beyond solution.

Earlier in the book, the author celebrates, on the one hand, the tolerance which leaves students "to arrive at answers by themselves" lest we fall into "rank indoctrination," and rejoices in the "greater questioning of traditional values," in the "richer profusion of life-styles," and the "reconsideration of tired dogmas," yet, on the other hand, he hesitates over "a certain loss of coherence and a weakening of the bonds of common belief and mutual trust" that "help to bind together . . . the claims of individuality and community." He quotes Daniel Bell to the effect that ". . . the real problem of modernity is the problem of belief."[23]

There is no doubt in my mind that Bell is correct. One may agree with Mr. Bok's perception of the problem and even sympathize with his balancing act while finding his comments on the solution to be evasive and unenlightening. As is typical with the liberal position, and I regard myself as a liberal on these matters, this one has no

---

[22]Bok, *Higher Learning*, pp. 170–171.
[23]*Ibid.*, 48, 54–56.

next move; it is frozen between liberal tolerance and classicist indoctrination. Flustered when faced by the fact that values and commitment are "beyond reason" and that he may be pressed "beyond tolerance" if he is going to meet the issue, he retreats to the praise of pluralism and concomitant handwringing over loss of social cohesion.

What might Mr. Bok do instead? To put it briefly, he might enter the fray. He might tell us how he thinks human life ought to be lived, why he lives it as he does, from what community he has drawn his understanding and where he gets support for it, why he doesn't live the way others do and what he thinks about their ways of life. It would also help if he would tell us whether he lives as he does because he thinks it true to his and our common humanity. He might tell us whether his mode of living has for him a religious horizon. And then a serious conversation could begin. Short of these acts of self appropriation whereby traditions become self-consciously matters "handed over," pluralism can only seem chaotic (to classicism) or an unmediable good without reasonable foundation (to the latest variety of empiricism, post-modernism).[24]

I do not wish to be misunderstood here. I am no fan of William Bennett or Allen Bloom.[25] Although I disagree with Bok's recourse to individualism in the American style and tolerance in the liberal style, I far prefer it to Bennett's neo-classicism and tolerance in the Enlightenment style, and to Bloom's nostalgic elitism. The following recognitions seem to me vital to any Catholic attempt to cope with pluralism:

1. That we are in tow to pluralism for the long haul and that rehearsals of the old liberal-conservative polemics, whether political or theological, are no longer helpful;

2. That the first step to meeting the problems of intellectual and moral pluralism in the university and outside it, among faculty as

---

[24]On the benefits and liabilities of structuralism and deconstruction, see David Tracy, *Plurality and Ambiguity: Hermeneutics, Religion, and Hope* (New York: Harper and Row, 1987).

[25]William J. Bennett, *To Reclaim a Legacy: A Report on Humanities in Higher Education* (Washington, D.C.: National Endowment for the Humanities, 1984), and Allan Bloom, *The Closing of the American Mind: How Higher Education Has Failed Democracy and Impoverished the Souls of Today's Students* (New York: Simon and Schuster, 1987). For critical assessments see Norman Birnbaum on Bennett, "A Misguided Call to Spiritual Renewal," *The Chronicle of Higher Education*, vol. 32, #1 (January 9, 1985), p. 128; and on Bloom, Martha Nussbaum, "Allan Bloom's 'American Mind,' " *The New York Review of Books*, v. 34, #17 (November 5, 1987), pp. 20–26.

well as among students, is to get the communities to clarify their positions and talk to one another about them, rather than evading both clarification and conversation;

3. That we must take responsibility for our positions both in their status as beliefs (rather than as supernaturally guaranteed knowledge) and in the search for intelligible explications of them;

4. That appropriation of one's own position involves criticism of it and the consequent probability of development and change in understandings, and so the possibility of trouble with our own religious community;

5. That there is a social reality of importance beyond one's own community of meaning and value, and that is the larger civic and human community the meaning of which religions reveal and of which the religious community, whatever its importance, is only a part.

And, thus, I say: if we are to find ways to cope with the realities of our civic and ecclesial life, we must press "beyond tolerance" to take responsibility, intellectual and spiritual, for our convictions with some courage in the political, the educational, and the ecclesial arenas. The American bishops have set us a splended example with their letters on peace and the economy, letters which are clearly public in their intent, their temper, and their rationale, and consequently open to disagreement and the criticism of Catholics and others.

Lonergan mentions in his lectures on education that in education these days we do not have too much use for the terms "true and false."[26] In part this is because of the etiquette of tolerance forced upon us by pluralism. Partly it is due to the implicit positivism of our academic life which ties the terms to what can be verified empirically and leaves everything else up for grabs. In part it is due to the epistemology of American pragmatists who maintain that what we are after in inquiry is not truth but ideas to use in changing situations. Lonergan himself describes the findings of scientific inquiry to be the best available opinion rather than the true and the false.[27] But since pluralism is the fact of our American life and we are to take it seriously, then the demand for clarification of the differences among us becomes paramount, and the issue of the true

---

[26]"Philosophy of Education," p. 152.

[27]The shift from the classical to the empirical understanding of science is described many times by Lonergan. See, for example, *Method in Theology*, pp. 314–318.

and the false is bound to reappear with a vengeance. We have to begin to practice what Lonergan calls dialectic, the search for the roots of the differences among us.[28]

The question of the true and the false will reappear not only in the classroom debates among the various moral and religious perspectives represented there, but in the relationship between the Catholic academic and the church. Roman Catholic higher education cannot avoid being critical of its own community—any more than the American university can avoid finding out about American life and politics what Americans and their politicians prefer not to hear. One is simply not able to avoid the hard questions of truth and falsity when one comes to one's own church traditions because it is irresponsible to exempt it from the scrutiny that every human institution must undergo. Questions occur to humanists, philosophers, social scientists, theologians and religionists, and the questions must be pursued. One is up against an absolute if there ever was one: the dynamic of human intelligence which, once it gets organized and under way, cannot be interfered with without serious damage to the individual and the institution. Charles Peirce wrote, in his own version of the transcendental imperative: "Do not block the way of inquiry."[29] Thus, the meaning and the truth of the doctrine of papal infallibility can no more escape scholarly examination than can the origins of and reasons for American policy toward central America. While special sensitivity is called for in matters of ecclesial doctrines, once one faces other traditions as human, one cannot afford to take one's own for granted, although one may take it to be true. But theology's task in the face of the pluralism of culture and the specializations of intelligence in the university is another topic, and I must return to ours.

Intellectual, moral, and religious differences cannot and should not be ignored (or excluded) by academic leaders. The educationists are responsible to make use of disagreements and differing versions for their students and the health of their institutions. I am thinking about issues that lie between humanists, scientists, and professionalists, between teachers and administrators, between students and

---

[28]On dialectic as a functional specialty in theology, see *Method in Theology*, pp. 235–267. On dialectic as method in metaphysics, see *Insight: A Study of Human Understanding* (New York: Philosophical Library, 1957), chapter XVII.

[29]*Philosophical Writings of Peirce*, ed. by Justus Buchler (New York: Dover, 1955), p. 54.

faculty, between theologians and bishops, between religious communities.[30]

Moral, spiritual, and religious pluralism among students and faculty should be taken advantage of rather than ignored, and for two good reasons. One is the good of the society, and the other is the good of the church. I think of the health of a society and a church in which intelligent disagreements and searching criticism, especially self-criticism, ought to replace repression and acrimony.

Not only should we use classrooms to explore the different worlds of students, but we should also utilize the public lecture forum. I think it is a mistake to exclude from that platform, and from public debate, positions which are *non grata* to the church, as it would be to exclude political questions. If the Pope can embrace Arafat and Jaruzelski and respectfullly hear out his Jewish critics, we and our students can afford to hear respectfully Charles Curran, Mario Cuomo, Daniel Maguire, and Eleanor Smeal. Above all, it is pedagogically vital that students, Catholic and otherwise, have a chance to feel out the differences in important positions as well as read them in textbooks.[31] A college which is interested only in formation in the Catholic tradition will not be interested in my suggestion; the college that is also convinced that its task is transformation of that tradition will be interested.[32] Again, from my own point of view, higher education sponsored by a church ought to be the mediator between the church and the culture, making as sure as it can that the

---

[30]On the issue of specialization and the consequent fragmentation of a faculty, my concern presumes my own experience and reflects my woeful interdisciplinary ignorance. Lonergan's transcendental method would help the university community enormously in this because it explains specialties to specialists in accessible universal terms, rendering classical laws and statistical probabilities intelligible in the same terms as history and hermeneutics. At the same level of generality he explains specialization as an historical phenomenon. See his discussion of "The Ongoing Discovery of Mind" in *Method in Theology*, pp. 300–319; and specialization and functional specialties, p. 125ff.

[31]This applies not only to students and faculty, but also to nonacademic participants in public debate. For example, an analysis of the abortion controversy leads one to the conclusion that the language of vilification employed extensively by both sides is manipulatory, misleading, and alienating, and has little to do with either the communication of fundamental values or reaching a common understanding even if disagreement cannot be avoided. See a soon to be published paper by Marsha Vanderford of the Department of Communication, University of South Florida, "Vilification and Social Movements: A Case Study of Pro-Life and Pro-Choice Rhetoric."

[32]For the distinction between formative and transformative functions of religious language, see Rosemary Haughton, *The Transformation of Man* (New York: Paulist Press, 1967).

maximum amount of clarity and charity is achieved between different belief and value systems.

In conclusion, let me tersely restate my position on the relationship between Catholic higher education and the church community.
Education is public because knowledge and wisdom are public, and
they are in no sense the property of a church community. An
educational institution sponsored by the church is not in existence
for the church alone, but for the society as well. Therefore, its
responsibility is to introduce the student not only to the world of
meaning of the church but also to the worlds of meaning available
in the society. It is against its very nature for higher education to be
exclusivist with regard to its community of students and teachers.
Yet its roots in the Catholic church community ought to support
strongly a critical as well as a constructive attitude toward the
intellectual and religious pluralism of our society.

CONTRIBUTORS

JOHN V. APCZYNSKI, editor of this volume, is professor in the Department of Theology at St. Bonaventure University. His doctorate is from McGill University in contemporary religious thought, and his publications have appeared in *Theological Studies*, *Zygon*, and *Studies in Religion*.

LILLIAN BOZAK-DeLEO is associate professor and chair of the Theology Department of Molloy College (Rockville Centre, N.Y. 11570). She received her Ph.D. from Marquette University and has presented papers on medieval women mystics at various conferences.

ALICE GALLIN, O.S.U., Ph.D. from the Catholic University of America, was a professor of history at the College of New Rochelle (1950–76). Currently she is the Executive Director of the Association of Catholic Colleges and Universities. She is the author of *German Resistance to Hitler* (1955) and *Mid-Wives to Nazism: University Professors in Weimar Germany, 1925–33* (1986).

JAMES L. HEFT, S.M. (Marianist) is a professor of theology and, since 1983, chair of the Department of Religious Studies at the University of Dayton. He has published in numerous journals, including the *Journal of Ecumenical Studies*, *Archivum Historiae Pontificiae*, and *One in Christ*, and is the author of a study of the origins of papal infallibility, *John XXII (1316–1334) and Papal Teaching Authority* (Edwin Mellen Press, 1986).

JAMES HENNESEY, S.J., is Rector of the Jesuit community and professor of the history of Christianity at Canisius College, Buffalo, N.Y. He is the author of *American Catholics: A History of the Roman Catholic Community in the United States* (Oxford, 1981) and co-author of the forthcoming *Il cattolecesimo del XX secolo* (Rome: Laterza, 1989).

PHYLLIS H. KAMINSKI, SSND, a doctoral student in theology at the Toronto School of Theology (University of St. Michael's College), holds Master's degrees from Georgetown University and Fordham University. In 1986 she was awarded the Canadian Theology Society's student essay prize and presented her paper "Blondel and the Christian Life" at the Society's meeting in Winnipeg.

GARY MACY is an associate professor of religious studies at the University of San Diego. Holding a Ph.D. in divinity from Cambridge University, he has published widely in the area of eucharistic theology, including *Theologies of the Eucharist in the Early Scholastic Period* (Oxford, 1984) as well as a contribution to the CTS annual volume for 1983.

WILLIAM MADGES received his Ph.D. in the area of historical theology from the University of Chicago, and he is currently an assistant professor at Xavier University. His publications include *The Core of Christian Faith: D. F. Strauss and His Catholic Critics* (Lang, 1987) and "Authority and Persuasion: Ignaz von Döllinger" in the 1986 annual volume of the College Theology Society.

TERENCE J. MARTIN, JR. is assistant professor of religious studies at Saint Mary's College, Notre Dame, Indiana. He is presently working on the uses of fictional dialogues in theological literature. His "The Social Rationality of Theological Discourse" appeared in *Horizons* in 1986.

JOHN McCARTHY is an assistant professor of theology at Loyola University of Chicago and chair for publicaitons and research for the College Theology Society.

PATRICK F. O'CONNELL is associate professor of Arts and Humanities at Villa Maria College, Erie, Pennsylvania. His publications include articles on patristic, medieval, and modern spiritual writers, on Renaissance and contemporary religious poetry, and on the spirituality of non-violence. He is a regular columnist for *Living Prayer* magazine.

STEVEN T. OSTOVICH is an assistant professor of religious studies at the College of St. Scholastica in Duluth, Minnesota. His Ph.D. is from Marquette University, and he also studied with J. B. Metz as a Fulbright Scholar in West Germany. His main scholarly interests are political theology, neo-Marxist philosophy, and historical philosophy of science.

WILLIAM L. PORTIER received his Ph.D. in theology from the University of St. Michael's College, Toronto, in 1980 and has published in the areas of historical and systematic theology. He is an associate professor of theology at Mount Saint Mary's College in Emmitsburg, Maryland. From 1986 to 1988 he served as Vice President of the College Theology Society.

WILLIAM M. SHEA has been professor of religious studies at the University of South Florida since 1980. In 1984–86 he was president of the College Theology Society, and in 1986–87 he was a fellow at the Woodrow Wilson Center in Washington, D.C. He is presently working on a book on American higher education and theology's role in it.

DAVID TRACY is the Andrew Thomas Greeley and Grace McNichols Greeley Distinguished Service Professor at the Divinity School, University of Chicago. His most recent book is *Plurality and Ambiguity: Hermeneutics, Religion, Hope* (Harper and Row, 1987).